Origami Ooh La La!

Action Origami
for Performance and Play

Jeremy Shafer

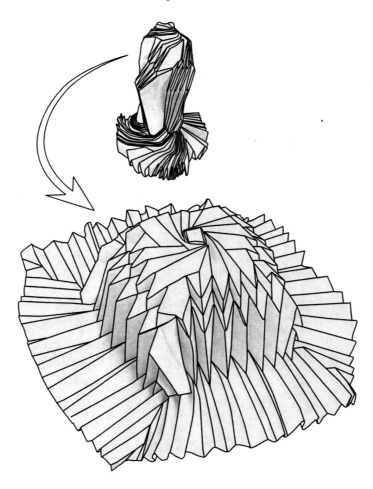

To Alicia

ORIGAMI OOH LA LA!
ACTION ORIGAMI FOR PERFORMANCE AND PLAY

ISBN 978-1456439644

Introduction

Freaky Fingers Finger Puppet
(page 155)

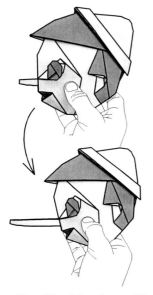

Familiar Liar (page 77)

Spinning Candy Cane
(page 81)

Unless you insist on being a closet folder, the art of origami boils down to a game of show and tell. Whether you are a seasoned origami artist or a first-time folder, at some time you are bound to show your origami. Whether it happens at the dinner table, on the playground, or at the office, you are still putting on a show! The aim of this book is to nurture the concept of origami as a performance art, and encourage origamists to not just show origami, but actually perform it! The book is filled with models that are well-suited to performing, and ideas for how to present them to an audience.

Ten years have passed since publishing my first book, *Origami to Astonish and Amuse*. During this time, I've been focusing on my career as an entertainer but still steadily designing and diagramming more origami models. For most of my performances, I'm billed as "Jeremy the Juggler," but at least ten minutes of my forty-minute Action Packed Act" is my origami show – a "Magical Box" stuffed with origami models, which I pull out and show one by one. For most of the models in this book I've included "Perform It" boxes with specific suggestions for how to present them to an audience. I also have a YouTube page **www.youtube.com/jeremyshaferorigami** with videos of my origami show. In this introduction, however, are some more general origami performing tips. My specialty is performing for kids, so the following tips are especially tailored to kids performances, but many of the ideas can also be applied to adult audiences who, I believe, are deep down still kids at heart.

From my experience performing origami, I've learned that the crowd reacts better to origami models that move than to models that are static. Except for the last chapter, all of the models in this book are 'action' models, which open, spin, fly, shoot out, or transform in some way. Most can also be flattened or squished allowing them to be stuffed in a "Magical Box" without getting destroyed. My current Magical Box is a cardboard box covered with brightly decorative washi paper and protected by a layer of clear packing tape. In the past, I've used fabric or acrylic paint to decorate the box. I recently added backpack straps to my origami box, which makes it even more portable! I can now unicycle around and juggle while transporting the origami act!

The first step to an Origami Show is to gather the audience. I gather the kids around me by saying, "Whoever wants to see what is in my Magical Box, come over here!" Once the kids are around me, I tell them to sit down; that way they will be less likely to wander off! When I perform, I like to be as close as I can to the audience so that I can more easily interact and connect with them, and keep their attention. One way to get closer to an audience is to fold bigger models; they grab more attention, but they also take up more space!

Cobra Pop-up (page 61)

When performing with origami, I try to keep the kids actively participating in any way I can. For example, as I pull out each model, I will first ask, what is this? When someone says, "It's a Cobra!," I'll say, "Yes! Who wants to get bitten by a Cobra?!" If it's a hat, I'll ask, "Who wants to wear this hat?" If it's a frog, I'll say, "Everyone, throw a kiss to the frog!" I will often pull out a model, and say, "Oh, no, this model is too scary!," and I'll put it back in the box and go on to the next model. This riles the kids up, and makes them really want to see more, in particular, the scary one! After I finally show the scary one, the very next model will be too big, too silly, or too profound, etc., so that the kids remain riled up the whole show.

Prince Not So Charming
(page 77)

Another way I keep the kids actively participating is to move the group in any which way I can. I will sometimes take my box and run to new location while calling out "Follow me!" This usually gives the kids a fresh attention span. Other times, I will say, "Everyone, come closer to check out this really small origami!" and then, soon after, I will say, "Watch out, here comes a big one! Move back!" When performing at birthday parties, especially when confronted with chattering parents, I'll have the kids chase me around the yard just to see the next model! This keeps the kids on their feet and the parental noise level under control. If the audience is too big to move or the performance space is too small, I'll achieve the same effect by jumping to different spots in and around the audience, sometimes right between the two chattering parents! Even for well-behaved audiences, moving around helps break the show into more manageable chunks.

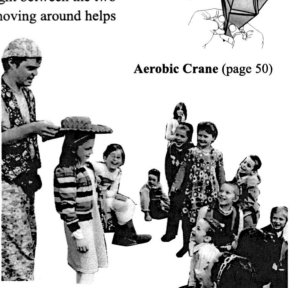

Aerobic Crane (page 50)

When I perform, I try to keep my excitement level at an all time high. I often fluctuate the level of my voice, but I'll keep the same high intensity level. For instance, I can whisper, "Watch out, here comes a scary one! Everyone, hold your hands up!," and then show the model while making a loud growling noise for extra impact. Another way I maintain a high excitement level is to make the transitions between the models at lightning speed. It only takes a couple seconds to lose an audience! In addition, I keep my patter going the whole time and I use a lot of call and response. If it's a heart model, I'll say, "Everyone say, "Ahhhhhh!" or if it's a monster, I'll say, "Everyone make the sound of a monster!" Near the end of my act, I ask, "Are you ready for the

A Volunteer Modeling a Flasher Hat (page 226)

Giant Origami Space Monster
Gobbling up Kids at a Birthday Party
(Venus Flytrap from *Origami to*
Astonish and Amuse)

grand finale?" No matter how loud they say yes, I respond, "You certainly don't sound ready, so I'll show you another small one." After doing that several times, I eventually do show my grand finale, which is a giant brightly-painted Flasher (for Flashers, see pages 201-236). Compared to juggling and unicycling, performing with origami is relatively easy because the work is already in the "Magic Box." I don't need to worry about dropping a torch or falling off the unicycle! Maintaining the audience's attention and interest is no small task, but one which can be made easier if you can relate to the audience and show them that you are having fun.

When I perform at birthday parties, libraries or schools, I like to follow my show with teaching origami. To me, teaching origami is like performing, so I try to make it as interactive and exciting as possible. When teaching young kids, I constantly use call and response to help maintain their attention and interest. One of my favorite calls is, "Everyone say, 'What's the next step teacher?'" This effectively announces over the loudspeaker that I'm about to go on to the next step and gets everyone to pay attention. Another favorite call is, "Everyone hold your model up and say, 'Is this right, teacher?'" This gets their attention, but also lets me see if anyone is lost. If the responses get too loud, I sometimes bring it down a notch with the call, "Everyone whisper, 'Sorry for being loud, teacher.'" When teaching adults and older kids, I tone down the call and response, but I still often use, "Everyone say, 'Next step!'" to get their attention, and I certainly use, "Everyone hold up your model!" to make sure everyone is following me correctly.

Call and response is useful for teaching origami, but it's especially useful for performing origami. My favorite way to end the origami show is with the call and response, 'Ooh La La!' which I have the audience exclaim as I open a giant origami Flasher. Then, as I close the Flasher, I have the audience exclaim, "La La Ooh!" The phrase, "Ooh La La!," is an exclamation of great surprise, excitement and intrigue that, to me, captures the essence of performing with origami.

And so, now, with no further ado or brouhaha, I present to you, **Origami Ooh La La!**

Performing with Origami is Easier than Riding a Flaming Unicycle!
(page 3)

CONTENTS

SIMPLE ACTION MODELS . . . 19

Contents **5**

SPINNIGAMI . . . 80

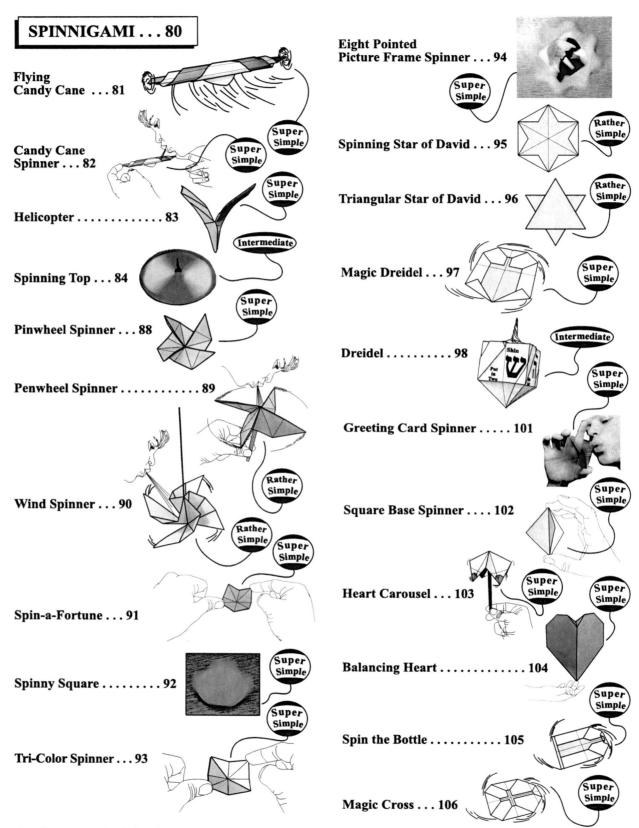

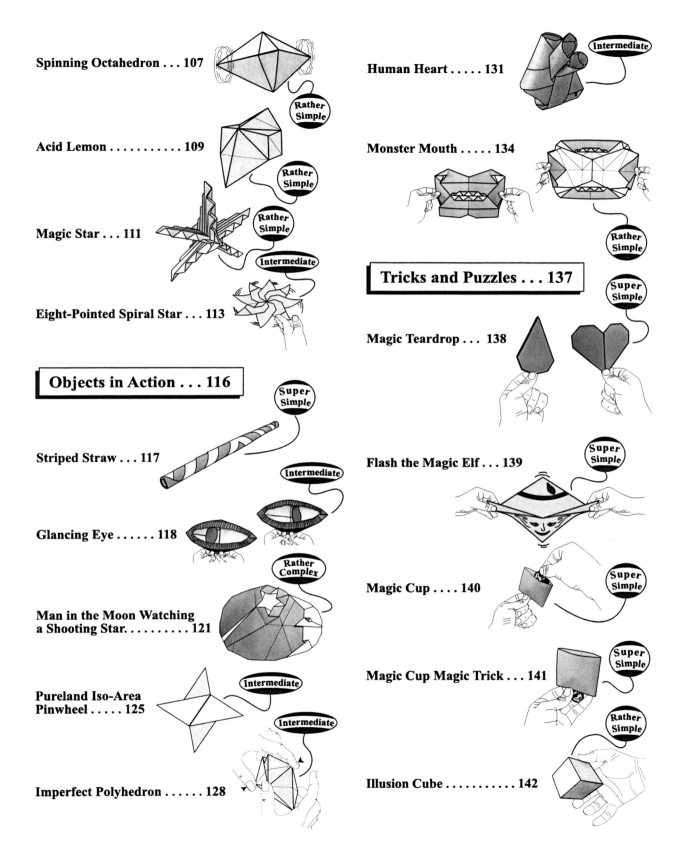

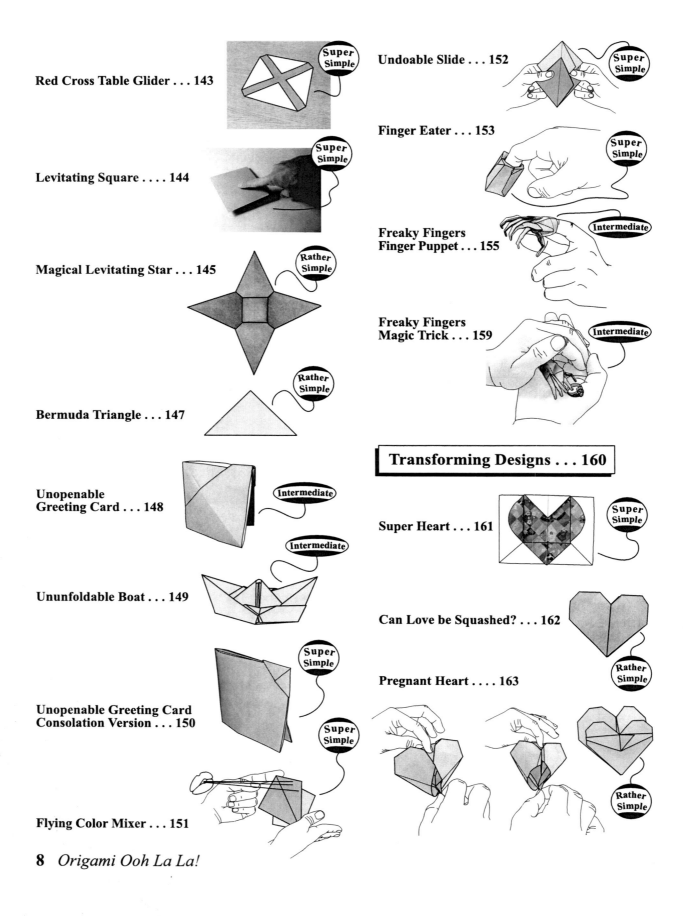

Transforming Designs . . . 160

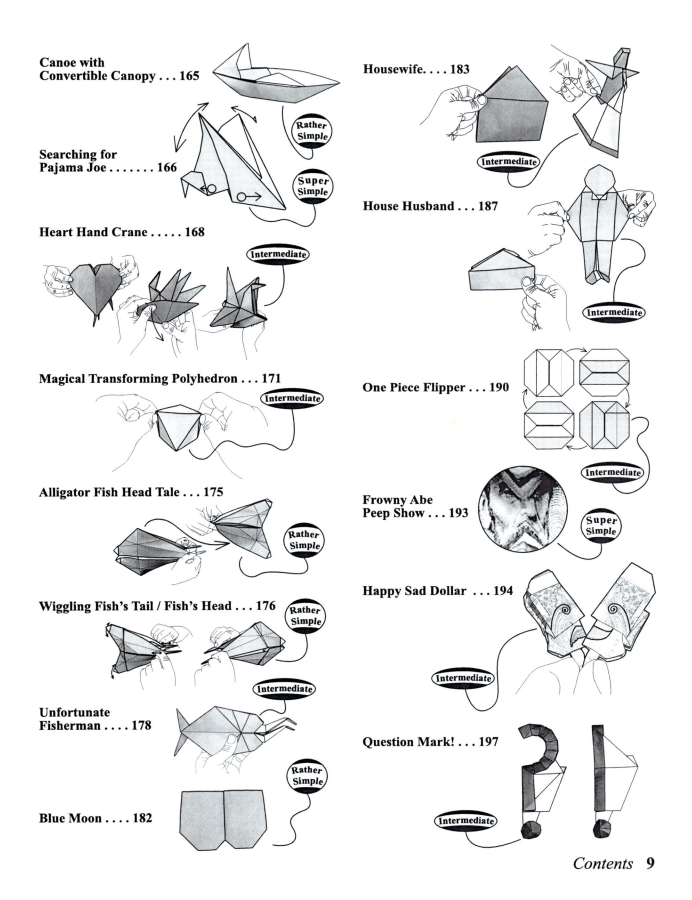

Contents **9**

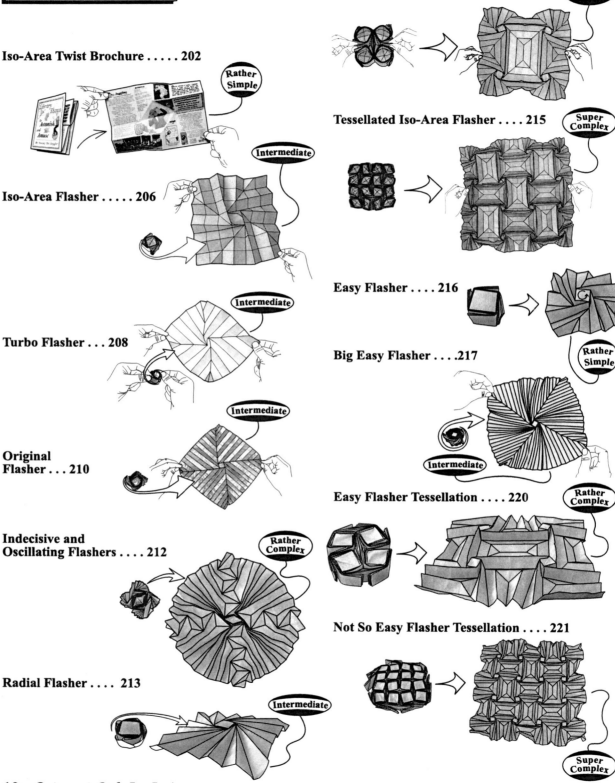

Contents **11**

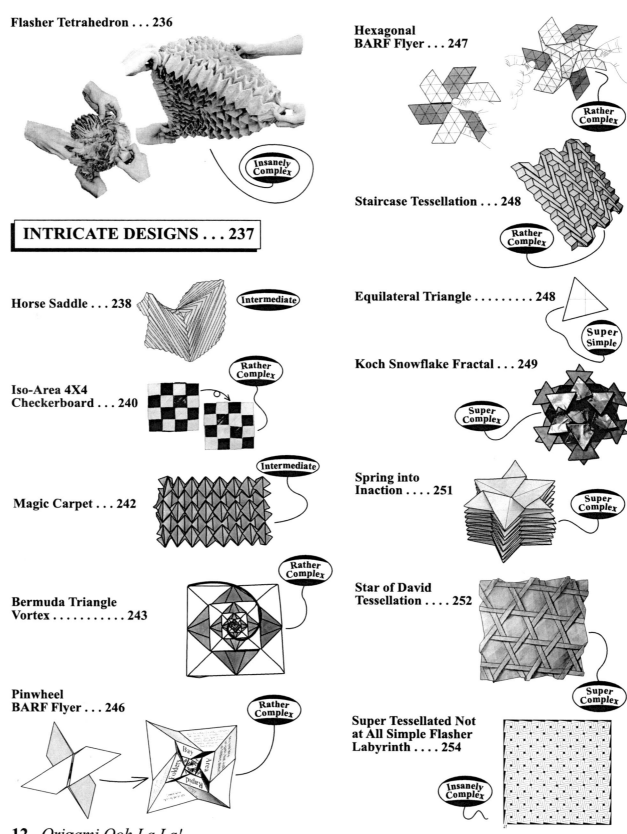

NOTATION

Line Styles

Valley Fold	‑ ‑ ‑ ‑ ‑ ‑ ‑ ‑ ‑ ‑ ‑ ‑
Mountain Fold	‑·‑··‑·‑··‑·‑··‑·‑
Crease	———————
Covered up edges or folds or where the paper ends up	·················

Arrows and Symbols

Fold from here to there	
Valley-fold and unfold	
Fold behind	
Fold behind and unfold	
Unfold	
Push in or Apply force	
Pleat-sink	
Open between these two layers	
Turn the model over	
Slide out paper from underneath	
Repeat once	
Repeat three times	
Rotate the model	180°
Exploded view—the next drawing will be larger	
Imploded view—the next drawing will be smaller	
Eyeball—the next drawing is from the point of view of this eyeball	
Focus on this spot	●
Inflate or blow	

Anatomy of the Origami Diagram

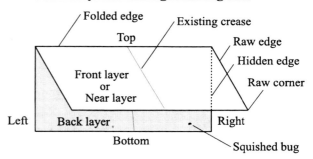

Tips for Following Diagrams

Make folds as precise as possible. Carefully line up each fold making sure it's exactly where it's supposed to be. Never approximate unless the diagram calls for it. Most of the models in this book are fully guidelined (i.e., there are landmarks for every fold). Any error made will get magnified; if the beginning folds of a model are off, the end folds will be REALLY off!

Look ahead to the next step. If, for instance, you're on step 4 of a model, your goal is to make the model look like the diagram in step 5. So before doing step 4, you should look at the diagram in step 5 to see what you're aiming for.

Orient the paper. Make sure the paper is oriented exactly as it is shown in the diagram.

Fold on a flat surface. Most folders, including myself, fold on a flat surface simply because it's easier.

Make sharp folds (unless otherwise stated). Fingernails are a good tool.

Don't get in over your head. All the models in the Contents are labeled Super Simple, Rather Simple, Intermediate, Rather Complex, Super Complex, and Insanely Complex.

If you are a beginning folder, it's a good idea to start with the super simple models. You're welcome to start out with the complex diagrams, but if you get stuck, before you tear up the paper out of frustration, please come back and attempt something easier.

Choosing Paper

There are thousands of varieties of paper, and most of them will work well for origami. A good test to find out if a certain paper is well-suited to origami, is to fold the corner of it back and forth ("Valley-fold, unfold, mountain-fold, unfold, valley-fold, etc."). If the paper doesn't break after 20 reverses, it's good for origami. If it does break, be thankful that you didn't buy a huge quantity! For the Flashers (pages 206-236), I recommend Wyndstone Marble paper, available at major art stores, but almost any paper that doesn't break easily is good.

For my show pieces I like to paint the paper with acrylic paint. This makes the model stronger, more colorful and also makes it water proof. Another technique to make the paper stronger is to laminate it. A cheap (but time consuming) method of laminating paper is to completely cover one side with clear packing tape.

Basics

This is a pictorial glossary showing how to do the basic folds which appear throughout origami diagrams. All origami maneuvers can be broken down into mountain folds and valley folds. Mountain folds, indicated by dot-dot-dash lines, are convex like a mountain ridge. Valley folds, indicated by dash-dash lines, are concave, like a valley.

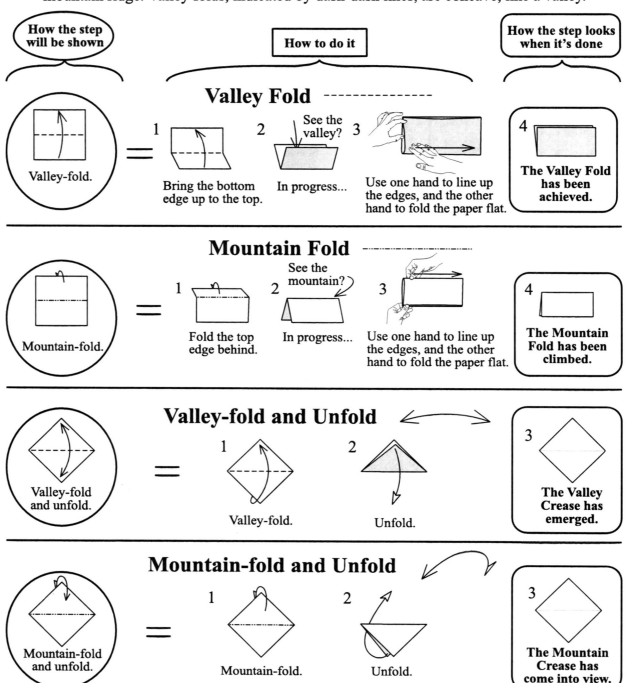

How the step will be shown

How to do it

How the step looks when it's done

Valley Fold

Valley-fold.

1 Bring the bottom edge up to the top.

2 In progress... See the valley?

3 Use one hand to line up the edges, and the other hand to fold the paper flat.

4 **The Valley Fold has been achieved.**

Mountain Fold

Mountain-fold.

1 Fold the top edge behind.

2 In progress... See the mountain?

3 Use one hand to line up the edges, and the other hand to fold the paper flat.

4 **The Mountain Fold has been climbed.**

Valley-fold and Unfold

Valley-fold and unfold.

1 Valley-fold.

2 Unfold.

3 **The Valley Crease has emerged.**

Mountain-fold and Unfold

Mountain-fold and unfold.

1 Mountain-fold.

2 Unfold.

3 **The Mountain Crease has come into view.**

Kite Base

 **=**

Fold a
Kite Base.

1

Begin with white side up.
Valley-fold and unfold in half.

2

Valley-fold to the
centerline.

3

**The Kite Base
has taken off.**

Rotate the model or

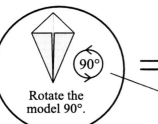 **=**

Rotate the
model 90°.

Note that the
arrows show which
direction to turn it.

**The model has
been rotated.**

To get ready for the next
fold, valley-fold the Kite
Base upward in half.

Inside Reverse Fold

 **=**

Inside-reverse-fold.

1

Valley-fold
and unfold.

2

Reach in and lift the point up
through the middle as shown.

3

Continue lifting.

4

Now flatten it along
the existing creases.

5

**The Inside Reverse
Fold has risen.**

Outside Reverse Fold

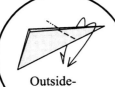 **=**

Outside-
reverse-fold.

1

Valley-fold
and unfold.

2

Unfold the kite
from behind.

3

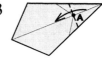

Valley-fold, so that the fold
line goes through point **A**.

4

Mountain-fold the
bottom half behind.

5

Rotate the small flap
counterclockwise in a hinge
action, so that the folds end
up on the existing creases.

6

**The Outside
Reverse Fold has
fallen into place.**

Pleat

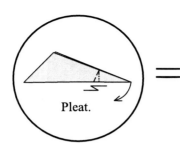 =

1

Valley-fold.

2

Valley-fold.

3

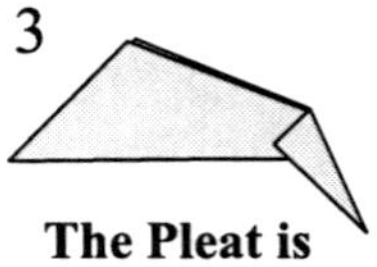

The Pleat is complete.

Crimp

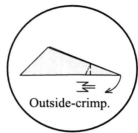 =

1

Pleat (shown above).

2

Unpleat. That means unfold the pleat.

3

Unfold the front layer downward.

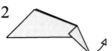

4

Valley-fold so that the fold goes through point **A.**

5

Valley-fold the point to the right on the existing crease.

6

Valley-fold the model in half.

7

Rotate the point down.

8

The Outside Crimp is created.

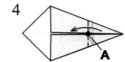

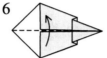

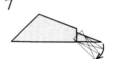

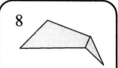

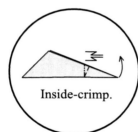 =

1

Perform steps 1–6 of the outside crimp.

2

Rotate the point up rather than down. To avoid tearing the paper it helps to open the model partially.

3

The Inside Crimp is crafted.

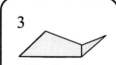

Squash Fold

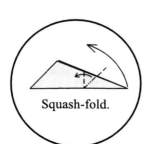 =

1

Valley-fold.

2

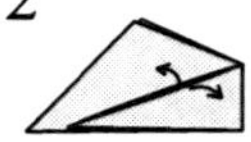

Puff out the pocket.

3

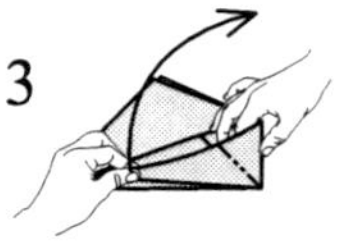

Lift the flap and squash it flat.

4

The Squash Fold has been committed.

Square Base

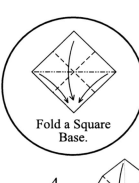

Fold a Square Base.

$=$

1

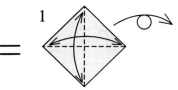

Colored side up. Valley-fold and unfold diagonally both ways. **Turn over.**

2

Valley-fold and unfold in half both ways.

3

Along existing creases, swing the three upper corners down to the lower corner. The following two steps show this fold in progress.

4

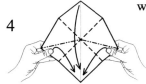

Step 3 slightly in progress. Continue bringing the three corners downward.

5

Step 3 further in progress. Flatten completely.

6

The Square Base has taken shape.

Note: For an alternate method of folding a Square Base, see page 102.

Petal Fold

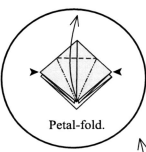

Petal-fold.

$=$

1

Begin with a Square Base. Valley-fold the left and right front flaps to the middle crease.

2

Valley-fold the top down.

3

Unfold the two flaps but leave the top folded down.

4

Lift the front flap slightly.

5

Keep lifting.

6

Here we have a boat. Collapse the sides of the boat to the middle line.

7

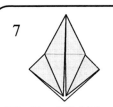

The Petal Fold has blossomed.

Fish Base or Rabbit Ear

Note: A rabbit ear is just one side of a Fish Base.

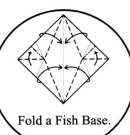

Fold a Fish Base.

$=$

1

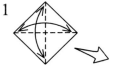

Begin with white side up. Valley-fold and unfold in half diagonally both ways.

2

Valley-fold.

3

Unfold.

4

Valley-fold and unfold.

5

Using existing creases, pinch the left and right corners so that they point toward you.

6

In progress.

7

Flatten the model.

8

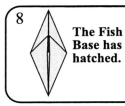

The Fish Base has hatched.

Waterbomb Base

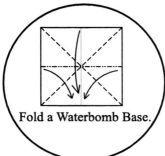

Fold a Waterbomb Base.

=

1

Begin colored side up. Valley-fold and unfold in half both ways. **Turn over.**

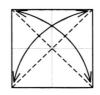

2

Valley-fold and unfold diagonally in half both ways.

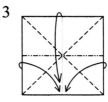

3

Bring the midpoints of the three upper sides down to the midpoint of the lower side.

4

In progress.

5

Even more progressive!

6

The Waterbomb Base has exploded into existence.

Sink ▼

Note: The sink arrowhead is also used when a point gets reverse-folded into the model.

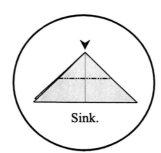

Sink.

=

1

Begin with a Waterbomb Base (see above). Valley-fold and unfold.

2

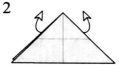

Completely unfold.

3

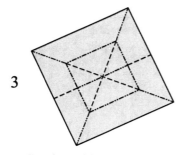

Starting with the mountains, make the indicated folds.

4

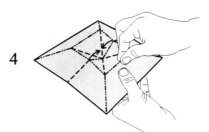

Mountain-pinching in progress. Return the paper to the configuration of step 1, but with the central portion pushed in.

5

The Sink is sunk.

Pleat Sink

Pleat-sinking is sinking a point multiple times. The Eight-Pointed Spiral Star (page 113) is a good model to learn pleat-sinking.

Simple Action

Could a performance captivate an audience if all the characters were frozen in space? Well, most exhibits in museums are as still as stone, and yet some do attract large audiences, but exhibits that have moving parts tend to grab even more attention. While origami is still primarily a still art, the performance of origami in this book is meant to be moving, and that does not mean making people cry!

Why are movies so popular? Because they move! Likewise, movement in origami adds another dimension and makes it that much more fun to watch and to do. Action models can be presented as a Show and Tell, or they can be incorporated into a story. They can also be taught, which in itself is like a performance. This chapter contains action models that are relatively simple to fold – a good place to begin! So now, on with the folds!

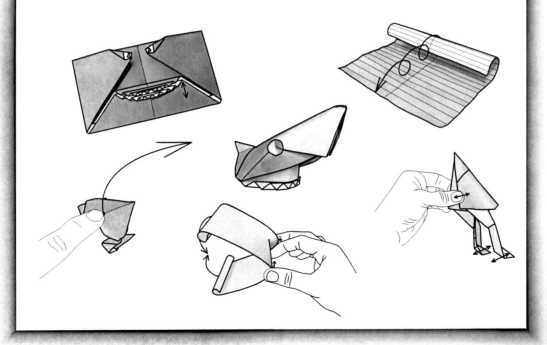

Monster Envelope

By Jeremy Shafer ©2004

Here's an envelope that's so scary, even the
mail carrier will be too scared to deliver it!

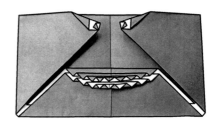

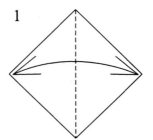

1

White side up,
valley-fold in half
vertically and unfold.

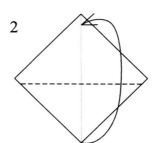

2

Valley-fold the
corner almost but not
all the way to the top.

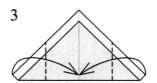

3

Valley-fold the
corners so that
they touch the
center crease.

4

Valley-fold the
shaded flap.

5

Valley-fold
the white flap
downward so
that all four
raw corners
are touching.

6

Valley-fold both
layers to the top.

7

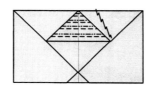

Pleat the double-layered flap
to taste, to form the mouth.
In other words, make lots of
mountains and valleys on the
flap so that the edges of the
flap form a zigzag monster
mouth.

8

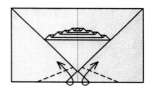

Valley-fold to taste
to form the eyes.

9

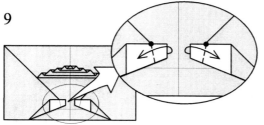

Valley-fold again to form pupils in the eyes.
The valley fold originates at the black dot.

10

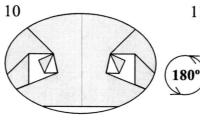

Like this. Rotate the
model 180°.

11

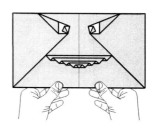

Holding as shown,
slide the top layer
downward, opening
the mouth slightly.

12

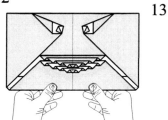

The Monster Envelope has appeared at your door step. To make the monster laugh hideously, slide the front layer up and down. Don't forget to add sound effects!

13

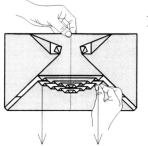

To make it extra scary, hold the outermost teeth as shown and pull the mouth down as far as it goes.

14

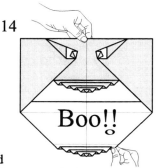

Boo!!

To make it super scary, write in big letters the word, *Boo!!*.

Note: To use as an envelope, insert a separate letter into the mouth of the beast. Who says envelopes need to open from the top?! If you really want to send it in through the mail, you'll probably need to secure it with clear tape.

PERFORM IT!

The Monster Envelope is one of my favorite models for teaching, which in itself can be like a performance, but you could also work the model into an act. Showing the back side of it, say to your audience, **"This envelope is alive! If you close your eyes, it will talk to you."** When they close their eyes, start talking in a monster voice, and then say in your normal voice, **"Open your eyes. Did you hear it?"** [Audience says, "That was you!"] Turn the model over and start talking again in the monster voice (using ventriloquism). Then say in your normal voice, **"You see, this Monster is real! I can even prove it to you."** Open it as shown in step 14 but with the word *REAL!* (instead of *Boo!*). After putting it back in the box, say, **"Wasn't that REAL scary?"**

Castanet (Super Simple) By Jeremy Shafer ©2005

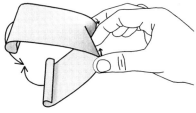

Make this model and bring sound to your fingertips!

1

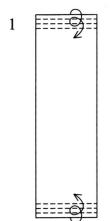

Begin with a rectangular sheet of **cardstock**, 8.5 inches by 11 inches. Roll both ends at least once around and do not flatten.

2

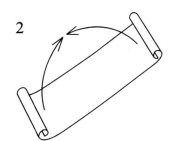

Bring both ends together so that they touch. Hold the model as shown in step three.

3

Done! Using your index finger make an indentation in the middle of the paper. Then, with your thumb and middle fingers, lightly squeeze the edges repeatedly. The two rolled up edges should repeatedly hit together and make a loud noise. If you practice enough, who knows, you might be able to join a Flamenco Band! If not, at least you'll be able to sufficiently annoy your friends.

PERFORM IT!

Say to the audience, **"Do you think you can clap faster than I can clap this castanet? Let's see. Ready, set, CLAP!"** [Audience claps as fast as they can.] Stop clapping the castanet, take a bow, and say, **"Thank you for the huge applause! What a wonderful audience!"**

Leaping Heart

By Jeremy Shafer ©2003

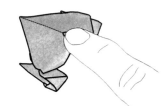

Here's a heart that thinks it's a frog. Fold this model and let your heart leap into love.

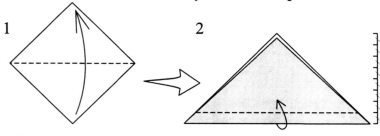

1. White side up, valley-fold in half diagonally.

2. Valley-fold. This fold does not need to be precise.

3. Valley-fold.

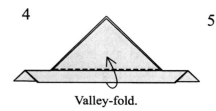

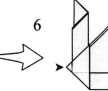

4. Valley-fold.

5. Valley-fold.

6. Reverse-fold the protruding paper. In other words, push in the tiny points.

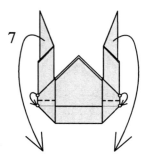

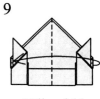

7. Valley-fold the legs dot-to-dot.

8. Valley-fold.

9. Valley-fold.

10. Reverse-fold. In other words, push in the point (with great force) and flatten.

11. **Done.** Open and place on a table as shown in step 12.

12.

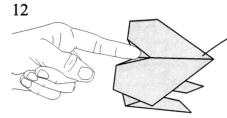

The leaping heart is ready to leap. Press downward as shown and release, and the heart will leap like a jumping frog.

PERFORM IT!

Choose a volunteer. Say to the audience, **"This is a leaping heart. It's going to make a dare-devil, death-defying leap off this human highdive and plunge over 1000 millimeters to the ground. Kids, don't try this at home! Get ready, set, everyone yell LEAP!"** [Audience yells, "LEAP!"] Make the heart leap off the volunteer's outstretched hand. Pick it up and exclaim, **"It survived!!! It sure is hearty!"**

Transforming Tent

By Jeremy Shafer ©2010

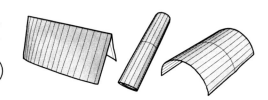

Super Simple

Here's a tent that transforms from the classical pointy tent into a totally tubular tube tent. And, if you fold it just right, it can transform into a stylishly arched round tent.

1

White side up, valley-fold in half and unfold.

2

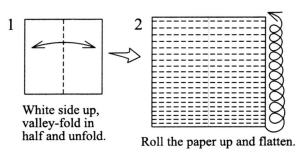

Roll the paper up and flatten.

3

Completely unroll the paper and rotate 90°. **90°**

4

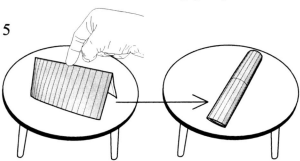

Valley-fold to form a tent and place it on the table as shown in the next step.

5

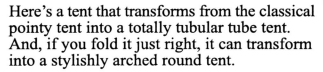

The Transforming Tent is ready to transform into a tube. Tap on the top edge of the tent and it will instantly transform into a tube. If the tent pops into a tube without touching it, then make the valley fold in step 4 sharper.

PERFORM IT!

Say to the audience, **"This is a magical pointy tent that turns into a telescope when you tap on it. Who wants to tap on it?"** Choose a volunteer to tap on it and when it transforms, hold it up, look through it and say, **"It's a telescope! I see a whole bunch of young stars! Everyone say, 'Totally Tubular!'"**

Tap Trap

This model can be used to play a game I made up called Tap Trap, in which players take turns tapping on top of the tent gradually moving it downward until – "Pop!" – the tent turns into a tube. Each tap has to visibly push the tent downward. The player that triggers the trap is eliminated! **Number of Players: 2 to ∞**

6

For the "pointy tent to round tent" effect, do steps 1-3 but when you unroll the model, flatten it out so much that its natural resting position is as shown above. Then, do step 4.

7

It's a pointy tent that, when you push down and release, turns into a round tent, or, perhaps, an airplane hangar for your imaginary miniature paper airplane collection, which just got squished when you pushed down!

Ocean Wave (Super Simple) By Jeremy Shafer ©2010

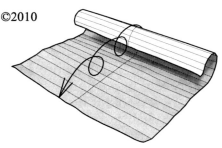

Here is an origami model that simulates how ocean waves form. How do they form? Wind blows across the ocean, which forms little ripples, and the little ripples join together to form bigger ripples, and they keep growing until they become full blown waves, which eventually crash upon the shore.

In this wave model, the ripples are represented by lots of valley folds, all of which are curving the paper in the same direction. Each valley fold on its own can't do much, but when they are all acting together, they join forces to trigger a giant crashing wave!

1

Colored side up, roll up the paper and flatten.

2

Completely unroll the paper.

3

Valley-fold the paper in half and unfold, but don't unfold completely; keep the valley fold folded just enough that the paper will not roll up on its own.

4

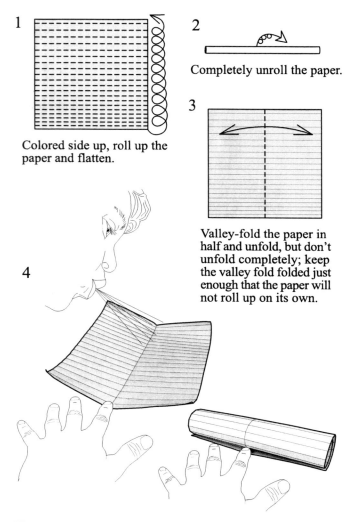

The ocean looks calm, but, beware, a storm is brewing, and a big wave is about to form. Here it comes! Holding as shown, blow onto the far side of the paper, which will trigger the wave to roll to shore and crash upon your finger.

Magic Reverse Fold

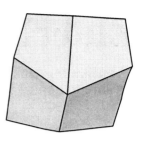

By Jeremy Shafer ©2010

This is a sister model to the Magic Cube (*Origami to Astonish and Amuse*, page 38), as they both make use of the same optical illusion.

1

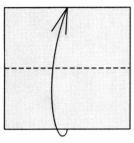

For a colored model, begin colored side up. For a white model, begin white side up. Valley-fold the square in half.

2

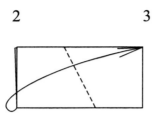

Valley-fold corner-to-corner.

3

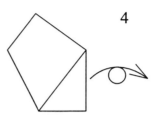

Completely unfold and **turn over**.

4

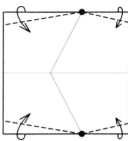

White side up, valley-fold on the black dots. These folds are "to taste," which means the exact placement of the folds is up to you.

5

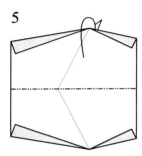

Mountain-fold.

6

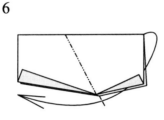

Reverse-fold.
(For help, see Inside Reverse Fold, page 15)

7

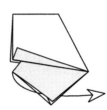

Unfold but do not flatten and do not unfold the folds made in step 4.

8

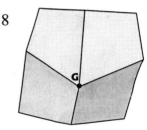

Done! Stare at the model with one eye closed, and try to visually invert it, making point **G** look as if it is convex instead of concave. When it is inverted, move left and right and the model will look as if it too is moving left and right.

PERFORM IT!

Performing with this model is really not appropriate for a kids show because kids probably won't be able to see the illusion. But for adult-only audiences, especially during cocktail hour, it should work like a charm. Have your audience stand over the model, and say to them, **"Close one eye, stare at the figure, and try to make spot G pop out at you. Once that's achieved, move left and right while still staring at the same spot. The whole figure should appear to rotate left and right as you move."** Say to whoever can't get it to work, **"That's OK, maybe you should try again later when you are more rested."**

Elderly Venus Flytrap

Super Simple

By Jose Tomas Buitrago

At just nine steps long, this two-toothed Flytrap
is sure to appeal to barflies.

1

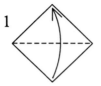

White side up,
valley-fold in
half diagonally.

2

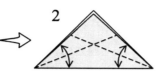

Valley-fold and unfold
on the front layer only.

3

Valley-fold the corners to the
black zits at the ends of the
creases made in the last step.

4

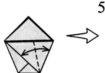

Valley-fold
and unfold,
bisectingly.

5

Squash!!!
(For help, see
Squash Fold,
page 16.)

6

Petal-fold.
(For help, see
Petal Fold,
page 17.)

7

A leaf has formed.
Mountain-fold the
right side of it behind.

8

Repeat steps
4-7 on the
left side.

9

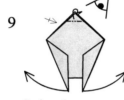

Swing the two
leaves apart. Form
two front teeth by
folding the tips of
the two raw corners.
Rotate 180°.

180°

10

The Elderly Venus Flytrap has
reached it's prime – only two teeth
left. When the flytrap is hungry,
simply pull the leaves apart...

Ready...

Set...

ATTACK of Grandpa Flytrap!
Now, let go and watch Grandpa try
to gum his prey.

PERFORM IT!

Say to the audience, **"This is a Grandpa
Venus Flytrap, because it has only two
teeth. Who wants to give Grandpa
Flytrap a BIG kiss?"** Open and close the
model in front of the kids and watch them
squirm to get away. Say, **"Why don't you
want to kiss Grandpa Flytrap? Let me
guess. It's because you all have cooties
and you don't want him to get them."**

Diagrammed by Jeremy Shafer, 1998.

Papercutter (Super Simple)

Ideal for Vampires with Toothaches

Here's a model that won't cut paper, but it can give you a fabulous paper cut. For best results, use razor sharp paper.

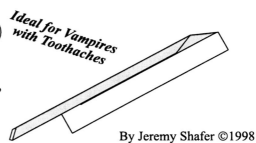

By Jeremy Shafer ©1998

1

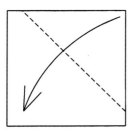

Begin white side up. Valley-fold to taste.

2

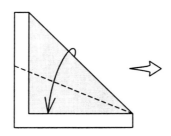

Valley-fold.

3

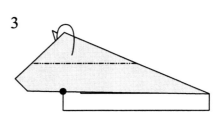

Mountain-fold. The top corner goes to the black dot.

4

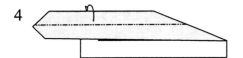

Mountain-fold.

5

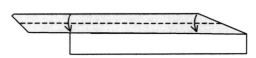

Valley-fold.

6

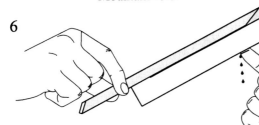

The Papercutter has been constructed. Tender uncallused fingers are the easiest to cut. In a quick motion, slide the blade across the surface to be cut. Repeat the above procedure as desired. Please donate the proceeds from this model to your local blood bank.

Warning: The Surgeon General has determined that repeatedly operating this model could be hazardous to your health or the health of those around you. Prolonged use is not advised.

Disclaimer: The Author will not be held responsible for unsupervised children who take this model seriously.

PERFORM IT!

Say to the audience, **"This is a papercutter because it's made out of paper. What shall we cut with the papercutter? How about an invisible watermelon? Ready, set... Everyone say, 'CUT!'"** Slice the invisible watermelon (or other imaginary object) into lots of pieces and say, **"Who would like a slice of invisible watermelon?"**

PERFORM IT!

Say to the audience, **"This is a papercutter. Everyone raise your hand..."** <pause> **"...if you would like a papercut?"** Pretend to cut everyone's raised hands.

Atom Smasher

A.K.A. Super Collider (Rather Simple)

By Jeremy Shafer ©2008

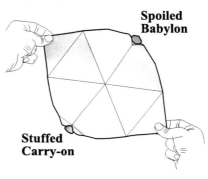

Spoiled Babylon

Stuffed Carry-on

Thanks to billion-dollar accelerators, A.K.A., atom smashers, all sorts of sub-atomic particles have been discovered – protons, neutrons, electrons, bosons, fermions, leptons, charmed baryons and anti-charmed baryons, etc. – but the question of whether they are dealing with particles or waves still can't be answered by even the best particle physicists (or, shall I say, wave physicists). Now, you can have your very own origami atom smasher, and you too can make up funny names for the particles that you smash.

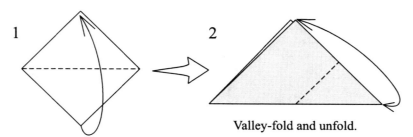

1

White side up, valley-fold diagonally in half.

2

Valley-fold and unfold.

3

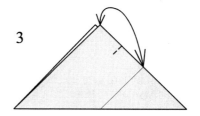

Valley-pinch and unpinch forming a creasemark.

4

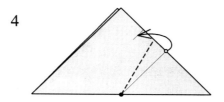

Valley-fold the white dot to the creasemark. The fold originates at the black dot.

5

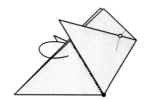

Mountain-fold on the black dot, lining up the fold with the edge of the front flap.

6

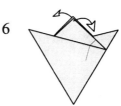

Completely unfold the model.

7

Valley-fold on the existing crease.

8

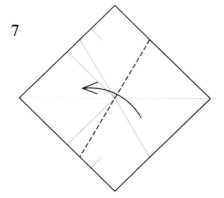

Valley-fold the left corner. **Repeat behind on the indicated corner.**

9

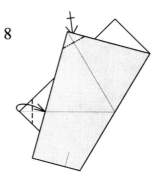

Valley-fold on the existing crease.

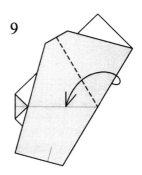

10

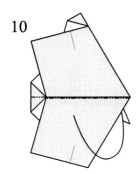

Mountain-fold on the existing crease.

11

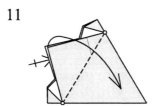

Valley-fold the front flap on the white dots. **Repeat behind.**

12

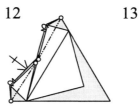

Mountain-fold the front flaps on the white dots, tucking them inside. **Repeat behind.**

13

Valley-fold on the white dots. These folds are perpendicular to the shaded edges.

14

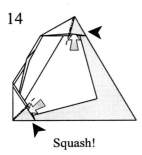

Squash!

15

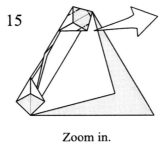

Zoom in.

16

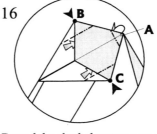

Round the shaded area to taste. To do this, first mountain-fold flap **A** (single layer). Then, reverse-fold points **B** and **C**; in other words, push in the corners and flatten.

17

Round the heptagon further with mountain folds if desired. One atom is done! Repeat steps 15-17 on the other side to form a second atom.

18

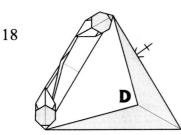

The Atom Smasher is constructed. To smash the atoms together, hold the front flap at point **D** with one hand, and with the other hand hold the rear flap similarly. Pull your hands apart and the dots will pass by each other and get into ready position.

19

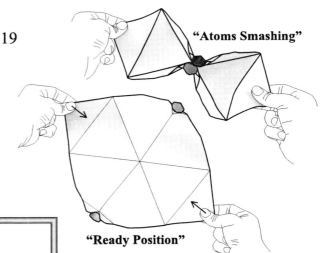

"Atoms Smashing"

"Ready Position"

Collide the dots by pushing your hands together. To make them pass by each other, rotate both hands clockwise (or counterclockwise) as you push them together. Who knows, if you push them together fast enough (at nearly double the speed of light) you could discover the elusive Higgs Boson particle! But, more likely, you'd just discover that both wrists are broken from jerking your hands together so quickly!

PERFORM IT!

Say to the audience, **"This is a giant atom smasher, and these are two giant atoms! They are trillions of times bigger than normal atoms, and they are going to collide in a few seconds!"** Explain to your audience that most atoms in atom smashers pass by very near to each other but don't collide. But if you fire billions of atoms at each other, eventually some of them do smash into each other and go "Boom!" Have the audience say, "BOOM!" as you collide the atoms, and finish by saying, **"And now you know what particle scientists do all day!"**

Fatal Attraction (Rather Simple)

By Jeremy Shafer ©2008

This model illustrates fundamental laws of electro-magnetism, particle physics, astrophysics, and, yes, even origami physics. Nobody knows for sure why oppositely charged particles attract one another, or why black holes eat up innocent little stars, or why *origami physics* isn't even on Wikipedia, but what is clear is that the attraction between the colored dot and white dot on this model is an undeniable, unavoidable, **fatal** attraction!

1

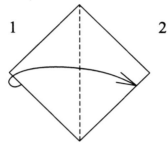

White side up, valley-fold diagonally in half.

2

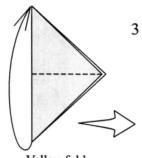

Valley-fold.

3

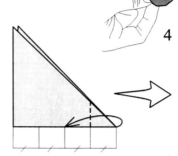

Valley-fold.

4

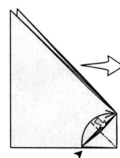

Open the pocket and squash it squarely.

5

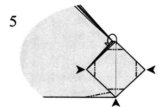

Close-up of the resulting square squash. Round the square to taste. To do this, first mountain-fold the top corner (both layers). Then reverse-fold (push in) the left and right corners and sink (push in) the bottom. (For help, see Sink, page 18)

6

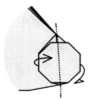

Rotate the octagon so that it faces to the right. The model will no longer lie flat.

7

Like this.

9

Fatal Attraction is finished! Pull the two dots apart, and let go of them, and they will not only snap back together, but the colored dot will consume the white dot, which is another reason why it's called Fatal Attraction! This model provides teachers with a model to illustrate various scientific phenomena, and provides kids with a fun, pseudo-magnetic toy. It could also prove to be a powerful romantic tool, especially if you turn the dots into hearts (see Heart Carousel, page 103).

8

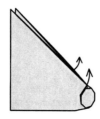

Reach in and, like a hero, free the trapped white octagon from the dark octagon's fierce, unyielding grip.

PERFORM IT!

Say to the audience, **"This model has a really long name. Let's all say it together, ELECTROMAGNETISM."** [Audience says, "ELECTRO-MAGNETISM"] **"But you can call it a MAGNET for short."** Holding the two dots apart, say, **"This blue atom has too many electrons and wants to get rid of them, while this white atom doesn't have enough and wants more. So they have to get together and make the trade. Here they go! Ready, set... everyone say 'GO!'"** [Audience says, "GO!"] Let go, making the two dots snap together and say, **"You see, they got pulled together by... what is it called? ELECTROMAGNETISM! Tell your parents that today at this show you learned about electromagnetism, and they should be very impressed."**

Running Nose (Rather Simple)

By Jeremy Shafer ©2004

Look out! From around the bend, comes the snot monster. Run while you still can!

"It's a bird! It's a plane! No, it's the BOOGER MONSTER! Please remain seated. It's snot about to get you!"

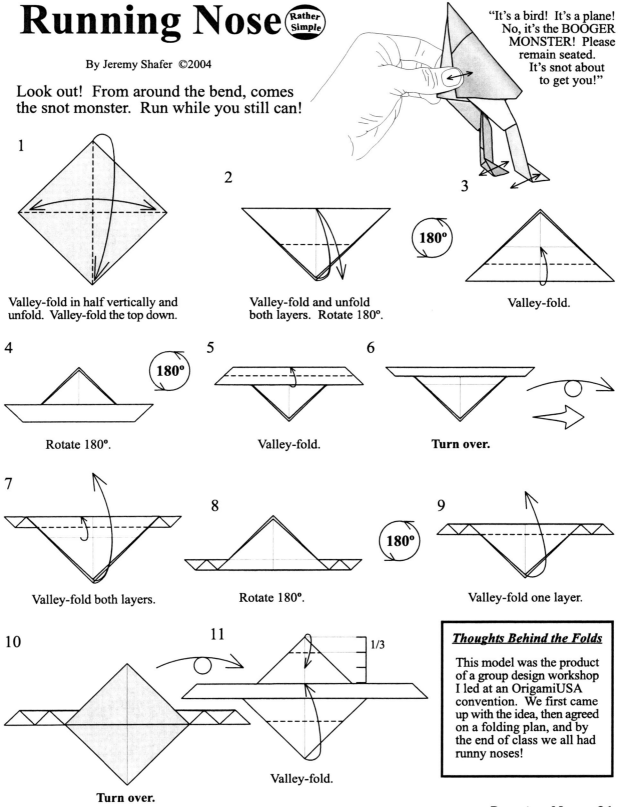

1
Valley-fold in half vertically and unfold. Valley-fold the top down.

2
Valley-fold and unfold both layers. Rotate 180°.

3
Valley-fold.

4
Rotate 180°.

5
Valley-fold.

6
Turn over.

7
Valley-fold both layers.

8
Rotate 180°.

9
Valley-fold one layer.

10
Turn over.

11
Valley-fold.

1/3

Thoughts Behind the Folds

This model was the product of a group design workshop I led at an OrigamiUSA convention. We first came up with the idea, then agreed on a folding plan, and by the end of class we all had runny noses!

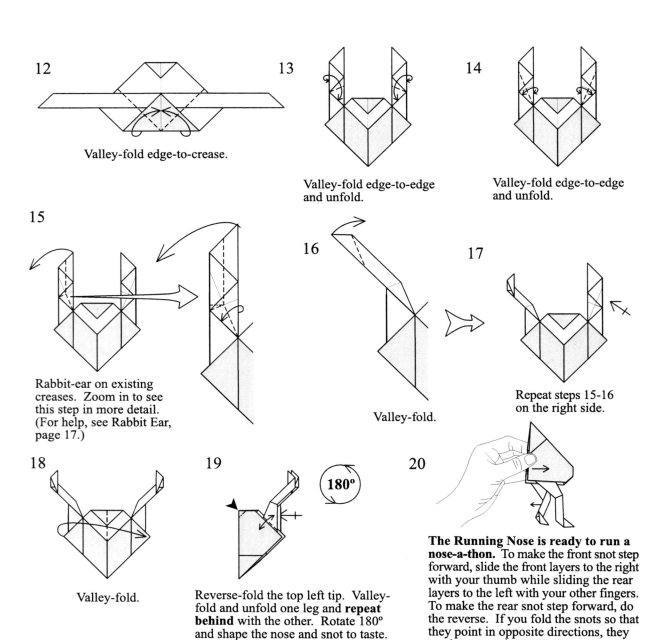

12

Valley-fold edge-to-crease.

13

Valley-fold edge-to-edge and unfold.

14

Valley-fold edge-to-edge and unfold.

15

Rabbit-ear on existing creases. Zoom in to see this step in more detail. (For help, see Rabbit Ear, page 17.)

16

Valley-fold.

17

Repeat steps 15-16 on the right side.

18

Valley-fold.

19

180°

Reverse-fold the top left tip. Valley-fold and unfold one leg and **repeat behind** with the other. Rotate 180° and shape the nose and snot to taste.

20

The Running Nose is ready to run a nose-a-thon. To make the front snot step forward, slide the front layers to the right with your thumb while sliding the rear layers to the left with your other fingers. To make the rear snot step forward, do the reverse. If you fold the snots so that they point in opposite directions, they can become wings. You can say, **"So you've heard of *the nose of a plane*... Well, this is just a *plane nose*."**

PERFORM IT!

Ask the audience, **"Who KNOWS what this is?"** Repeat the question until someone guesses, *nose*. Ask, **"What kind of nose?"** After the audience (or you) answers *Runny Nose*, say, **"We'd better wipe it with a tissue!"** As you are wiping it, point to the legs and ask the audience, **"What are these?"** To whatever the audience guesses, respond, **"No, it'S NOT!   Get it? No, it's snot!"** If you have any Spanish speakers in the audience you can say this joke: **"How do you say nose in Spanish? No se."**

Talking Fortune Cookie (Rather Simple)

This fortune cookie might not be as tasty as those in the restaurant, but it can tell many more fortunes!

By Jeremy Shafer ©2003

Inspired by Madeline Schiller's search for origami fortune cookie diagrams

Note: If you can find or make circular paper, you can skip steps 2 and 3. Or, you can skip all of the steps by folding the crease pattern shown to the right, but the model might not stay closed unless it's wetfolded. This model ends up with the same folds as a real fortune cookie, so if you want to see a finished model, simply go to a Chinese restaurant and ask for the check!

1

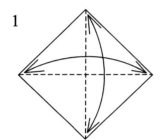

For the most realistic fortune cookie, begin with a three-inch square, white side up. Valley-fold and unfold both ways in half.

2

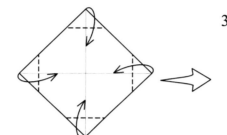

Valley-fold the four corners, estimating a regular octagon.

3

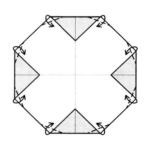

Valley-fold the eight corners estimating a regular 16-gon.

4

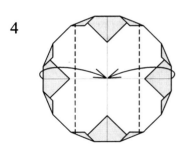

Valley-fold.

5

Turn over.

6

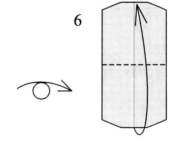

Valley-fold in half.

7

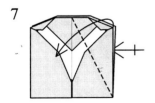

Valley-fold.
Repeat behind.

8

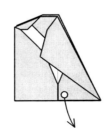

Hold at the white dot and pull down all the way.

9

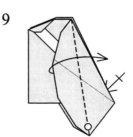

Valley-fold.
Repeat behind.

10

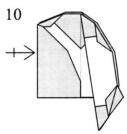

Repeat steps 7-9 on the left side.

11

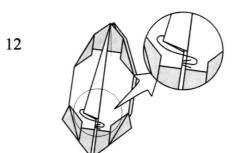

Pleat. This fold, which will come undone when the mouth opens (step 17), serves to enhance the snapping-closed action of the mouth.

12

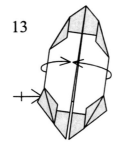

Hide the flap.

13

Fold the two flaps together. **Repeat behind.** The model will not lie flat.

14

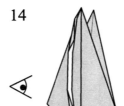

Look from the left side.

15

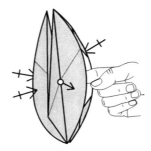

Reach in and push the white circle outward to round the fortune cookie. **Repeat on the other three such edges.**

PERFORM IT!

Say to the audience, "**This is a talking fortune cookie. Who would like to have their fortunes told?**" Go up close to your volunteer and ventriloquistically make the fortune cookie say, "**You will see some very unusual origami models that will make you smile...**" You say, "**Hey, your fortune is already coming true! How about another fortune...**" Fortune cookie says: "**You will give the entertainer your next 10 allowances!**" You say to the volunteer, "**Gosh, that is so nice of you! Thank you! Your next 10 allowances – that really is a fortune! I'll be rich!**"

16

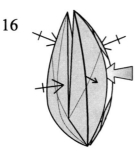

Reach in and puff out the boldly diagrammed edge. **Repeat on the other three such edges,** sculpting the perfect fortune cookie. For an even more perfect fortune cookie, fold the model again, but avoid making the extra creases (steps 1, 4, 7, 9).

17

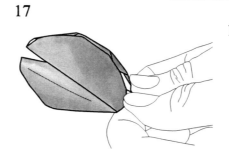

The Fortune Cookie is ready to tell fortunes. Holding from the back of the model as shown, pull the two sides apart, and the mouth snaps open.

18

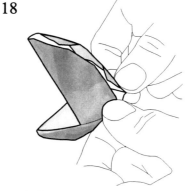

Push the two sides together and the mouth snaps closed. This model can also be called Hungry Fortune Cookie, Pac Man, or Hungry Moon.

34 *Origami Ooh La La!*

By Jeremy Shafer ©2005

Pregnant Mountain (Super Simple)

Fertile Origami!

This model is ideal for storytime or Show and Tell.
The mountains seem to come out of nowhere!

1

Begin by folding a white
Waterbomb base. (For help, see
Waterbomb Base, page 18, but
remember to reverse the color).

2

Completely unfold
the model.

3

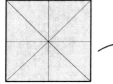

Turn over.

4

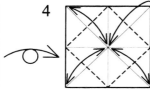

Valley-fold the top right corner
to the center. Valley-fold and
unfold the other three corners.

5

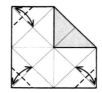

Valley-fold
and unfold.

6

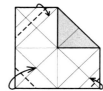

Valley-fold the bottom corners
to the indicated creases.
Valley-fold the top left corner
so that the shorter crease
touches the longer crease.

7

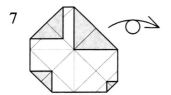

Turn over.

8

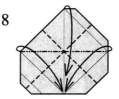

On the existing
creases, reform the
Waterbomb Base.

9

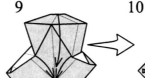

Step 8 in
progress.

10

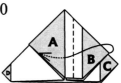

Valley-fold, inserting
triangle **B** completely into
the pocket of triangle **A**.

PERFORM IT!

Hold up the finished model (step 15) and ask the audience, **"What's this?"** [Audience guesses, "Triangle."]
Say, **"No, it's a mountain. But what kind of mountain?"** [Audience guesses, "Purple Mountain."]
Say, **"No, it's a pregnant mountain! And look, it's going into labor! Everyone shout, 'PUSH!'"**
[Audience shouts, "PUSH!"] Perform step 15 and exclaim, **"It's a girl! A girl mountain. Millions
of years later... guess what... the girl is pregnant! Everyone, shout, 'Push!'** [Audience shouts
"PUSH!"] Pull out the next triangle and exclaim, **"It's a girl! Another girl mountain. Millions of
years later... now this girl mountain is pregnant. Everyone, shout, 'Push!'"** [Audience shouts
"PUSH!"] Pull out the last triangle and exclaim, **"It's a boy! Don't worry, it won't get pregnant.
And, that is your geology lesson for today."**

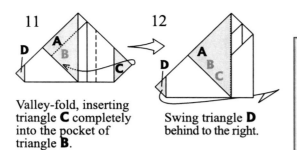

11

Valley-fold, inserting triangle **C** completely into the pocket of triangle **B**.

12

Swing triangle **D** behind to the right.

13

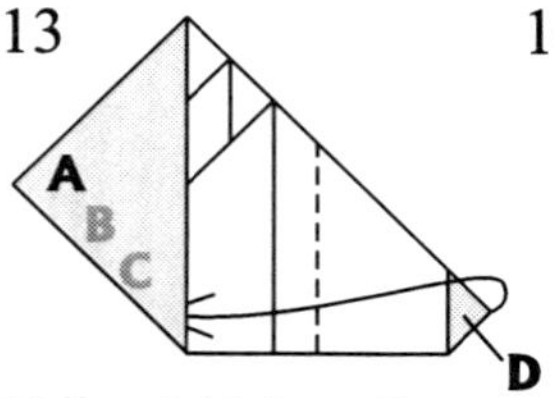

Valley-fold, inserting triangle **D** completely into the pocket of triangle **C**.

14

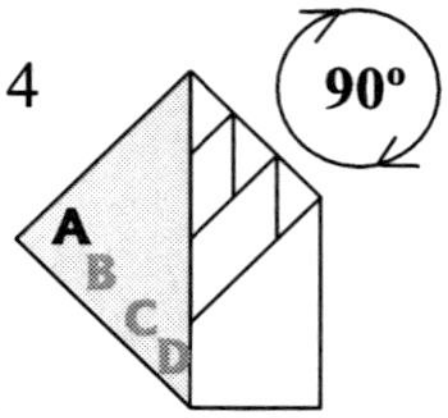

90°

Rotate 90°.

15

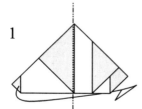

It's a labor of love!

The Pregnant Mountain is ready to give birth. Pull out Triangle **B**.

16

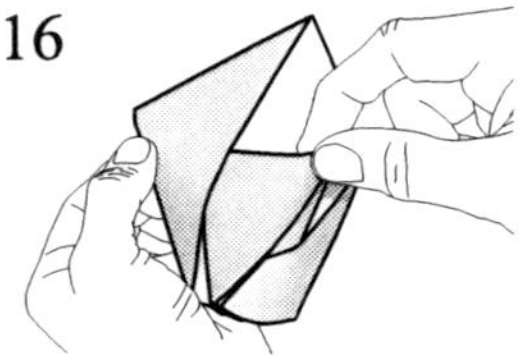

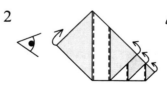

The Pregnant Mountain is giving birth! It's a girl! Repeat until all four mountains are visible.

Mountain Range (Super Simple)
By Jeremy Shafer ©2005

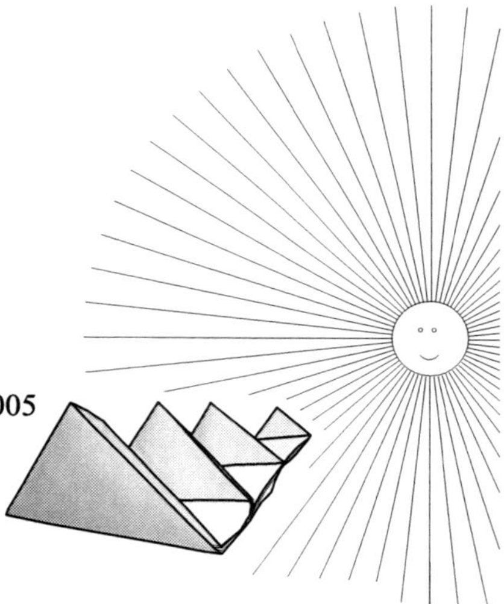

1

Begin by folding steps 1-9 of the Pregnant Mountain. Fold the left flap behind to the right.

2

Fold all of the triangles so that they stick out, and view the model from the left.

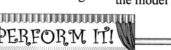

3

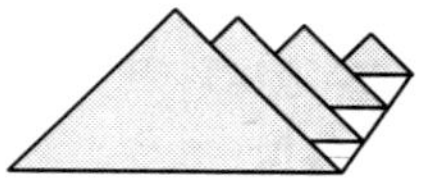

The Mountain Range has evolved, and it didn't even take 200 million years! This is also an action model. For the action, move the model very very slowly as to simulate continental drift.

Folding Chair By Jeremy Shafer ©2001

This chair is about as portable as it gets, but, if made out of paper, will probably only support the weight of the lightest paper dolls. For a sturdier chair, use heavy-duty sheet metal and a blow torch, but do so at your own risk. Apply hinges to all the joints to allow it to fold up. To avoid the headache of such a mammoth project, you might want to simply go out and buy a standard metal folding chair or settle for this paper version.

1

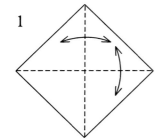

White side up, valley-fold and unfold diagonally in half both ways.

2

Valley-fold and unfold.

3

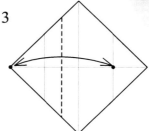

Valley-fold dot-to-dot and unfold.

4

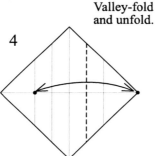

Valley-fold dot-to-dot and unfold.

5

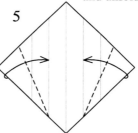

Valley-fold edge-to-crease.

6

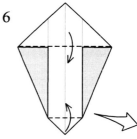

Valley-fold.

7

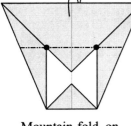

Mountain-fold, on the two black dots.

8

Valley-fold edge-to-edge.

9

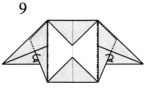

Mountain-fold the flaps behind, going underneath the front layer.

10

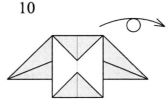

Turn over.

11

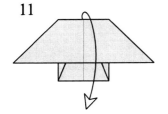

Unfold the front flap.

12

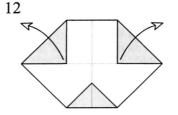

Unfold the two flaps.

13

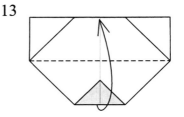

Valley-fold.

Folding Chair **37**

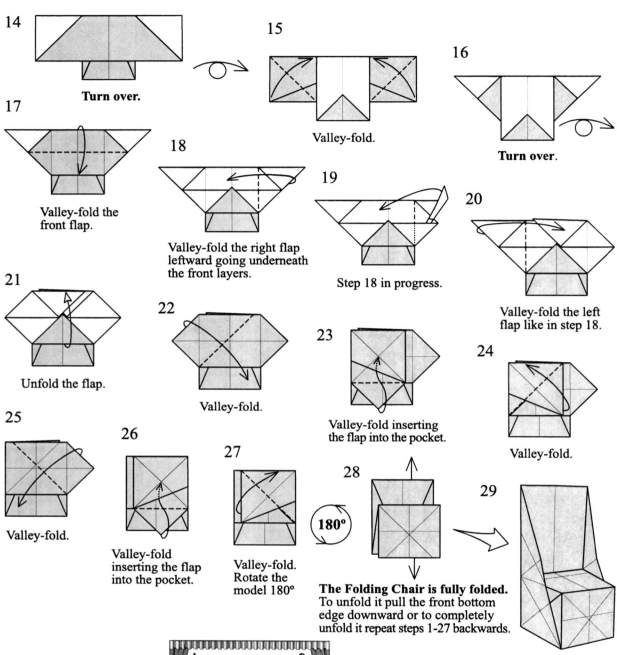

14

Turn over.

15

Valley-fold.

16

Turn over.

17

Valley-fold the front flap.

18

Valley-fold the right flap leftward going underneath the front layers.

19

Step 18 in progress.

20

Valley-fold the left flap like in step 18.

21

Unfold the flap.

22

Valley-fold.

23

Valley-fold inserting the flap into the pocket.

24

Valley-fold.

25

Valley-fold.

26

Valley-fold inserting the flap into the pocket.

27

Valley-fold. Rotate the model 180°.

28

180°

The Folding Chair is fully folded. To unfold it pull the front bottom edge downward or to completely unfold it repeat steps 1-27 backwards.

29

The Folding Chair has been folded and unfolded!

PERFORM IT!

Say to the audience, **"This is an origami folding chair and I am going to now demonstrate what a wonderful folding chair it is by sitting in it. Ready, set... Everyone say, 'SIT!'"** [Audience says, "SIT!"] Sit on the chair, crumpling it flat. Pull it out and say, **"Uh oh, I guess I must weigh too much for this chair because I completely squashed it!"** Try to open it out into a chair again and say, **"It still works! It's now just a very complex folding chair!"**

Shark Attack

Rather Simple

By Jeremy Shafer ©2002

Watch out! Here comes a pair of jaws that will rip your papers to bits and pieces! Three-inch kami is particularly at risk, but even six-inch foil has been devoured on more than one occasion.

1

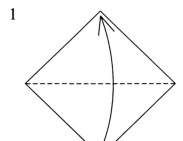

White side up, Valley-fold in half diagonally.

2

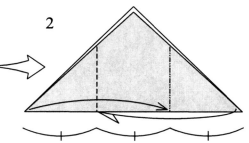

Divide the base of the model into thirds by folding the left side in front and the right side behind.

3

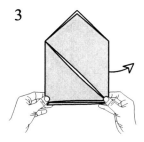

Fiddle with the folds until the thirds are exact. Then unfold the back flap.

4

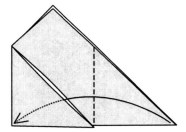

Valley-fold, inserting the flap into the pocket.

5

Valley-fold on the left. Valley-fold and unfold on the right.

6

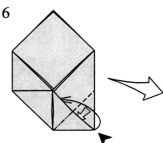

Reverse-fold.

7

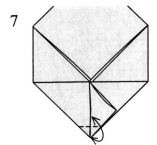

The bottom point will form the nose of the shark which needs to be less pointy. So, valley-fold to taste and unfold.

8

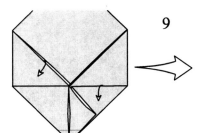

Pull the indicated edges so that they stick out.

9

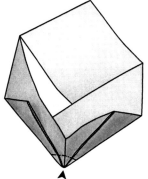

3D View. Closed-sink the bottom point. In other words, shove it inward.

Shark Attack **39**

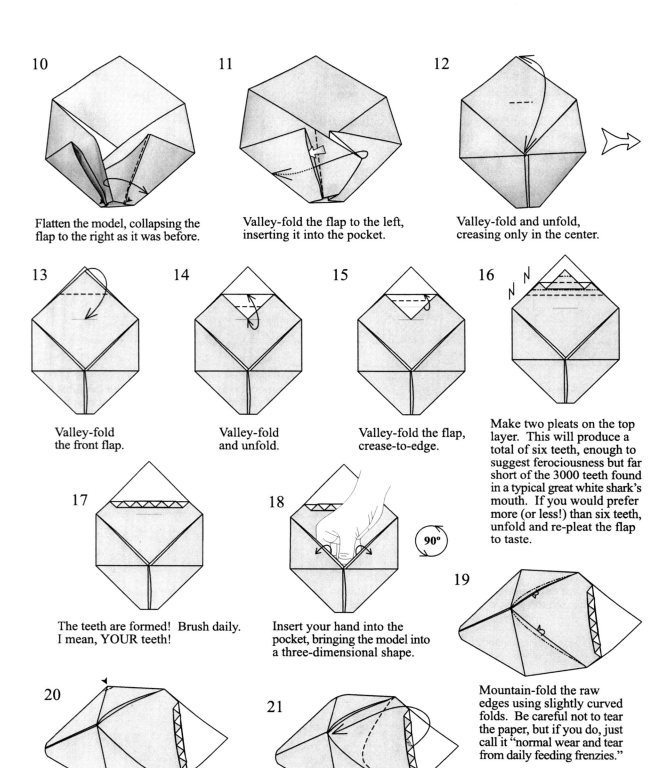

10

Flatten the model, collapsing the flap to the right as it was before.

11

Valley-fold the flap to the left, inserting it into the pocket.

12

Valley-fold and unfold, creasing only in the center.

13

Valley-fold the front flap.

14

Valley-fold and unfold.

15

Valley-fold the flap, crease-to-edge.

16

Make two pleats on the top layer. This will produce a total of six teeth, enough to suggest ferociousness but far short of the 3000 teeth found in a typical great white shark's mouth. If you would prefer more (or less!) than six teeth, unfold and re-pleat the flap to taste.

17

The teeth are formed! Brush daily. I mean, YOUR teeth!

18

Insert your hand into the pocket, bringing the model into a three-dimensional shape.

90°

19

Mountain-fold the raw edges using slightly curved folds. Be careful not to tear the paper, but if you do, just call it "normal wear and tear from daily feeding frenzies."

20

Closed-sink the two corners. In other words, push them in.

21

Valley-fold the jaw flap, making a curved fold. The more curved the fold, the more round the back of the shark will be.

22

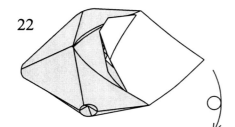

Turn over top to bottom.

23

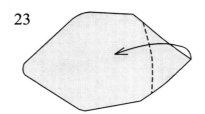

Valley-fold.

24

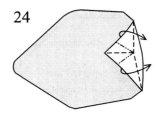

Rabbit-ear the flap to taste
to form a dorsal fin.

25

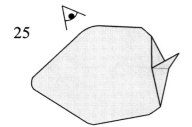

Look at the model
from the side.

26

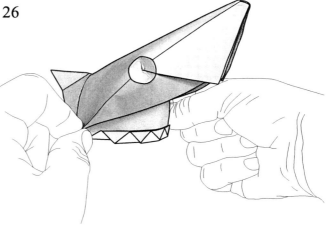

> **Note:** This model can also be fashioned
> into a stylish Shark Attack Hat.

The Shark Attack is ready to be orchestrated.
Holding at the sides as shown, push your hands
together and the jaws will shut. Adjust the curved
valley-fold in step 21 to optimize the jaw movement.

PERFORM IT!

Hold the completed model up and ask the audience,
"What is this?" [Audience says, "A Shark."] Say, **"No,
it's a shark attack! Everyone shout, 'SHARK
ATTACK!'"** [Audience shouts, "SHARK ATTACK!"]
Make the shark attack the audience as you say, **"Quick,
everyone out of the water!"** Put the Shark back in the
box and say, **"Is everyone out? Looks like everyone
IS out of the water. I'm glad we all got out of the
water safely!"** If any kids call out, **"But there is no
water!,"** then spraying them with your bottle of water is
the correct thing to do.

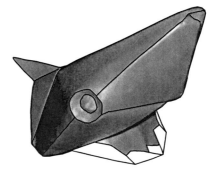

Here's an earlier version of the
Shark Attack featuring double
sunk eyes and pleatless teeth.

The Chomper

By Jeremy Shafer ©2010

Rather Simple

This model will dutifully fulfill all of your chomping needs!

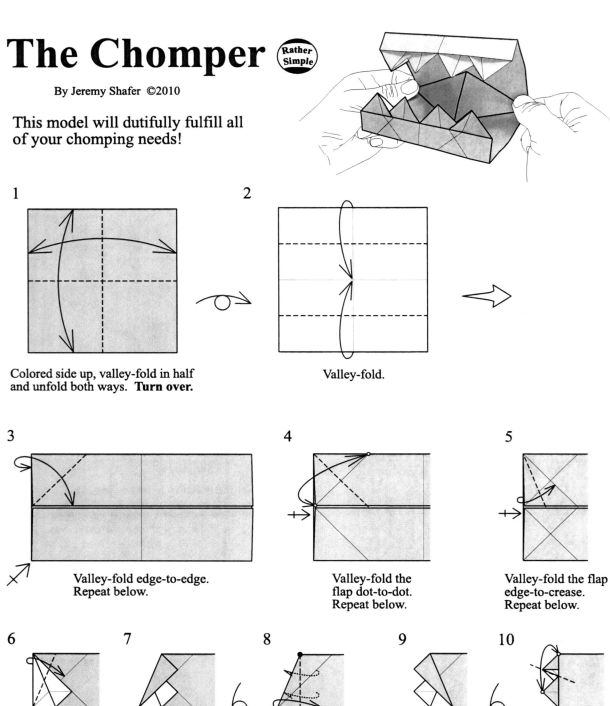

1
Colored side up, valley-fold in half and unfold both ways. **Turn over.**

2
Valley-fold.

3
Valley-fold edge-to-edge. Repeat below.

4
Valley-fold the flap dot-to-dot. Repeat below.

5
Valley-fold the flap edge-to-crease. Repeat below.

6
Valley-fold edge-to-crease. Repeat below.

7
Turn over top to bottom.

8
Valley-fold on the black dots letting the rear flaps swing into view.

9
Turn over.

10
Valley-fold dot-to-dot.

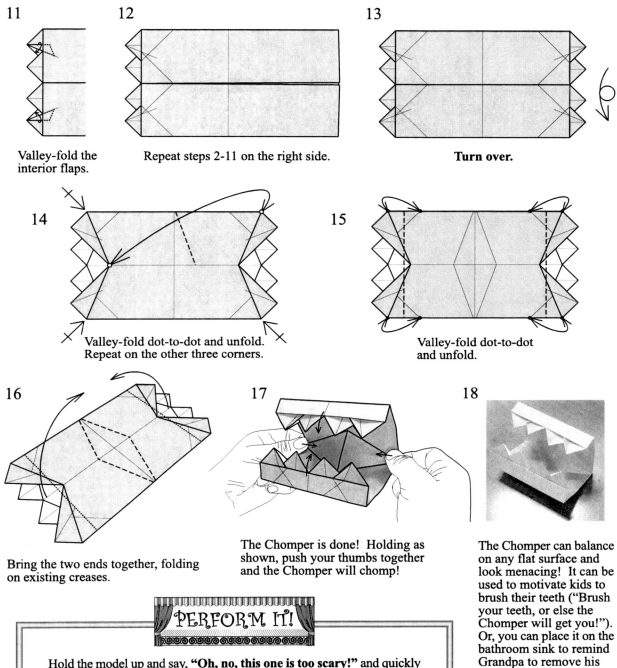

11

Valley-fold the interior flaps.

12

Repeat steps 2-11 on the right side.

13

Turn over.

14

Valley-fold dot-to-dot and unfold.
Repeat on the other three corners.

15

Valley-fold dot-to-dot and unfold.

16

Bring the two ends together, folding on existing creases.

17

The Chomper is done! Holding as shown, push your thumbs together and the Chomper will chomp!

18

The Chomper can balance on any flat surface and look menacing! It can be used to motivate kids to brush their teeth ("Brush your teeth, or else the Chomper will get you!"). Or, you can place it on the bathroom sink to remind Grandpa to remove his dentures at night.

PERFORM IT!

Hold the model up and say, **"Oh, no, this one is too scary!"** and quickly put it back in the box. [Audience protests, "We want to see it!"] Ask, **"Do you really want to see it? Alright then..."** Back away from the audience and say, **"...Everyone hold up your hands and SCREAM!"** As they scream, run toward them while making the model open and close. Exclaim, **"Wow! Wasn't that SO scary?!"** [Audience shouts "NO!"] **"Who said it wasn't scary?"** Pick one kid who said, "No," and ask them, **"Why didn't you think it was scary?"** To whatever they say, respond, **"No, it's because it's really just a hat!"** Stick it on their head and say, **"It's a hungry hat – eating a yummy head!"**

Food Grinder (Rather Simple)

By Jeremy Shafer ©2010

This is not your conventional food grinder, but people do grind food like this on a daily basis. It's called eating!

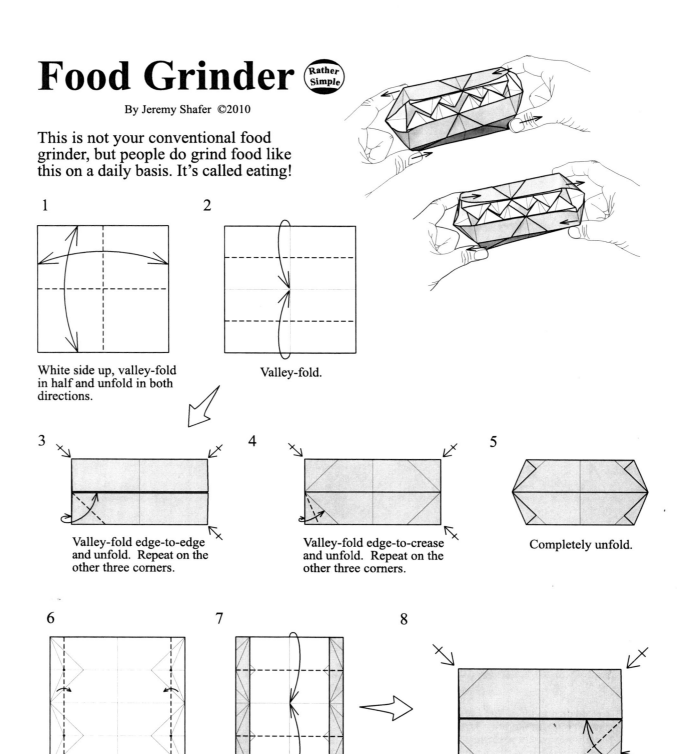

1

White side up, valley-fold in half and unfold in both directions.

2

Valley-fold.

3

Valley-fold edge-to-edge and unfold. Repeat on the other three corners.

4

Valley-fold edge-to-crease and unfold. Repeat on the other three corners.

5

Completely unfold.

6

Valley-fold on the black dots.

7

Valley-fold.

8

Valley-fold edge-to-edge and unfold. Repeat on the other three corners.

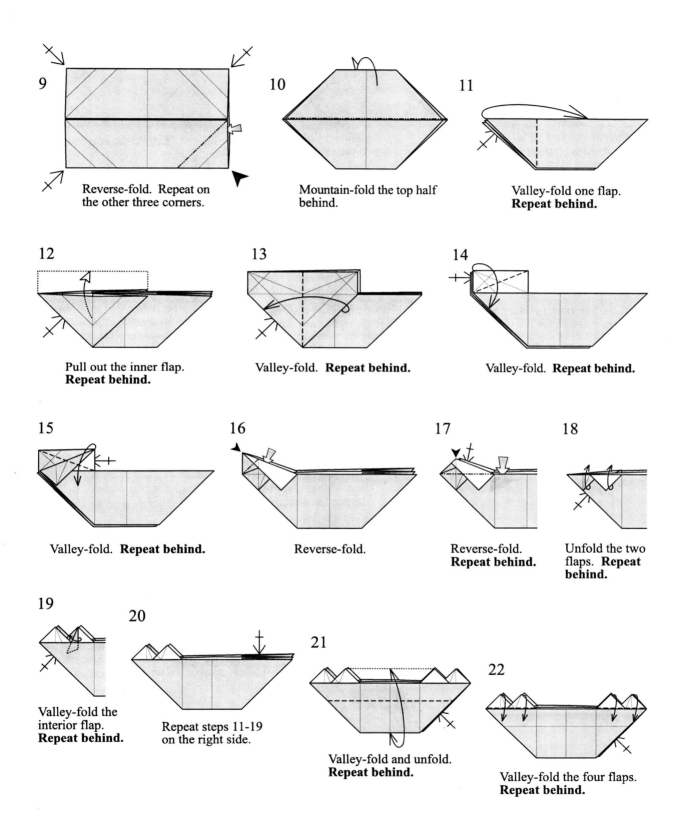

9 Reverse-fold. Repeat on the other three corners.

10 Mountain-fold the top half behind.

11 Valley-fold one flap. **Repeat behind.**

12 Pull out the inner flap. **Repeat behind.**

13 Valley-fold. **Repeat behind.**

14 Valley-fold. **Repeat behind.**

15 Valley-fold. **Repeat behind.**

16 Reverse-fold.

17 Reverse-fold. **Repeat behind.**

18 Unfold the two flaps. **Repeat behind.**

19 Valley-fold the interior flap. **Repeat behind.**

20 Repeat steps 11-19 on the right side.

21 Valley-fold and unfold. **Repeat behind.**

22 Valley-fold the four flaps. **Repeat behind.**

23

Valley-fold on all layers and unfold. **Turn over.**

24

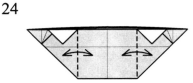

Valley-fold on all layers and unfold again.

25

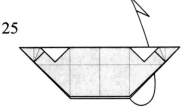

Unfold the rear flap.

26

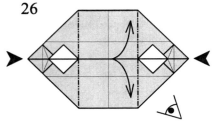

Pull the horizontal middle edges apart, and open and shape the model to form an open rectangular box.

27

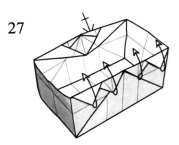

Unfold four flaps and **repeat behind.** Once all eight flaps are pointing straight up, you can call them teeth.

28

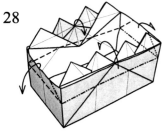

Fold the eight teeth toward the inside of the box on existing creases, so that they overlap. The left and right edges move apart.

29

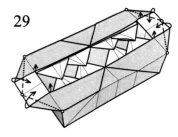

Valley-fold dot-to-dot on only the rear layer.

30

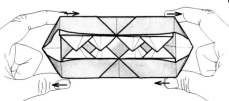

The Food Grinder is ready to grind food. Move your index fingers to the right and thumbs to the left.

31

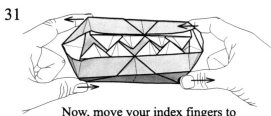

Now, move your index fingers to the left and thumbs to the right.

32

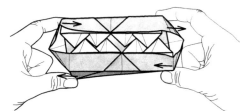

Continue grinding your teeth until you are no longer stressed. **Challenge:** To relieve more stress, try to design an origami mouth that bites its lip or chews on a fingernail.

PERFORM IT!

Say to the audience, **"This is an origami food grinder. It can grind just about anything, even this carrot!"** Place a carrot into the mouth and grind. Take the carrot out and say, **"This seems to be a very tough carrot... Anyone have any mashed potatoes and gravy?"**

Animals in Action

I would venture to guess that 68% of all origami is on the subject of animals. I'm probably wrong, but it doesn't hurt to guess. What is for sure is that animal folding in origami is hugely popular. So, in order to satisfy all you animal aficionados, the next section is dedicated to animal action models. No action animal section would be complete without arguably the most amazing and popular action model ever: the Traditional Flapping Bird. But why stop there?! There are many fun variations that can take the origami crane one step further and, of course, there are endless moving subjects in the animal kingdom. So get your animal instincts in gear, and set off on the road of origami action animals!

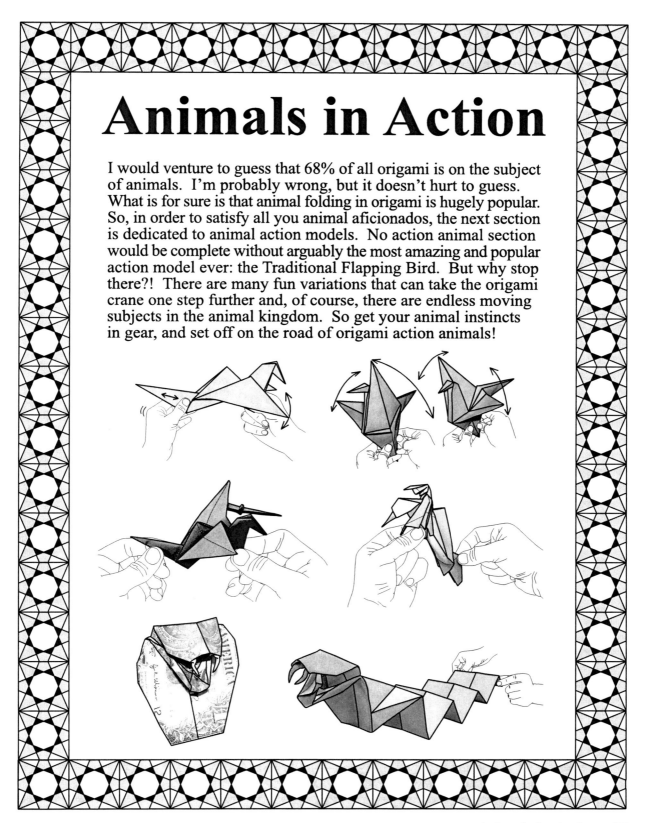

Traditional
Flapping Bird

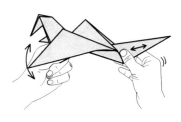

Origami underwent huge advances in the latter half of the 20th century, but if there is one traditional origami model that has withstood the ravages of time, it is the Flapping Bird. The look of wonder on kids' faces when I hand them a flapping bird confirms to me that it still ranks as one of the most amazing origami models ever designed, and certainly deserves a spot in this chapter on origami action animals.

1

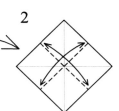

Colored side up.
Valley-fold and unfold
diagonally both ways.
Turn over.

2

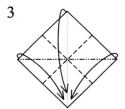

Valley-fold and
unfold in half
both ways.

3

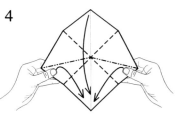

Bring the three corners
down to the lower corner
folding on existing creases.
The following two steps
show this fold in progress.

4

Step 3 slightly in
progress. Continue
bringing the three
corners downward.

5

Step 3 further
in progress.
Flatten completely.

6

Valley-fold the left
and right front flaps
to middle crease.

7

Valley-fold the
top down.

8

Unfold the two
flaps but leave the
top folded down.

9

Now it's time to do a
Petal Fold. Lift the
front flap slightly.

10

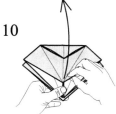

Keep lifting.

11

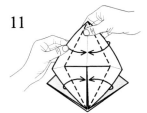

Here we have a boat. Collapse the
sides of the boat to the middle line.

12

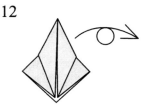

The Petal Fold
is complete.
Turn over.

PERFORM IT!

Hold up the finished Flapping Bird and ask the audience, **"What is this?"** [Audience says, "A bird."]
Make the wings flap and say, **"It's a flapping bird! Everyone flap your wings like a bird!"**
[Audience flaps their arms.] **"Stop! That was close! You guys almost flew away!"**

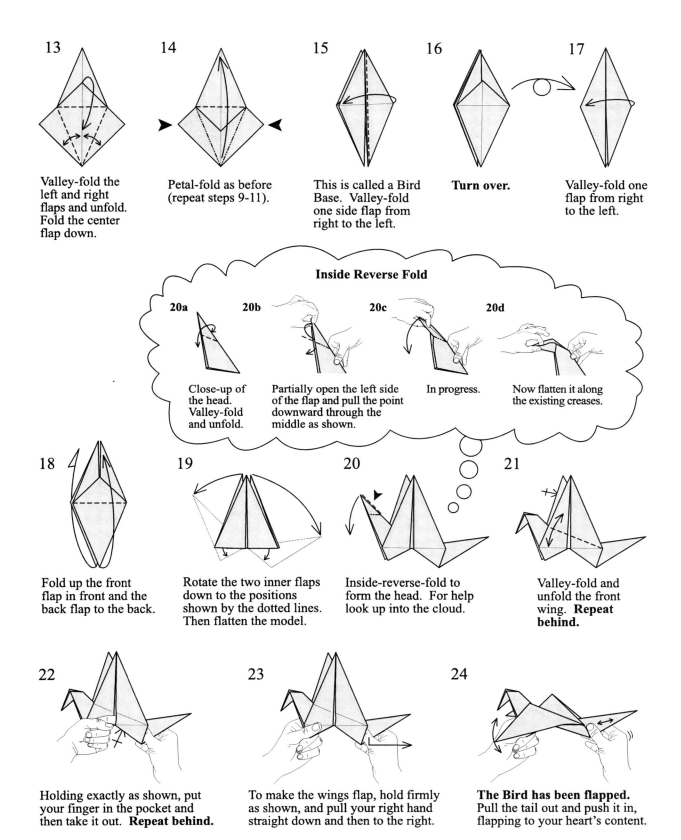

13

Valley-fold the left and right flaps and unfold. Fold the center flap down.

14

Petal-fold as before (repeat steps 9-11).

15

This is called a Bird Base. Valley-fold one side flap from right to the left.

16

Turn over.

17

Valley-fold one flap from right to the left.

Inside Reverse Fold

20a

Close-up of the head. Valley-fold and unfold.

20b

Partially open the left side of the flap and pull the point downward through the middle as shown.

20c

In progress.

20d

Now flatten it along the existing creases.

18

Fold up the front flap in front and the back flap to the back.

19

Rotate the two inner flaps down to the positions shown by the dotted lines. Then flatten the model.

20

Inside-reverse-fold to form the head. For help look up into the cloud.

21

Valley-fold and unfold the front wing. **Repeat behind.**

22

Holding exactly as shown, put your finger in the pocket and then take it out. **Repeat behind.**

23

To make the wings flap, hold firmly as shown, and pull your right hand straight down and then to the right.

24

The Bird has been flapped. Pull the tail out and push it in, flapping to your heart's content.

Aerobic Crane (Rather Simple)

By Jeremy Shafer ©2002

It's time to get in shape! Operating this model is great exercise... at least digitally speaking!

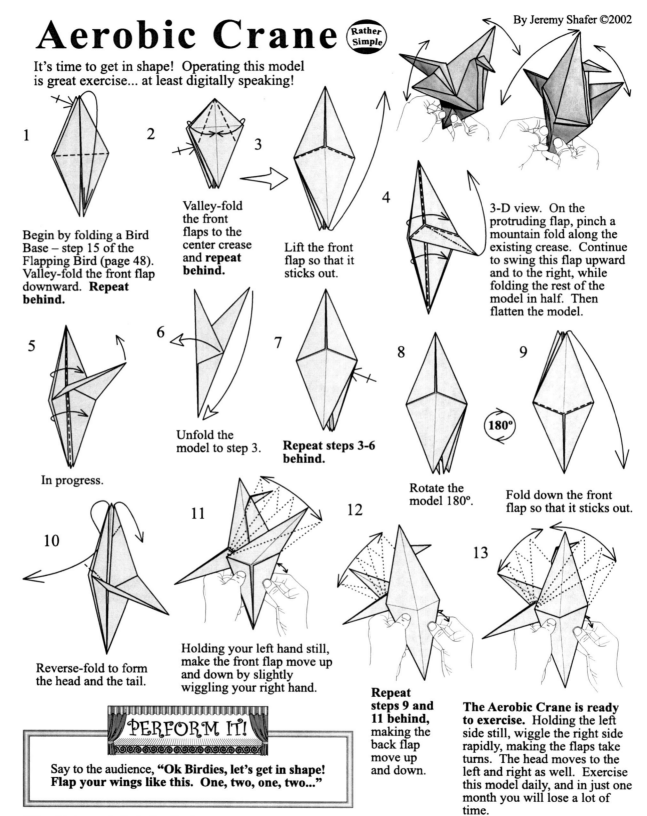

1 Begin by folding a Bird Base – step 15 of the Flapping Bird (page 48). Valley-fold the front flap downward. **Repeat behind.**

2 Valley-fold the front flaps to the center crease and **repeat behind.**

3 Lift the front flap so that it sticks out.

4 3-D view. On the protruding flap, pinch a mountain fold along the existing crease. Continue to swing this flap upward and to the right, while folding the rest of the model in half. Then flatten the model.

5 In progress.

6 Unfold the model to step 3.

7 **Repeat steps 3-6 behind.**

8 Rotate the model 180°.

180°

9 Fold down the front flap so that it sticks out.

10 Reverse-fold to form the head and the tail.

11 Holding your left hand still, make the front flap move up and down by slightly wiggling your right hand.

12 Repeat steps 9 and 11 behind, making the back flap move up and down.

13 The Aerobic Crane is ready to exercise. Holding the left side still, wiggle the right side rapidly, making the flaps take turns. The head moves to the left and right as well. Exercise this model daily, and in just one month you will lose a lot of time.

PERFORM IT!

Say to the audience, **"Ok Birdies, let's get in shape! Flap your wings like this. One, two, one, two..."**

Semi-Traditional

Contorted Crane

By Jeremy Shafer ©2003

Most contortionists can put their heads between their legs. Well, this crane can swallow its head, digest it, and have it come out still looking like a head!

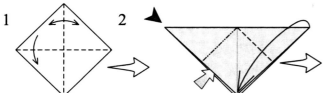

1

Prerequisite: Fold the Traditional Flapping Bird (page 48). White side up, valley-fold and unfold vertically. Valley-fold horizontally.

2

Valley-fold the right corner. Reverse-fold. the left corner.

3

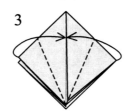

On the right side, valley-fold through all layers. On the left side valley-fold the front flap only.

4

Valley-fold the top down.

5

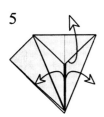

Unfold to step 3.

6

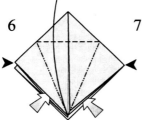

Petal-fold.

7

Outside-reverse-fold.

8

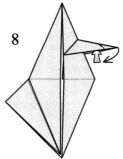

Inside-reverse-fold to form the head.

9

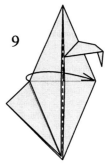

Valley-fold one flap to the right.

10

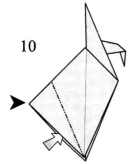

Reverse-fold.

11

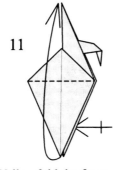

Valley-fold the front flap. **Repeat behind.**

12

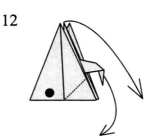

Holding the model firmly at the black dot, slide the tail (and head) rightward.

13

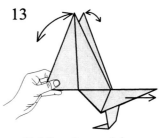

Holding the model firmly as shown, pull the tail rightward, and the wings will flap.

PERFORM IT!

Hold up the model, but hide the head from the audience, as shown at the top right of this page. Make the model flap and say to the audience, **"Here's a crane that has lost its head! Can anyone find it?"** Show the head and say, **"I found it! Look, it's coming out of its butt! Everyone say, 'Knarly dude!'"**

Warrior Crane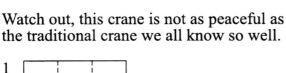

By Jeremy Shafer ©2004

Based on the model "Crane with a Knife" by Grayson Penfield

Watch out, this crane is not as peaceful as the traditional crane we all know so well.

1

Prerequisite: Fold the Traditional Flapping Bird (page 48). White side up, valley-fold and unfold in thirds.

2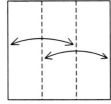

Here's one way to fold thirds. Holding as shown, fiddle with the folds until they line up.

3

Valley-fold diagonally and unfold.

4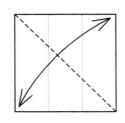

Valley-fold to the black dot and unfold.

5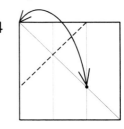

Valley-fold the top edge to the black dots and unfold.

6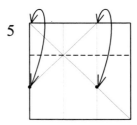

Valley-fold edge-to-crease and unfold. **Turn over.**

7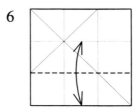

Valley-fold and unfold. **Turn over.**

8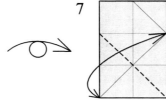

On the existing creases fold an off-centered Square Base. (For help, see Square Base, page 17)

9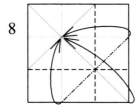

Petal-fold. (For help, see Petal Fold, page 17)

10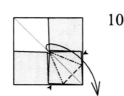

Valley-fold.

11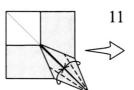

Rabbit-ear, reaching underneath the top layer. (For help see Rabbit Ear, page 17).

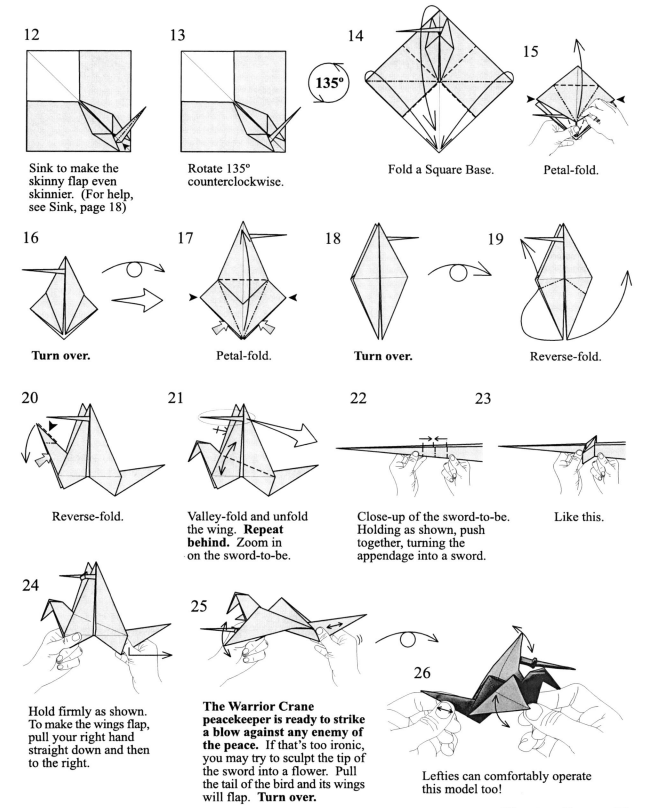

12

Sink to make the skinny flap even skinnier. (For help, see Sink, page 18)

13

Rotate 135° counterclockwise.

135°

14

Fold a Square Base.

15

Petal-fold.

16

Turn over.

17

Petal-fold.

18

Turn over.

19

Reverse-fold.

20

Reverse-fold.

21

Valley-fold and unfold the wing. **Repeat behind.** Zoom in on the sword-to-be.

22

23

Close-up of the sword-to-be. Holding as shown, push together, turning the appendage into a sword.

Like this.

24

Hold firmly as shown. To make the wings flap, pull your right hand straight down and then to the right.

25

The Warrior Crane peacekeeper is ready to strike a blow against any enemy of the peace. If that's too ironic, you may try to sculpt the tip of the sword into a flower. Pull the tail of the bird and its wings will flap. **Turn over.**

26

Lefties can comfortably operate this model too!

By Jeremy Shafer ©2004

Extra-large Crane

Rather Simple

You've heard of a big fish in a small pond...
Well, this is a big bird in a small sky. Forget
Weight-Watchers, this birdie was born to be big!

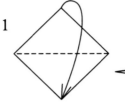

1

For an extra heavy set crane,
begin with a sheet of
heavyweight paper or
cardstock. White side up,
valley-fold diagonally in half.

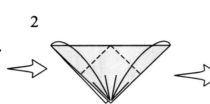

2

Valley-fold.

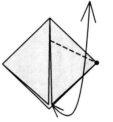

3

Valley-fold the flap on the
black dot and unfold. The
angle of this crease is to taste.

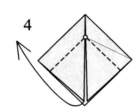

4

Valley-fold
the flaps on
the white dot.

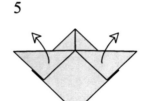

5

Unfold to step 2.

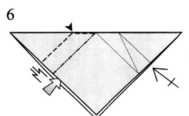

6

Crimp. Repeat
on the right side.

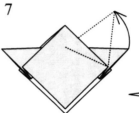

7

Pull the flap upward and
flatten on existing creases.

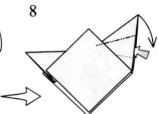

8

Reverse-fold to form
the head.

9

**The Extra Large Crane is ready to
fly into an extra large tree.** Holding
as shown, pull your hands apart and
the wings will flap.

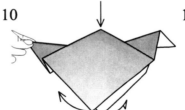

10

To make the Extra Large Crane
swim, push downward on the
center, flipping the wings upward.

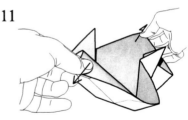

11

**X-Large Crane
Swimming.** Pull the wings
apart and the head and tail
will bob back and forth in
a swimming motion.

Note: Although the
Extra Large Crane does
not flap its wings as
well as the Traditional
Flapping Bird (page 48),
it does fly about as well!

PERFORM IT!

Before showing the model, ask the audience, **"What happened when the crane
ate too much fish?"** Hold the model up and say, **"That about sums it up!"**

Flapping Hummingbird

Rather Simple

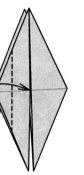

Based on the Traditional Flapping Bird

Thousands of origami flapping birds are folded each year. How about some variety?! With just a few more folds you can make a Flapping Hummingbird!

1

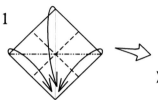

Begin by folding a colored Square Base. (For help, see Square Base, page 17.)

2

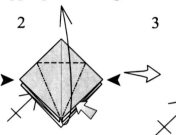

Petal-fold and **Repeat behind**, to form a Bird Base. (For help, see Bird Base, page 17.)

3

Valley-fold. **Repeat behind.**

4

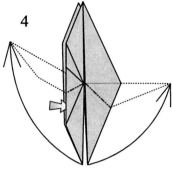

Reverse-fold the left flap at a 60 angle. Reverse-fold the right flap even with the horizontal crease.

5

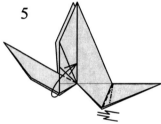

Valley-fold on the left and crimp on the right.

6

Valley-fold on the left. On the right, hide the small flap in the pocket.

7

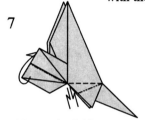

Mountain-fold on the left and crimp on the right.

8

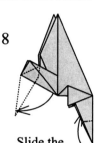

Slide the flap out on the left and reverse-fold on the right.

9

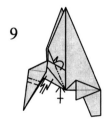

Crimp to form the head and beak. Mountain-fold the middle flap, tucking into the pocket. **Repeat behind.**

10

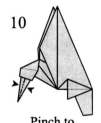

Pinch to narrow the beak.

11

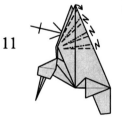

Moving upward, make three pleats and one valley fold on the wing. **Repeat behind.**

12

PERFORM IT!

Ask the audience, **"What bird flaps its wings the fastest?"** [audience says, "Hummingbird."] **"Everyone flap your wings really fast like a hummingbird."**

The Hummingbird is ready to fly out in search of nectar. Holding firmly as shown, pull your right hand down and then to the right. The crimp made in step 7 will unfold in the process of flapping. For a more realistic-looking hummingbird, flap the wings at about fifty times per second.

Frog Tongue By Jeremy Shafer ©2007

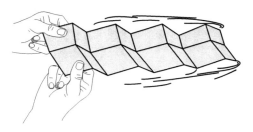

This is a simplified version of the Frog tongue published in *Origami to Astonish and Amuse*. It is included here as a prerequisite to folding the Attacking Cobra (page 57). The model requires starting out with a 2½-inch by 8½-inch rectangle of **cardstock** or **construction paper.** Normal paper just won't work. Cardstock, which is available at any office supply or copy store, comes in letter size paper (8½-inch by 11-inch). So, just use the extra strip you cut off when making a square, or you can cut off a 3-inch by 11-inch rectangle to create a longer more impressive tongue.

1
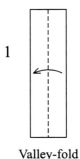

Valley-fold in half.

2

Valley-fold the lower right corner to the upper left.

3
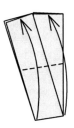

Valley-fold bottom to top. Try to be as centered as possible.

4

Valley-fold the front flap to the bottom.

5

Mountain-fold, lining up with fold made in step 4.

6

Completely unfold.

7

8
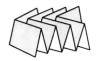

In progress.

9

The Frog Tongue is ready for action. To operate, hold the outermost layer between your thumb and index finger where the black dot is. Hold the back similarly with the other hand. Abruptly pull your hands apart and the model will spring out. Slam your fingers together and the model will retract making a loud snap. The faster you oscillate the tongue, the louder the noise, and the further the extension. The extension also improves the more the tongue is exercised.

Make the indicated folds on the existing creases. **IMPORTANT:** Do not alter the angle of any of the slanted creases. They need to be slightly slanted, **NOT** horizontal.

10

PERFORM IT!

Before showing the model, say to the audience, **"Everyone stick your tongue out at me!"** [Audience sticks out tongues] **"Such short tongues! My tongue is five times as long as yours. You want to see it?"** Demonstrate the Frog Tongue and pretend to attack the audience with it.

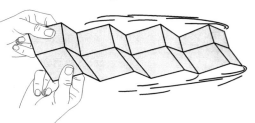

The Frog Tongue fully outstretched in attack mode. Fold a multitude of them and you can call yourself a master of many tongues.

Attacking Cobra

By Jeremy Shafer ©2007 Intermediate

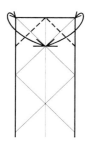

This model is so scary that it will make origami animals of all sizes stop dead in their tracks out of fear.

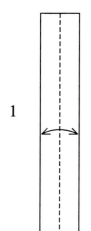

1

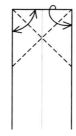

2

Valley-fold and unfold diagonally in one direction. In the other direction, valley-fold diagonally and don't unfold.

3

Valley-fold edge-to-edge and unfold in both directions.

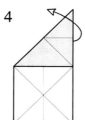

4

Unfold.

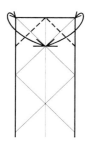

5

Valley-fold and unfold.

Begin with a 9X1 rectangle of cardstock preferably at least 17-inches long. Valley-fold and unfold.

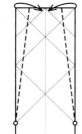

6

Valley-fold the corners to the existing diagonal creases. The folds originate at the white dots.

7

Unfold.

8

Valley-fold and unfold on the white dots.

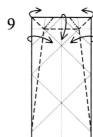

9

On existing creases fold the three edges toward the middle while rabbit-earing the two corners and folding them upward.

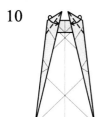

10

Valley-fold.

11

Turn over.

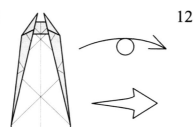

12

Valley-fold the black dots to the diagonal creases.

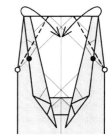

13

Valley-fold the corners to the center line. The folds originate at the white dots.

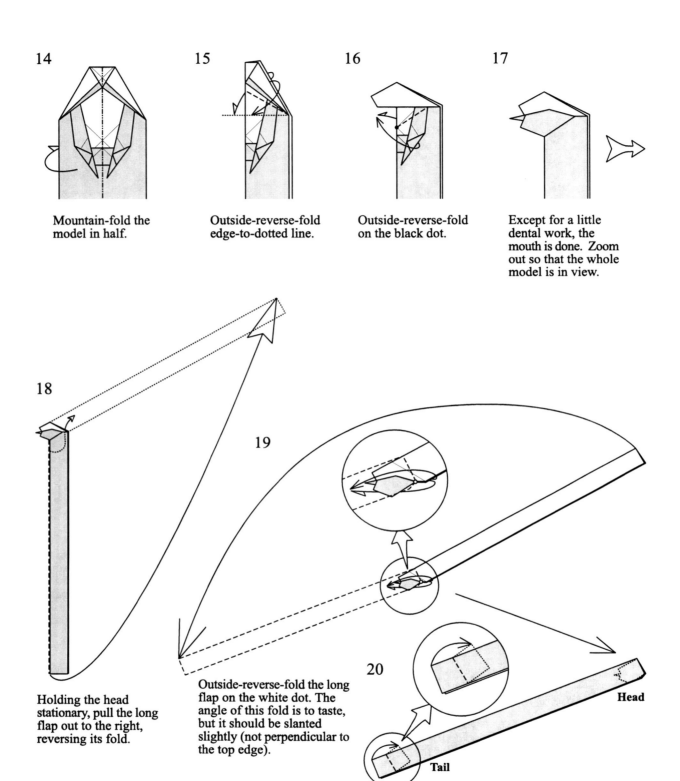

14

Mountain-fold the model in half.

15

Outside-reverse-fold edge-to-dotted line.

16

Outside-reverse-fold on the black dot.

17

Except for a little dental work, the mouth is done. Zoom out so that the whole model is in view.

18

Holding the head stationary, pull the long flap out to the right, reversing its fold.

19

Outside-reverse-fold the long flap on the white dot. The angle of this fold is to taste, but it should be slanted slightly (not perpendicular to the top edge).

20

Head

Tail

Outside-reverse-fold the end of the tail. The position and angle of this fold is to taste, but it does have to be angled a little (not perpendicular to the top edge).

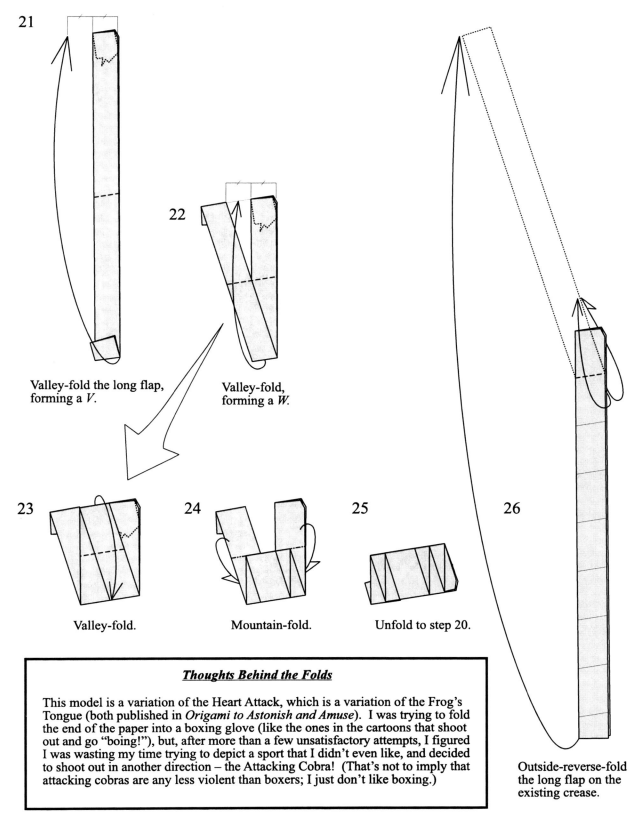

21

Valley-fold the long flap, forming a *V*.

22

Valley-fold, forming a *W*.

23

Valley-fold.

24

Mountain-fold.

25

Unfold to step 20.

26

Outside-reverse-fold the long flap on the existing crease.

Thoughts Behind the Folds

This model is a variation of the Heart Attack, which is a variation of the Frog's Tongue (both published in *Origami to Astonish and Amuse*). I was trying to fold the end of the paper into a boxing glove (like the ones in the cartoons that shoot out and go "boing!"), but, after more than a few unsatisfactory attempts, I figured I was wasting my time trying to depict a sport that I didn't even like, and decided to shoot out in another direction – the Attacking Cobra! (That's not to imply that attacking cobras are any less violent than boxers; I just don't like boxing.)

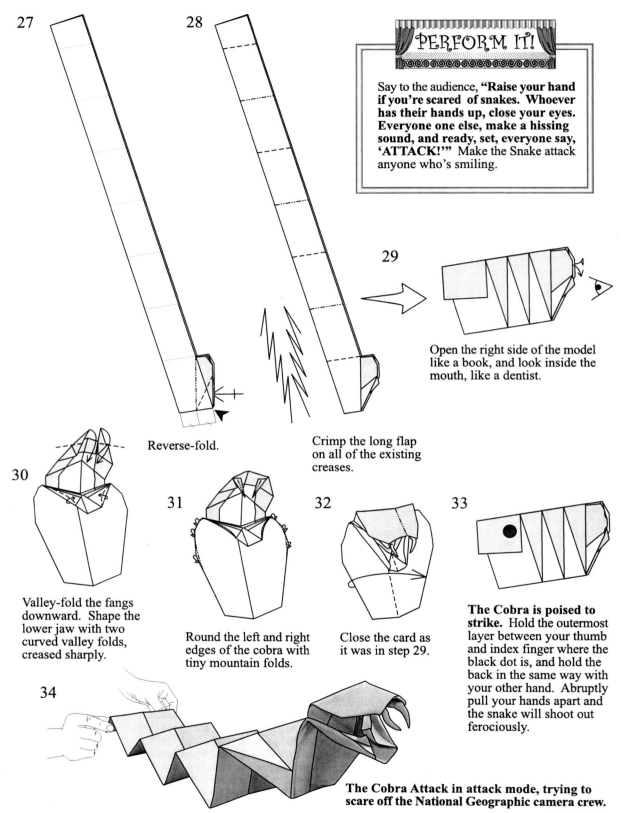

27

28

PERFORM IT!

Say to the audience, **"Raise your hand if you're scared of snakes. Whoever has their hands up, close your eyes. Everyone one else, make a hissing sound, and ready, set, everyone say, 'ATTACK!'"** Make the Snake attack anyone who's smiling.

29

Open the right side of the model like a book, and look inside the mouth, like a dentist.

Reverse-fold.

Crimp the long flap on all of the existing creases.

30

Valley-fold the fangs downward. Shape the lower jaw with two curved valley folds, creased sharply.

31

Round the left and right edges of the cobra with tiny mountain folds.

32

Close the card as it was in step 29.

33

The Cobra is poised to strike. Hold the outermost layer between your thumb and index finger where the black dot is, and hold the back in the same way with your other hand. Abruptly pull your hands apart and the snake will shoot out ferociously.

34

The Cobra Attack in attack mode, trying to scare off the National Geographic camera crew.

$ Cobra Pop-Up Card Intermediate

Although any 3 X 1 rectangle works, Using a U.S. One Dollar Bill is ideal because it results in a cobra with white fangs and spiral eyes!

By Jeremy Shafer ©2007

Note: If you do use a 1-by-3 rectangle instead of a dollar, make sure the paper is the same color on both sides and begin at step 2.

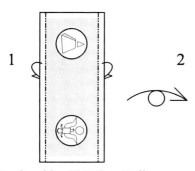

1 Begin with a U.S. One Dollar Bill, eagle and pyramid side up. Mountain-fold the left and right borders (the white part), resulting in a roughly 1-by-3 rectangle. **Turn over.**

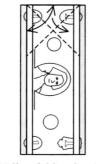

2 Valley-fold and unfold diagonally in one direction. In the other direction, valley-fold diagonally and don't unfold.

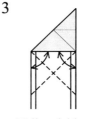

3 Valley-fold edge-to-edge and unfold in both directions.

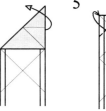

4 Unfold.

5 Valley-fold and unfold.

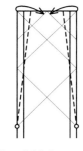

6 Valley-fold the corners to the existing diagonal creases. The folds originate at the white dots.

7 Unfold.

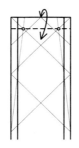

8 Valley-fold and unfold on the white dots.

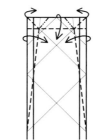

9 On existing creases fold the three edges toward the middle while rabbit-earing the two corners and folding them upward.

10 Valley-fold.

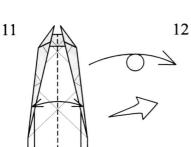

11 Valley-fold in half and unfold. **Turn over.**

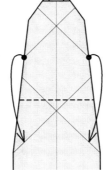

12 Valley-fold the black dots to the diagonal creases.

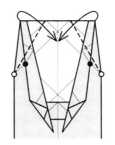

13 Valley-fold the corners to the center line. The folds originate at the white dots.

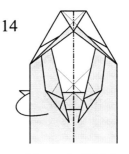

14 Mountain-fold the model in half.

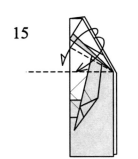
15

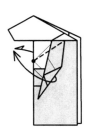
16

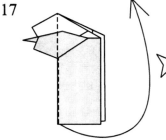
17

18

Outside-reverse-fold to the imaginary horizontal line.

Outside-reverse-fold on the black dot.

Pull the bottom flap out to the right, undoing the reverse fold.

Wrap the raw edge around to the interior of the model; the corner at the black dot needs to be turned inside out. **Repeat behind.**

19

20

21

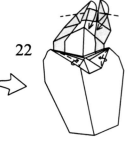
22

Outside-reverse-fold the long flap on the white dot. The angle of this fold is to taste. The closer the fold is to being perpendicular to the top edge, the better the cobra's head will fit inside the card, but the less the head will "pop up" when the card is opened.

Valley-fold. This fold is also to taste.

Open the card and look into the mouth like a dentist.

Valley-fold the fangs downward. Shape the lower jaw with two sharply creased, curved valley folds.

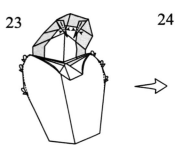
23

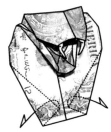
24

Round the left and right edges of the cobra with tiny mountain folds. Narrow and shape the fangs to taste... YUM!

Like this! To make the card stand, unfold the two rear flaps.

PERFORM IT!

Say to the audience, **"This is a scary dollar. Ready, set, everyone say 'Pop-up!'"** [Audience says "Pop-up!"] Open the model and ask, **"What is it?"** [Audience says, "It's a snake."] **"But what kind of snake?"** [Audience says, "Cobra."] **"Who wants to get bitten by a cobra?"** Attack all willing victims and yell, **"Oh no, we have lots of snake bites! Does anyone have any anti-venom?"** Stick the model on your finger, shake it around, and shout, **"Aaah! It's got my finger!"**

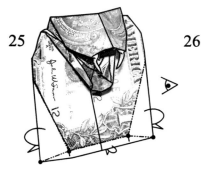
25

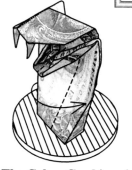
26

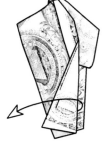
27

28

Pinch a mountain fold on the black dots, and then fold the two flaps behind again. This will enable the Cobra Card to stand.

The Cobra Card is poised to strike, or, perhaps, just striking a pose. Now, close the card.

The Cobra Card is closed. Open again.

The Cobra Pop-up Card is finished, and waiting to snack on some pop-up mice.

62 *Origami Ooh La La!*

Serpent Monster Mouth Intermediate

By Jeremy Shafer ©2010

This Serpent Monster Mouth is so scary that it scared the rest of the snake away!

1

Begin with step 20 of the Food Grinder (page 44). Valley-fold the four flaps. **Repeat behind.**

2

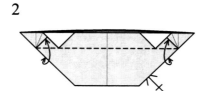

Valley-fold edge-to-edge and unfold.

3

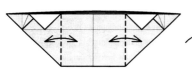

Valley-fold on all layers and unfold. **Turn over.**

4

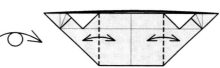

Valley-fold on all layers and unfold again.

5

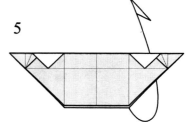

Unfold the rear flap.

6

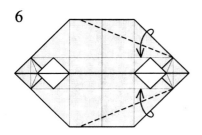

Valley-fold edge-to-crease.

7

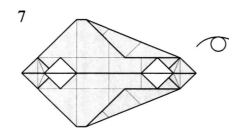

Turn over.

8

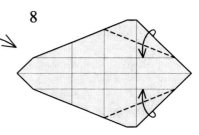

Valley-fold edge-to-crease.

9

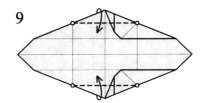

Valley-fold on the white dots.

10

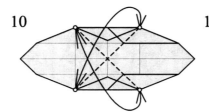

Valley-fold dot-to-dot and unfold in both directions.

11

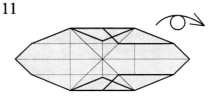

Turn over.

12

Lift and spread open the two raw edges, so that the model resembles a boat.

13

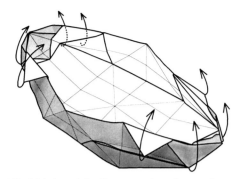

Unfold the eight flaps, so that they point upwards like teeth.

15

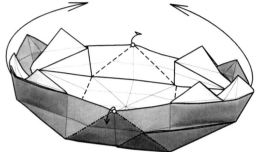

Bring the two sets of teeth together, folding on existing creases. The two white dots move apart.

16

Spread apart the two layers and shape them to form an eye (socket). **Repeat behind.**

17

It already looks like a snake, but there is one more step which will improve the action mechanism and allow the model to stand. Look at the back side of the head.

18

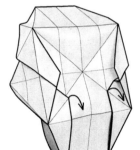

Freeing the trapped layers, pull the two flaps so that they stick out.

19

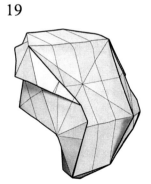

Stand the model on a table so that only the boldly-diagrammed edges are touching the surface of the table. You may need to close the mouth more in order for the model to stay standing.

20

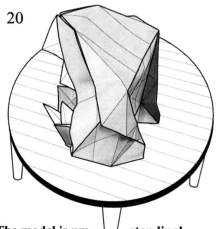

The model is um... ⊔ **...standing! And, it's also um...** ⊔ **... DONE!**
See the next page for more pictures of the completed Serpent Monster Mouth and how to make it move!

21

Side View

22

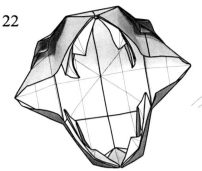

Front View

24

Holding the model as shown, press backward with your thumbs while pressing forward with your other eight fingers, and the mouth will shut. Alternatively, you can close the mouth by pulling the left and right sides of the mouth apart.

23

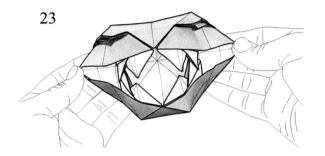

The Serpent Monster Mouth is nearly closed! Let go and the mouth should snap open on its own. If not, then reform the stand made in step 18, and try again.

PERFORM IT!

Say to the audience, **"This is my pet snake. His name is Sneaky, because he likes to sneak up and eat people. So, who would like to feed Sneaky today?"** Pick a volunteer and say, **"So, what would you like to feed him? How about, your nose or your foot, or perhaps a few fingers? I mean you do have 10 of them, you could certainly spare two or three."** If the volunteer is willing, have Sneaky nibble on their fingers. If not, choose another volunteer. After Sneaky is well-fed, exclaim, **"Those sure were some yummy fingers..."** Close Sneaky's mouth and say, **"...because look, Sneaky is smiling!"**

PERFORM IT!

Ask the audience, **"Raise your hand if you're NOT scared of snakes?"** Choose someone with their hand up and say, **"Well then look into the eyes of this Serpent Monster."** Make a loud hissing snake noise and make the serpent pretend to eat the volunteer. Exclaim, **"Wow! You sure are tough! This serpent can only eat soft, tender people."**

Swiveling Snake...

Rather Complex

By Michael Kan ©2001   Diagrams by Jeremy Shafer ©2001

...Or, maybe it's the tail of a dinosaur skeleton

Michael Kan happened upon this model while at a Bay Area Rapid Folders (BARF) meeting. He was trying to fold Jeff Beynon's Spring into Action, but accidentally got the dimensions wrong. I told him to cut off a two-unit strip so that it might still work. He came back to me a half-hour later with the folded two-unit strip, and said, couldn't fold the Spring into Action, but this thing is kind of cool!" And that's how the Swiveling Snake came to be. It's a weird model that when fully extended can swivel to the left and right without collapsing. Begin with a 1 by 13 rectangle. Don't worry about the exact length. just make sure it is at least 1 by 13, because you can cut off any extra length after doing step 5.

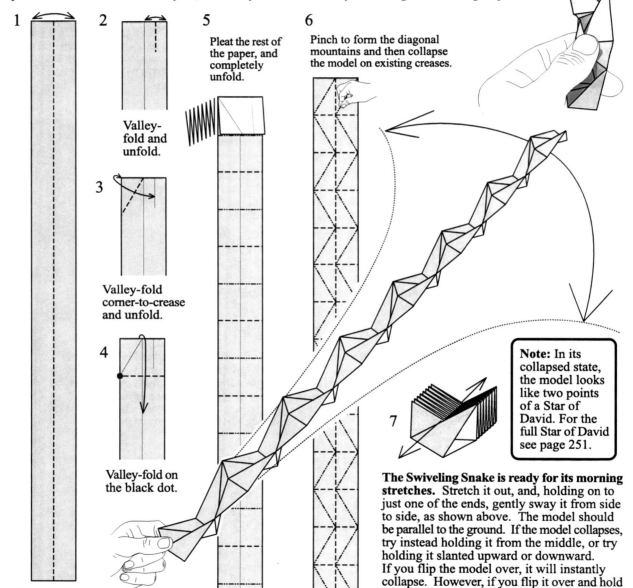

1

Colored side up, valley-fold and unfold.

2

Valley-fold and unfold.

3

Valley-fold corner-to-crease and unfold.

4

Valley-fold on the black dot.

5

Pleat the rest of the paper, and completely unfold.

6

Pinch to form the diagonal mountains and then collapse the model on existing creases.

7

Note: In its collapsed state, the model looks like two points of a Star of David. For the full Star of David see page 251.

The Swiveling Snake is ready for its morning stretches. Stretch it out, and, holding on to just one of the ends, gently sway it from side to side, as shown above. The model should be parallel to the ground. If the model collapses, try instead holding it from the middle, or try holding it slanted upward or downward. If you flip the model over, it will instantly collapse. However, if you flip it over and hold it from both ends, it makes for a remarkably sturdy bridge. I suspect structural engineers will be very interested in this model, and, if so, I have a bridge to sell them!

66 *Origami Ooh La La!*

Scary Snake Intermediate

By Jeremy Shafer ©2009

This snake is scary because its mouth
is as big as the snake itself!

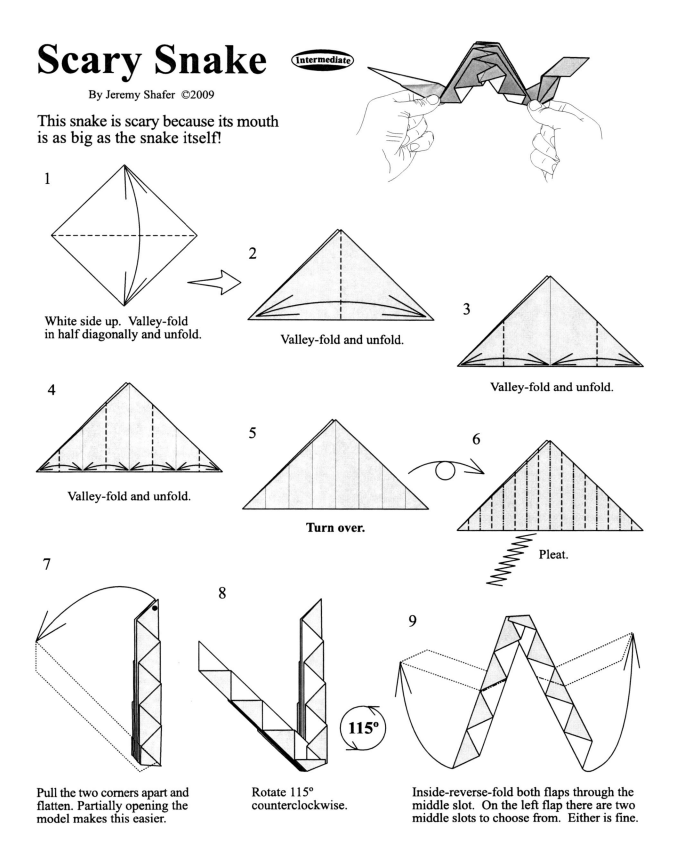

1 White side up. Valley-fold
in half diagonally and unfold.

2 Valley-fold and unfold.

3 Valley-fold and unfold.

4 Valley-fold and unfold.

5 Turn over.

6 Pleat.

7 Pull the two corners apart and
flatten. Partially opening the
model makes this easier.

8 Rotate 115°
counterclockwise.

115°

9 Inside-reverse-fold both flaps through the
middle slot. On the left flap there are two
middle slots to choose from. Either is fine.

10

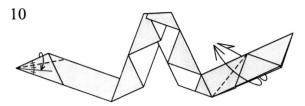

Valley-fold the left flap. Outside-reverse fold
the right flap.

11

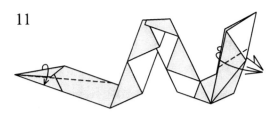

Valley-fold the left flap. Outside-reverse fold
the right flap.

12

**The scary snake is ready to scare some unsuspecting
ophidiophobic zoo goers.**

13

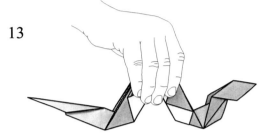

Think safety first! Here is the proper way to
hold the model in order to avoid getting bitten.

14

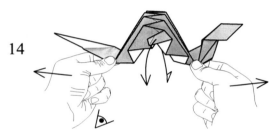

On the other hand, if you would like to get bitten,
hold the model as shown above, and pull your hands
apart. The middle of the snake will spread open and
downward, forming a scary mouth.

15

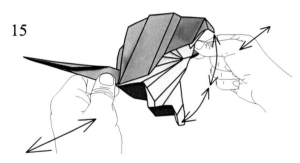

The Monster Mouth has appeared out of nowhere!
Pull you hands apart and it will go chomp! Repeat
over and over until your chomping needs are satisfied.

16

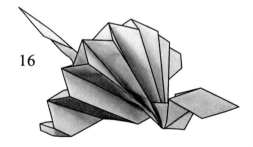

After an afternoon of chomping,
the Scary Snake is full.

PERFORM IT!

Hold up the model to the audience as shown in step 13 and
ask for a volunteer: **"Is there anyone who is not afraid of
snakes?"** Once you have a volunteer, say, **"Ok, I need you
to close your eyes and imagine that you're trapped in the
Amazon Jungle. It's so dark out that you can't even see!
Suddenly, you hear all around you the hissing sounds of
snakes – 'sssssssss!'"** Gesture to anyone with their eyes
open to join you in the hissing and continue, **"They're coming
closer and closer, and you hold out your hand to stop them,
and..."** Hold up a sign to the audience that reads, *"On the
count of three, SCREAM!"* Mouth the words, **"1-2-3,"** and,
as everyone screams, make the snake chomp on the kid's hand!
"Wasn't that scary? That's an applause moment!"

Another Flapping Bird

By Jeremy Shafer ©2009

Rather Simple

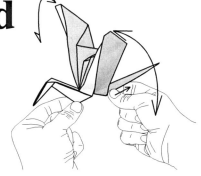

As an origami environmentalist, I feel it is my duty to help spawn new varieties of flapping birds. It is better that we are prepared should the Traditional Flapping Bird ever go extinct.

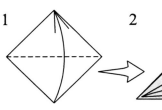

1 White side up, valley-fold in half diagonally.

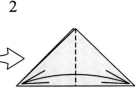

2 Valley-fold and unfold.

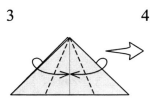

3 Valley-fold.

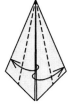

4 Valley-fold.

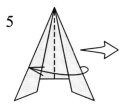

5 Valley-fold.

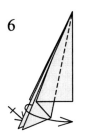

6 Valley-fold. **Repeat behind.**

7 Slide out the interior white flap and flatten the model.

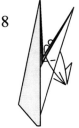

8 Outside-reverse-fold the white flap.

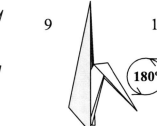

9 Rotate 180°.

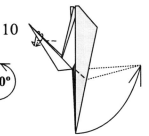

10 Outside-reverse-fold the left flap to form the head. Inside-reverse-fold the right flap to form the tail.

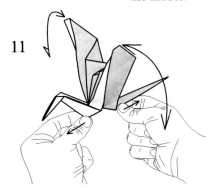

11 Holding the model as shown, pull your hands apart and the wings will flap.

PERFORM IT!

Say to the audience, **"This is an Accordion Crane. It plays the accordion as it flaps its wings!"** Flap the wings and say, **"It plays so quiet that you can't hear the song, but if you would like I could sing it!"** Start singing loudly any song that you think the whole audience will know, while flapping the bird like an accordion. When you're done, take a bow, and have the birdie take a bow too!

Tadpole Finger Puppet

By Jeremy Shafer ©2007

Now with a few folds you can have your very own pet tadpole. It's easier to catch than a real one, and it's a lot more fun to play with!

Super Simple

1
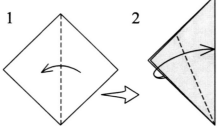

Begin with a 6-inch square white side up. Valley-fold diagonally in half.

2

Valley-fold on both layers.

3
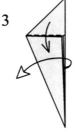

Valley-fold the top corner down. Unfold the fold made in step 2.

4
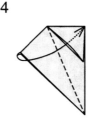

Valley-fold, inserting the flaps into the pocket.

5
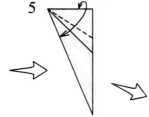

Valley-fold and unfold.

6
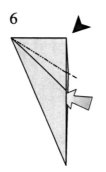

Open the right pocket and squash.

7
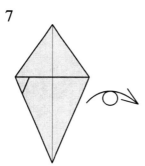

Turn over.

8
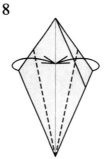

Valley-fold.

9
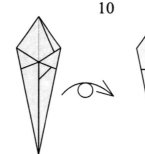

Turn over.

10
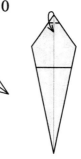

Valley-fold the tip to taste.

11
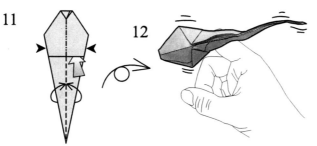

Valley-fold the bottom flap in half to form the tail and shape it to taste. Open the pocket and shape the body to taste. **Turn over.**

12

The Tadpole has hatched. Insert your index finger into the pocket and wiggle it to make the Tadpole swim. Throw it in the air to make the Tadpole fly.

PERFORM IT!

Put the model on your finger and wiggle it as shown to the left and say, **"This is a baby frog. A baby baby frog! Does anyone know what it is called?"** [Audience says, "Tadpole."] **"Everyone wiggle like a tadpole!"** [Audience wiggles] **"Oh my, what a squirmy, wormy audience! Watch out, if you keep it up you might all turn into frogs!"**

Prince Charming

By Jeremy
Shafer ©2007

Intermediate

This origami frog not only talks, it breathes!
What more can a princess ask for?!

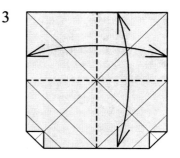

1

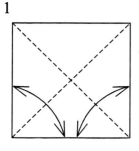

White side up, valley-fold
and unfold. **Turn over.**

2

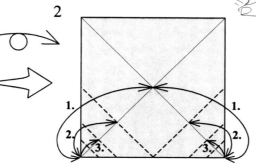

Make the indicated series
of creases and folds.

3

Valley-fold and unfold in half
both ways.

4

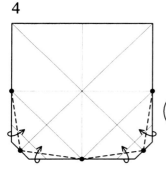

Valley-fold on the black dots.
Rotate the model 180°.

5

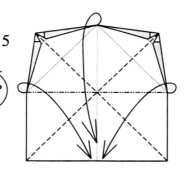

On existing creases,
form a Waterbomb Base.
(Basics, page 18).

6

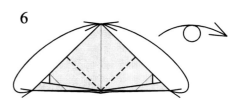

Valley-fold ON ALL LAYERS.
Turn over.

7

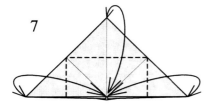

Valley-fold and unfold.

8

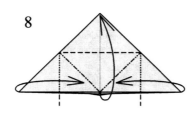

Petal-fold on
existing creases.

9

Petal-fold in
progress.

10

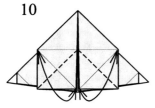

Valley-fold and unfold
the two front flaps.

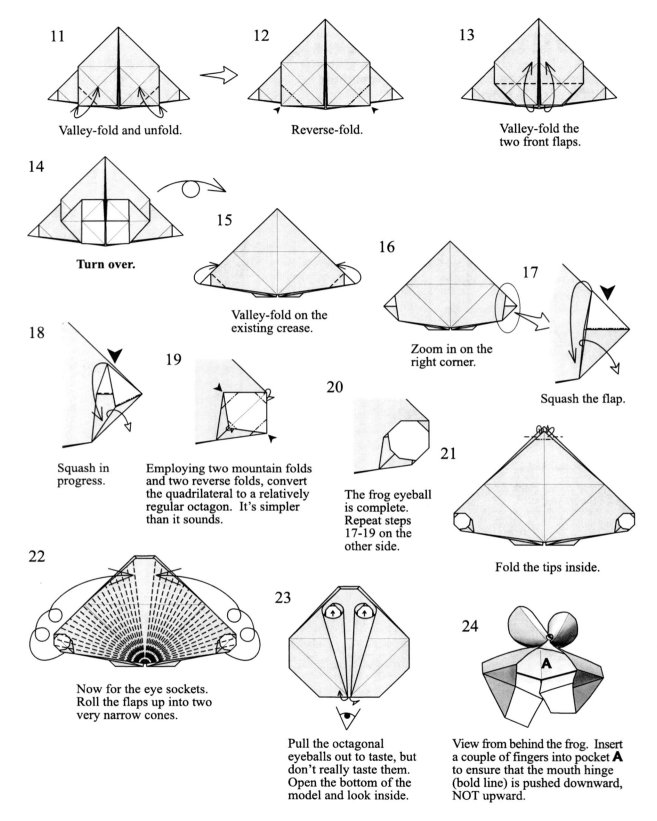

11
Valley-fold and unfold.

12
Reverse-fold.

13
Valley-fold the
two front flaps.

14
Turn over.

15
Valley-fold on the
existing crease.

16
Zoom in on the
right corner.

17
Squash the flap.

18
Squash in
progress.

19
Employing two mountain folds
and two reverse folds, convert
the quadrilateral to a relatively
regular octagon. It's simpler
than it sounds.

20
The frog eyeball
is complete.
Repeat steps
17-19 on the
other side.

21
Fold the tips inside.

22
Now for the eye sockets.
Roll the flaps up into two
very narrow cones.

23
Pull the octagonal
eyeballs out to taste, but
don't really taste them.
Open the bottom of the
model and look inside.

24
View from behind the frog. Insert
a couple of fingers into pocket **A**
to ensure that the mouth hinge
(bold line) is pushed downward,
NOT upward.

25

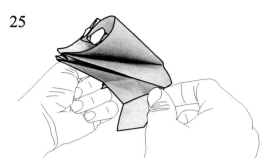

Prince Charming is ready for action.
Holding as shown, push your hands together...

26

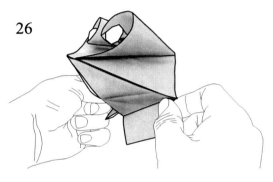

...and Prince Charming will take a deep breath.

27

Pull your hands apart and Prince Charming
will open his mouth. Start singing and the
Prince will lip-sync.

28

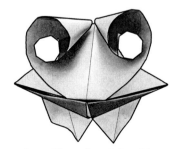

Prince Charming doing his
Kermit the Frog impersonation.

Here's a ventriloquism routine I perform
with Prince Charming:

Jeremy Shafer: Hi, my name is Jeremy
and this is my good friend Prince Charming

Prince Charming:
(to audience) Hi Cutie, Whata ya say, one
little kiss, and see what I turn into.
(To Jeremy) Hey Dogface, do you honestly
think that you are a ventriloquist?

JS: Look, Prince, I'm doing the best that
I can; now can we just get on with...

PC: Well you stink!

JS: Give me a break. It's my first time!

PC: You STINK!

JS: Stop! Why don't you act like you're
supposed to... Prince CHARMING.

PC: Why don't you stick to juggling
unicycling and that weird folding you do,
what do you call it Org, Orig...

JS: Origami and for your information, you
ARE origami.

PC: Get outta here!

JS: No really, you came from a single sheet
of 6-inch paper.

PC: Did not. Liar. Jerk.

JS: Hey, you should be a lot nicer to me.
I am like your father (well not literally –
that would be gross), but I folded you,
I made you, and I could very easily
squish you.

PC: You stink. Ventriloquist... Ha! More
like Loooser. Loser, Loser...[pause]...Jerk!

JS: OK time to unfold you.

PC: [While getting unfolded] Aaaaaaaaaah!

JS: Gosh I guess I am a Jerk. I miss my
friend. [JS refolds PC].

PC: Jerk! Loser, Dogface...[JS flattens PC].

Prince Not So Charming

By Jeremy Shafer ©2009

(Intermediate)

This origami frog might not be so charming
as the two-eyed prince, but is certainly as
beautiful, for, as they say, "Beauty is in the
EYE of the beholder!"

Hey you! Look me
straight in the eye!

1

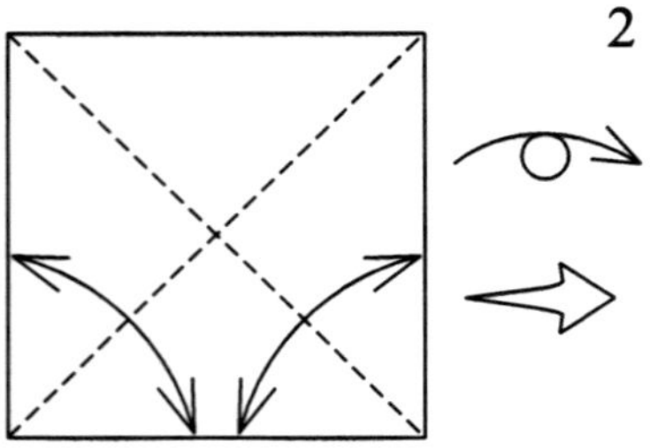

White side up, valley-fold
and unfold. **Turn over.**

2

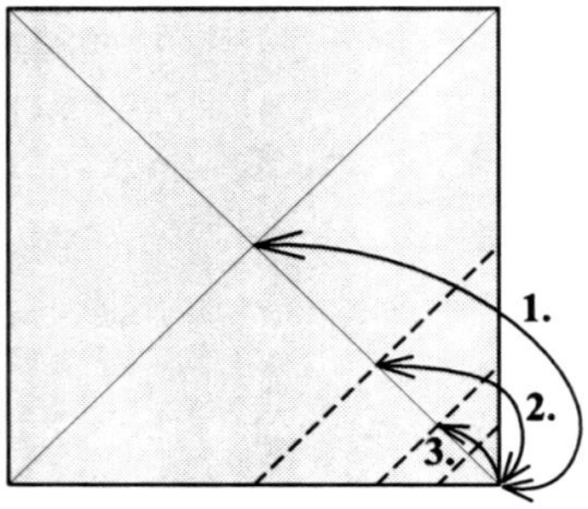

Make the indicated series
of creases and folds.

1.
2.
3.

3

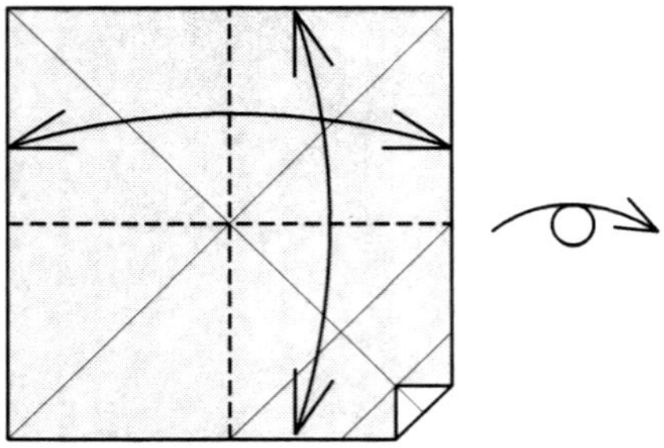

Valley-fold and unfold in half
both ways. **Turn over.**

4

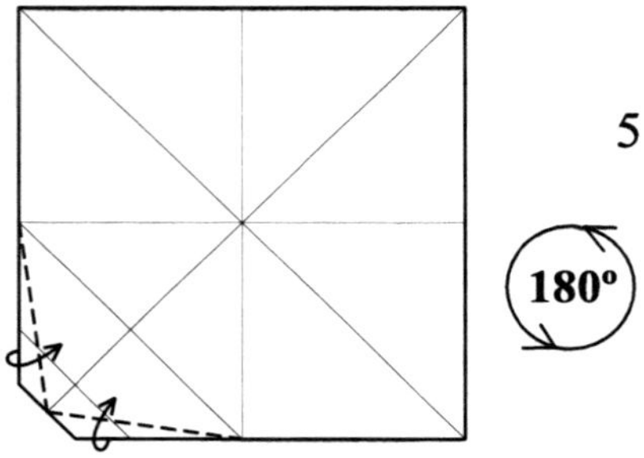

Valley-fold. Rotate the
model 180°.

5

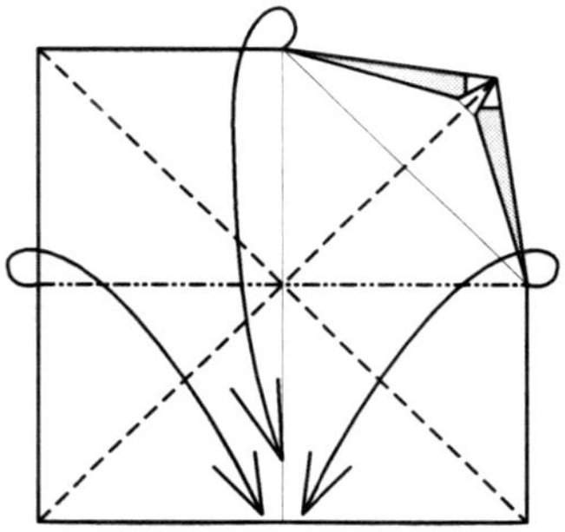

180°

Form a Waterbomb Base on
existing creases.

6

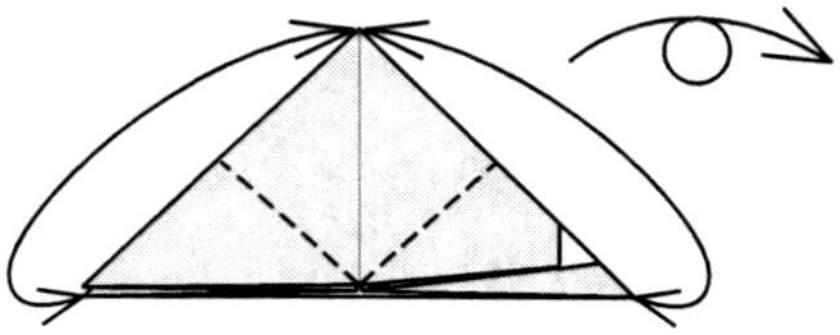

Valley-fold ON ALL LAYERS!
Turn over.

7

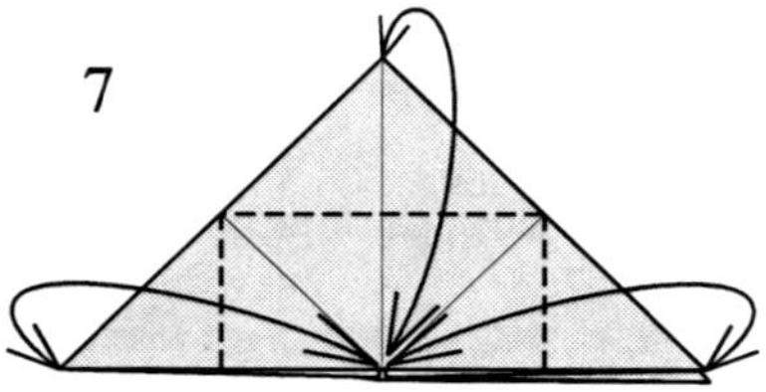

Valley-fold and unfold on the
top layer only.

8

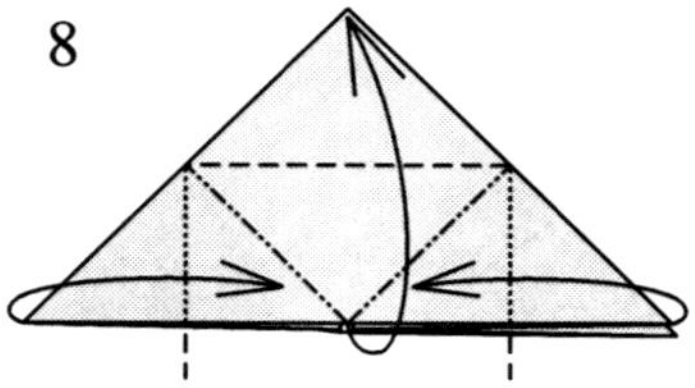

Petal-fold on existing creases.

9

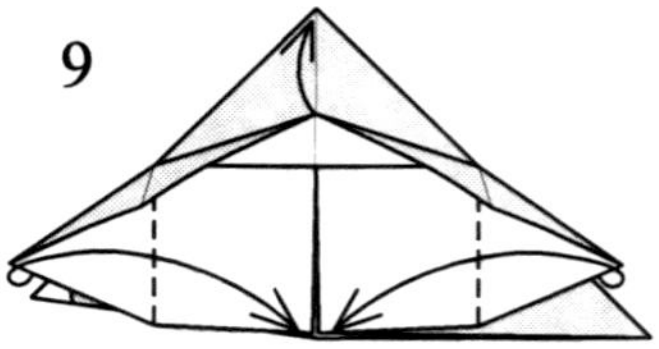

Petal-fold in progress.

10

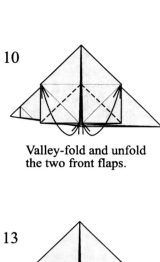

Valley-fold and unfold
the two front flaps.

11

Valley-fold and unfold.

12

Reverse-fold.

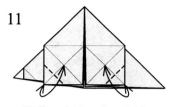

PERFORM IT!

Say to the audience, **"This is Prince Not So Charming. He's still charming, just not SO charming, but boy, does he see well! He has half the eyes but twice the vision, and has been used on occasion by blind princesses as a seeing eye frog."**

13

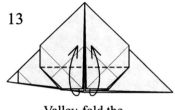

Valley-fold the
two front flaps.

14

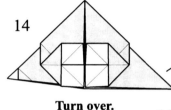

Turn over.

15

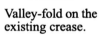

Valley-fold on the
existing crease.

16

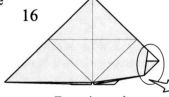

Zoom in on the
right corner.

17

Squash the flap.

18

Squash in progress.

19

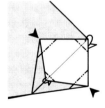

Employing two mountain
folds and two reverse folds,
convert the quadrilateral to
a relatively regular octagon.
It's simpler than it sounds.

20

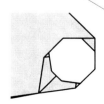

The frog eyeball is
complete.

Prince Not So Charming **75**

21

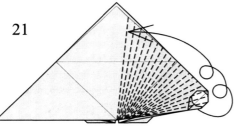

Now for the eye socket. Roll the flap up into a narrow cone.

22

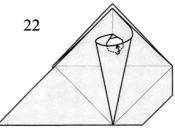

Pull the octagonal eyeball out to taste.

23

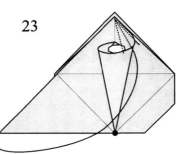

Insert the into flap into the slot, being careful not to tear the paper at the black dot. The next step will lock the flap into place.

24

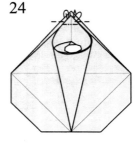

Fold the tips inside. Crease extra sharply to ensure the lock stays in place.

25

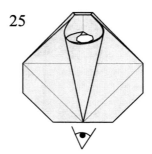

Focus on the behind of the model and don't giggle.

26

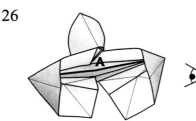

View from behind the frog. Insert a couple of fingers into pocket **A** to ensure that the mouth hinge (bold line) is pushed downward, NOT upward.

27

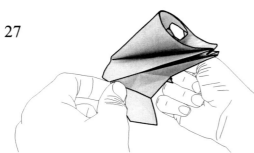

Prince Not So Charming is ready for action.
Holding as shown, push your hands together...

28

...and Prince Not So Charming will take a deep breath.

29

Pull your hands apart and Prince Not So Charming will open his mouth and, with the help of a ventriloquist, declare, **"EYE love you!"**

Prince Not So Charming singing a duet with Prince Charming

Familiar Liar

By Jeremy Shafer ©2003 **Intermediate**

Designing an origami face with a protractible nose was a completely original idea. It really was! It really was!....

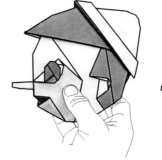

1
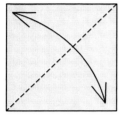
Colored side up, valley-fold and unfold.

2
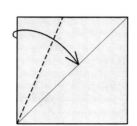
Valley-fold.

3
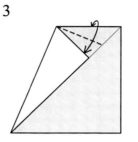
Make the indicated valley crease.

4
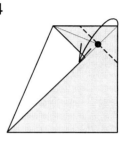
Valley-fold on the black dot.

5
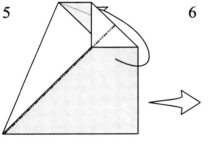
Mountain-fold.

6
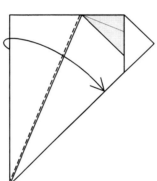
Valley-fold.

7
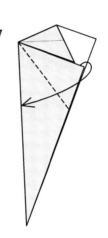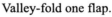
Valley-fold one flap.

8
Valley-fold one flap.

9

Valley-fold and unfold.

10
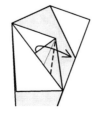
Valley-fold, so that the crease touches the edge.

11

Valley-fold.

12
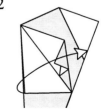
Unfold the flap.

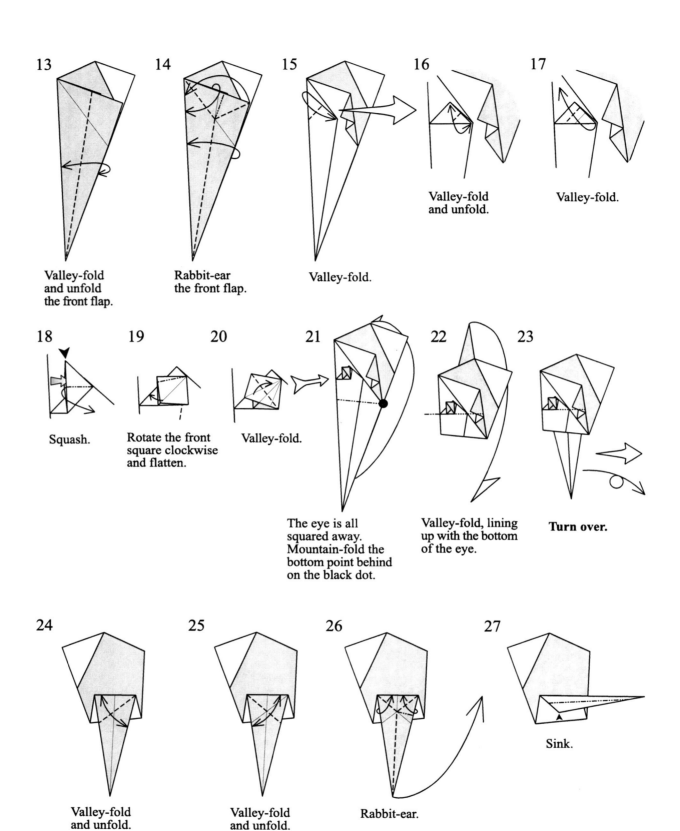

13

Valley-fold
and unfold
the front flap.

14

Rabbit-ear
the front flap.

15

Valley-fold.

16

Valley-fold
and unfold.

17

Valley-fold.

18

Squash.

19

Rotate the front
square clockwise
and flatten.

20

Valley-fold.

21

The eye is all
squared away.
Mountain-fold the
bottom point behind
on the black dot.

22

Valley-fold, lining
up with the bottom
of the eye.

23

Turn over.

24

Valley-fold
and unfold.

25

Valley-fold
and unfold.

26

Rabbit-ear.

27

Sink.

28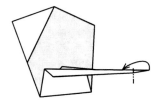

Reverse-fold the tip.

29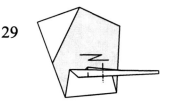

Pleat to make the nose
a respectable length.

30

Turn over.

31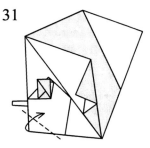

Valley-fold the mouth
to taste.

32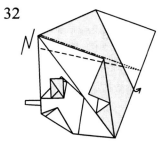

Pleat to define the hairline.
The pleat goes underneath
the white triangle.

33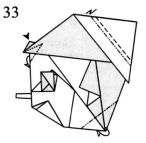

Squash to shape the forehead. Pleat
the white triangle to form the hat.
Mountain-fold the bottom corner
of the head.

34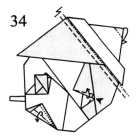

Mountain-fold the tip of
the hat. Pleat below the
base of the hat. Squash
to shape the ear. Slide
the single layer below
the mouth downward.

35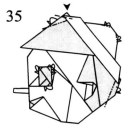

Make the indicated
mountain folds to
shape the hair, hat
and eye.

36

"I did not
tell a lie,
I swear..."

**The Familiar Liar is crafted and ready
to fib.** Holding from behind as shown,
extend the nose using four fingers.

37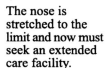

My, what a
long nose I
have! Cool!
I should lie
more often!"

The nose is
stretched to the
limit and now must
seek an extended
care facility.

38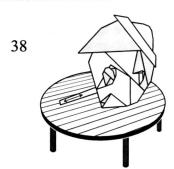

You can also get the growing/shrinking nose effect
without even touching the model. Simply balance
the model upright on a table by using the nose as
a stand. Then close one eye and move left and
right, to see the nose grow and shrink.

Ask the audience, **"Does anyone know who
this is?"** To whatever they say, respond in a
ventriloquist voice, **"No, I'm Elvis Presley!"**
Elongate the nose and say, **"OK, I was lying,
but will you still love me tender and love
me true?"**

Spinnigami

From the merry-go-round, to the Ferris wheel, to the simple top, people have long exhibited a fascination with spinning objects. This chapter focuses on origami that goes 'round and 'round. So get ready to get dizzy!

Shin

Put in Two

Flying Candy Cane

Super Simple

By Jeremy Shafer ©2009

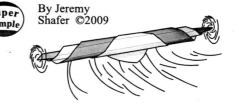

This model is so fun and easy, I imagine it will someday get mass-produced on playgrounds around the world!

1

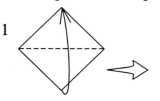

For a traditional red and white candy cane, use paper that is red on one side and white on the other. White side up, valley-fold in half diagonally.

2

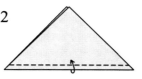

Valley-fold as near to the bottom as possible. Please fold evenly!

3

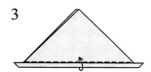

Valley-fold again and flatten.

4

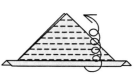

Continue rolling up the paper and flattening as you go. Roll it up all the way. Try to make the folds as perfectly horizontal as possible.

5

The paper is all rolled up and flattened. Now start unrolling the model by pulling apart the two middle corners.

6

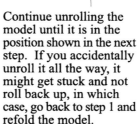

PERFORM IT!

This model is so quick and simple, I recommend folding it in front of your audience, so that they can learn how to fold it. Open and close the finished model a couple times so that it looks like the picture at the top right of this page. Say to the audience, **"This is the Intergalactic Flying Candy Cane rocket. Whoever can catch it can keep it, but be gentle, because you don't want to squish it or tear it. Three, two, one, everyone yell, 'Blast off!'"** Launch the model, throwing it like a rocket over their heads. When somebody grabs it, announce, **"The Next Generation Space rocket has landed safely! The International Origami Space Program is no longer in jeopardy!"**

Continue unrolling the model until it is in the position shown in the next step. If you accidentally unroll it all the way, it might get stuck and not roll back up, in which case, go back to step 1 and refold the model.

7

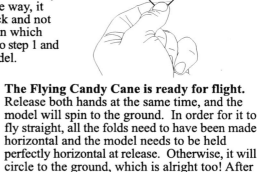

Thoughts Behind the Folds

I discovered this model while free-folding (folding without any aim in mind). It's so simple I wouldn't be surprised if it has been designed before, but if so, I'm surprised that I haven't seen it before! It has become one of my favorite models to teach – even kids as young as four can make it.

The Flying Candy Cane is ready for flight. Release both hands at the same time, and the model will spin to the ground. In order for it to fly straight, all the folds need to have been made horizontal and the model needs to be held perfectly horizontal at release. Otherwise, it will circle to the ground, which is alright too! After opening and closing it a couple of times, you should be able to simply throw it up in the air and it will spin down. To throw it up the highest, throw it up as if you were throwing a dart. When it reaches the apex it will start spinning down. **Warning:** Eating the Flying Candy Cane is not advised, unless you are a silverfish insect.

Flying Candy Cane **81**

Candy Cane Spinner (Super Simple)

By Jeremy Shafer ©2009

This wind powered variation of the Flying Candy Cane will take your breath away! Make sure you can fold the Flying Candy Cane (previous page) before trying this model.

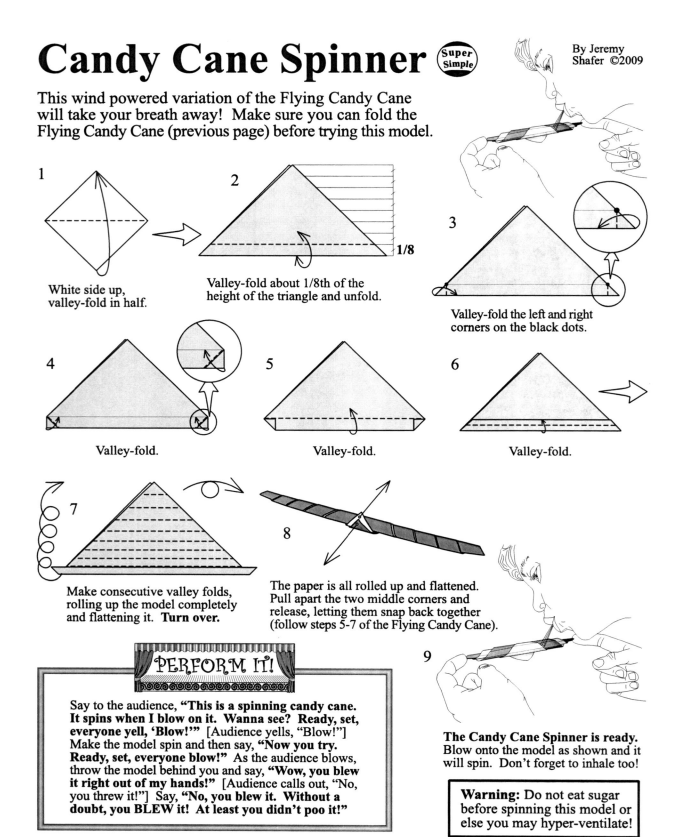

1 White side up, valley-fold in half.

2 Valley-fold about 1/8th of the height of the triangle and unfold. 1/8

3 Valley-fold the left and right corners on the black dots.

4 Valley-fold.

5 Valley-fold.

6 Valley-fold.

7 Make consecutive valley folds, rolling up the model completely and flattening it. **Turn over.**

8 The paper is all rolled up and flattened. Pull apart the two middle corners and release, letting them snap back together (follow steps 5-7 of the Flying Candy Cane).

9 The Candy Cane Spinner is ready. Blow onto the model as shown and it will spin. Don't forget to inhale too!

PERFORM IT!

Say to the audience, **"This is a spinning candy cane. It spins when I blow on it. Wanna see? Ready, set, everyone yell, 'Blow!'"** [Audience yells, "Blow!"] Make the model spin and then say, **"Now you try. Ready, set, everyone blow!"** As the audience blows, throw the model behind you and say, **"Wow, you blew it right out of my hands!"** [Audience calls out, "No, you threw it!"] Say, **"No, you blew it. Without a doubt, you BLEW it! At least you didn't poo it!"**

Warning: Do not eat sugar before spinning this model or else you may hyper-ventilate!

Helicopter By Jeremy Shafer ©2009

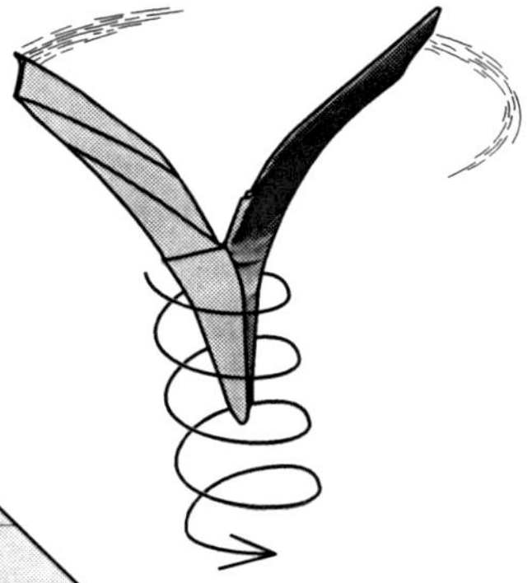

This simple model spins to the ground just like a helicopter...
...crash landing!

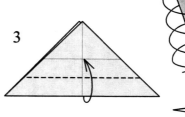

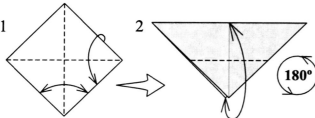

1

White side up, valley-fold in half vertically and unfold. Valley-fold in half horizontally.

2

Valley-fold on both layers and unfold. Rotate the model 180°

180°

3

Valley-fold.

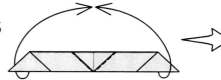

4

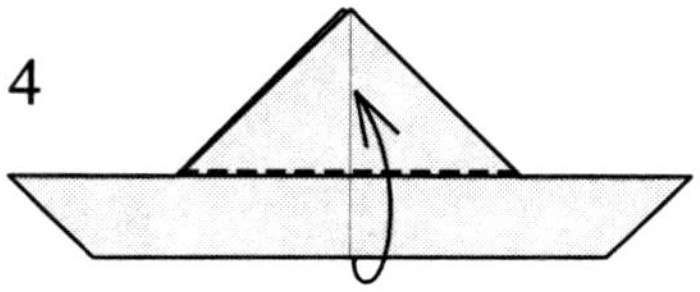

Valley-fold.

5

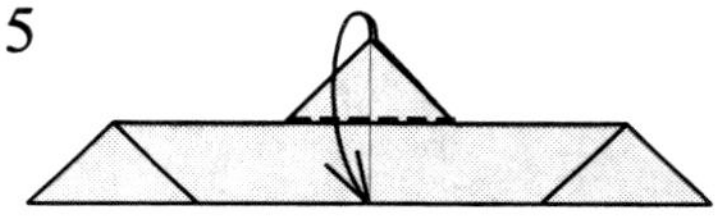

Valley-fold.

6

Valley-fold the right flap and mountain-fold the left flap.

7

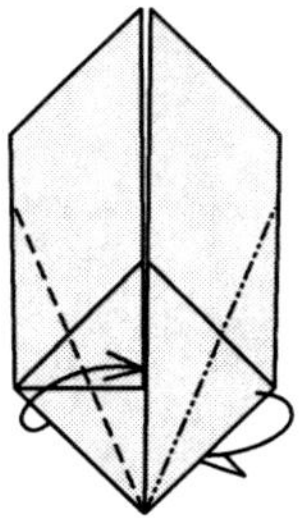

Valley-fold on the left side and mountain-fold on the right side.

8

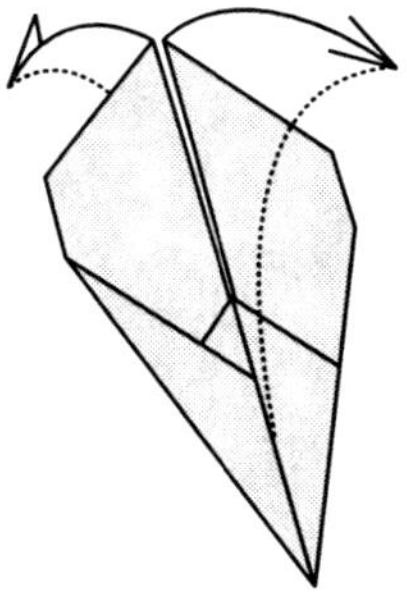

Bend the right flap forward and bend the left flap backward.

9

10

The Helicopter is complete. Throw it in the air and watch it spin to the ground. Adjust the amount of curvature on the wings to find the optimum spin.

The Helicopter in Flight. It's a lot easier to throw in the air and make it spin than it is to take a picture of it in midflight! The above pictures look more like some sort of UFO.

PERFORM IT!

Say to the audience, **"This is a helicopter. When I throw it up, it'll spin down. Whoever catches it gets to throw it up again. Ready, set, everyone say, 'Throw it up!'"** [Audience says, "Throw it up!"] Throw it up to the audience. When someone catches it or picks it up, say, **"Here we go again. Ready, set, everyone say, 'Throw it up!'"** Continue taking turns throwing it up until the game starts getting old or until the model no longer spins. Then say, **"OK, my turn again. Give it to me. Ready, set, everyone say "Throw it up!"** [Audience says, "Throw it up!"] This time, rather that throw it up in the air, pretend to regurgitate it, and then say, **"I threw it up! But I still feel sick!"** Pretend to barf all over the audience.

Spinning Top By Jeremy Shafer ©2009

If origami spinning tops ever become as popular as hit songs, this one might spin to the top of the charts! But until then, it'll just spin on the table.

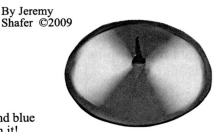

Note: If you fold this model from paper that is yellow on one side and blue on the other, the top of the top will appear to turn green as you spin it!

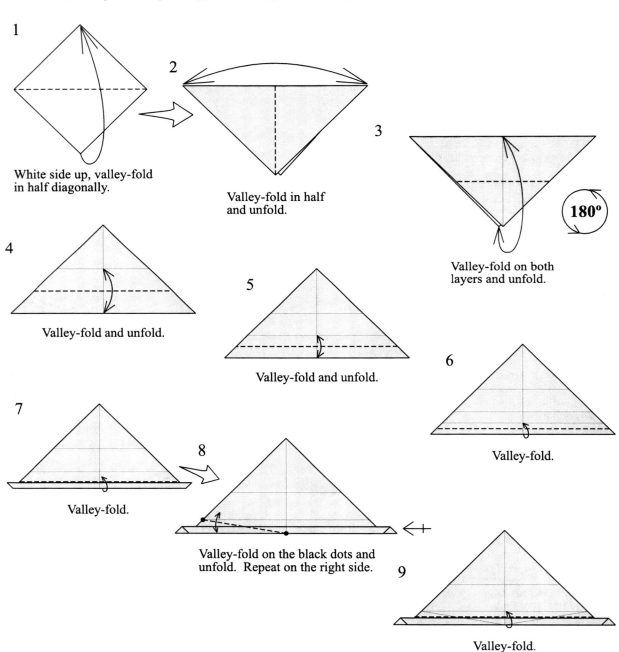

1
White side up, valley-fold in half diagonally.

2
Valley-fold in half and unfold.

3
Valley-fold on both layers and unfold.
180°

4
Valley-fold and unfold.

5
Valley-fold and unfold.

6
Valley-fold.

7
Valley-fold.

8
Valley-fold on the black dots and unfold. Repeat on the right side.

9
Valley-fold.

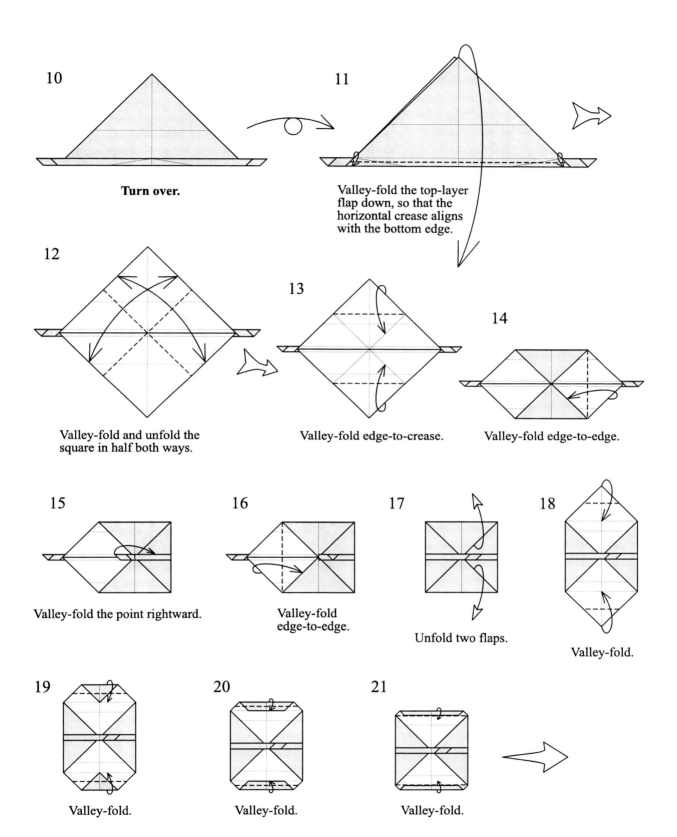

10

Turn over.

11

Valley-fold the top-layer flap down, so that the horizontal crease aligns with the bottom edge.

12

Valley-fold and unfold the square in half both ways.

13

Valley-fold edge-to-crease.

14

Valley-fold edge-to-edge.

15

Valley-fold the point rightward.

16

Valley-fold edge-to-edge.

17

Unfold two flaps.

18

Valley-fold.

19

Valley-fold.

20

Valley-fold.

21

Valley-fold.

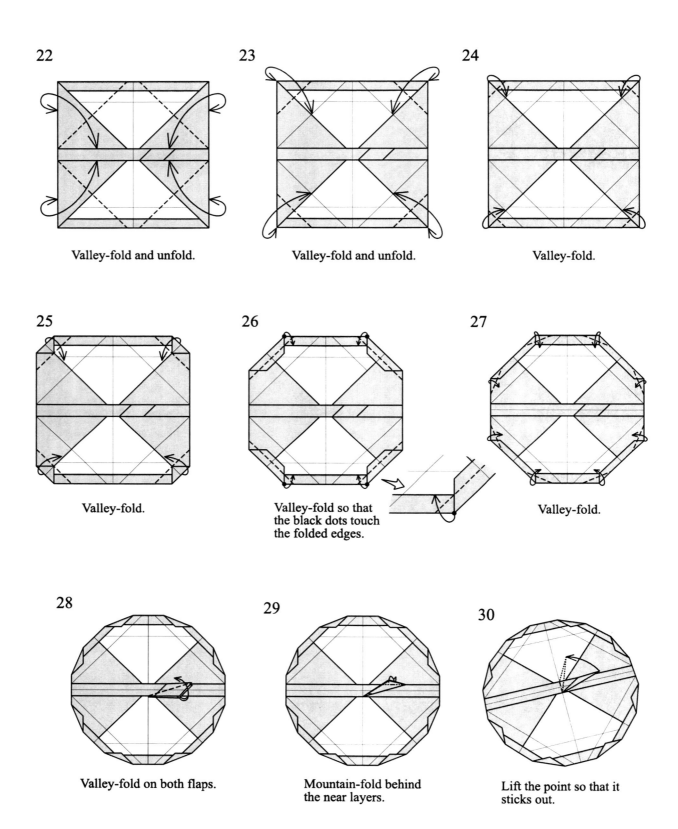

22

Valley-fold and unfold.

23

Valley-fold and unfold.

24

Valley-fold.

25

Valley-fold.

26

Valley-fold so that
the black dots touch
the folded edges.

27

Valley-fold.

28

Valley-fold on both flaps.

29

Mountain-fold behind
the near layers.

30

Lift the point so that it
sticks out.

31

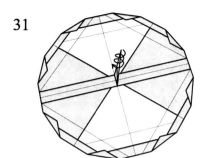

Twist the point clockwise.

32

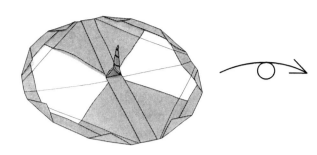

Turn over.

33

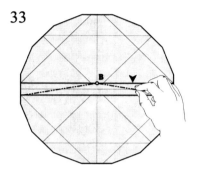

Point **B** is the point on which the Spinning Top will spin. Pinch on existing mountain folds, so that point **B** sticks out. The model will not lie flat.

34

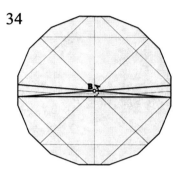

Reach behind point **B** and pull one layer upward. This will make point **B** sturdier and better able to support the weight of the Spinning Top.

35

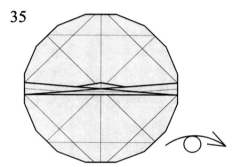

Turn over.

36

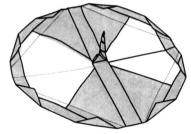

The Spinning Top is ready to spin on a table! Or if you're bald, you can spin it on your head, and call it a "Spinning **Top Hat**."

37

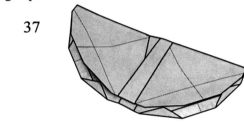

Fold it in half, and you have a taco, which will fit in a pocket.

38

The Spinning Top in action

Pinwheel Spinner

By Jeremy Shafer ©2009

This origami pinwheel spins on an ordinary table... so perhaps it should be called a 'Tablewheel Spinner!'

Inspired by Yami Yamauchi's Little Blow Top, and of course, the Traditional Origami Pinwheel!

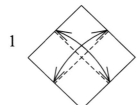

1

White side up, valley-fold and unfold in half in both directions.

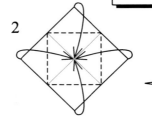

2

Blintz.

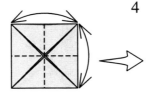

3

Valley-fold and unfold in half both in both directions.

4

Valley-fold.

5

Valley-fold.

6

Valley-fold and unfold in half on all layers.

7

Valley-fold the four flaps (if they are not already folded).

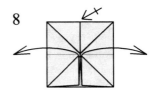

8

Pull the two points apart as far as they will go, and flatten. Repeat on the top.

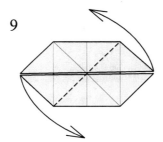

9

Valley-fold two flaps.

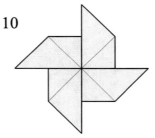

10

Flatten! **Turn over.**

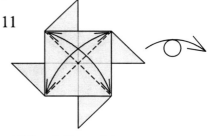

11

Valley-fold on all layers and unfold. **Turn over.**

PERFORM IT!

Place the model on top of a package of foil origami paper and say to the audience, **"This is a Wind Turbine. It spins in the wind to generate electricity. This package of origami foil is highly conductive, which means that by holding it in my hand I am risking getting a huge shock. But I'll be brave! Ready, set, every one say, "BLOW!"** Blow on top of the model, making it spin on the package of origami foil. After a few seconds of spinning it, intentionally blow the model off the package of foil and into the audience. Just as someone grabs it, cry out, **"No! Don't touch it! You could have gotten electrocuted! But you didn't! You're still alive! I'm shocked! I told you I might get shocked."**

12

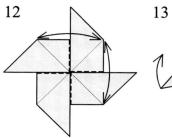

Valley-fold and unfold.

13

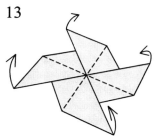

Lift the four flaps so that they stick up a little.

14

The Pinwheel Spinner is complete. Put the model on a smooth table and blow down onto it and it will spin counterclockwise. I find it spins best if you blow down from a foot above the model.

15

Spinning! If you happen to blow the model off the table, you can call it, "Gone with the Wind!"

Penwheel Spinner (Rather Simple)

By Jeremy Shafer ©2009

This model couldn't be named Pinwheel Spinner because that name is already taken (previous model), and because it's too big to spin on a pin, but with the slight name change, spinning is a cinch!

1

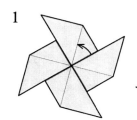

Begin by folding steps 1-12 of the Pinwheel Spinner. Pull the indicated flap so that it touches the crease, as shown in the next step. Make sure the model stays convex. Do not flatten yet!

2

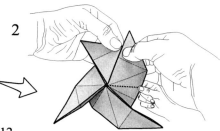

3-D View of the edge touching the crease. Using your third hand, flatten sharply on the dotted line through all layers, so that the model holds its position.

3

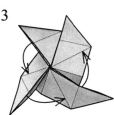

Repeat steps 1-2 on the other three flaps.

4

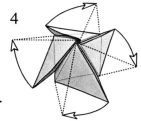

Unfold the flaps so that they stick out.

5

The Penwheel Spinner is Complete. Insert a ball-point pen (without its cap) into the hollow space under the model. Blow down onto the model and it will turn counterclockwise. I find, it works best if your mouth is a foot away from the model, or at least 5 toes!

PERFORM IT!

Say to the audience, **"This is called a Pinwheel Spinner because it will spin on a pin. But this one is too big for a pin. So we have to call it a..."** Pull out a ball point pen without top and continue, **"...a Pen-wheel Spinner! Who wants to make it spin?"** Find a volunteer and have them blow onto the model, making it spin. Quickly say, **"Wow that was some breath! Did you eat garlic and onions for breakfast? Just kidding! Give this kid – and his/her powerful breath – a big hand!"**

Wind Spinner By Jeremy Shafer ©2009

What's another way for origami to spin?
The answer is blowing in the wind.

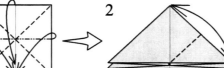

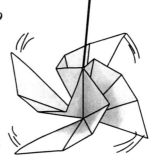

1. Begin by folding a Waterbomb Base (Basics, page 18).

2. Valley-fold and unfold.

3. Valley-fold and unfold.

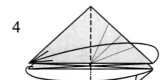

4. Valley-fold the front right flap to the left. Fold the rear left flap behind to the right, balancing the model.

5. Repeat steps 2-4 three times, so that all of the flaps have creases.

6. Like this.

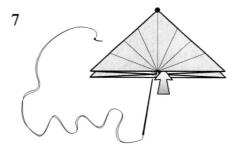

7. Now comes the moment where origami and acupuncture become one! Like they say... "This won't hurt a bit!" Thread a needle and tie a big knot at the end of the thread. Insert the needle into the bottom of the Waterbomb Base and pull it out through the top point (black dot).

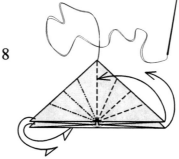

8. Refold the mountains and valleys so that they curl up as shown to the right.

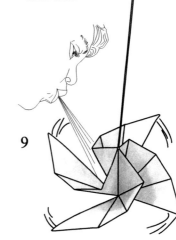

9. **The Wind Spinner is ready to spin.** Letting the model hang from the thread, blow down onto the top of it or hang it outside in the wind. You can also make it spin by running with it like a kite. As it spins, the thread will wind up and when the wind stops it will unwind, spinning the model in the opposite direction. For an ideal windspinner that does not wind and unwind, attach the tread to a ball-bearing swivel, like the kind used at the end of fishing lines. For a neat effect, try using invisible thread (available at magic shops).

PERFORM IT!

Before showing the model, ask the audience, **"How many tentacles does an octopus have?"** [Audience answers, "Eight."] **"Well I have an origami octopus in this box that lost 4 legs in battle, so now I call it a quadropus. But it's really cool; it can swim in the air and do spinning tricks. You want to see it?"** [Audience answers, "Yes!"] Reach in the box, grab the end of the thread and pull, so that the model comes out of the box spinning. Declare, **"That's a clapping moment!"** This routine works best if you use magician's invisible thread, so that the model looks like it's swimming and spinning all by itself.

Spin-a-Fortune

By Jeremy Shafer ©2009

With a little luck, this model will allow you to give up your day job and fulfill your dream of becoming a full time fortune teller.

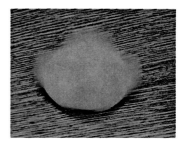

1

White side up, valley-fold in half diagonally and unfold in both directions.

2

Blintz.

3

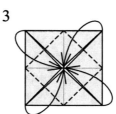

Blintz again.

4

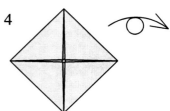

Turn over.

5

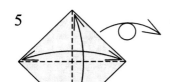

Valley-fold and unfold. **Turn over.**

6

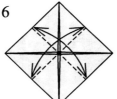

Valley-fold and unfold.

7

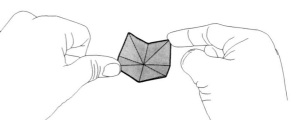

The Spin-a-Fortune is ready to spin. Holding as shown, flick your fingers to spin the model. To turn it into a fortune teller, go on to step 8.

8

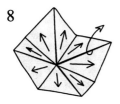

Draw eight arrows as shown. Unfold one flap.

9

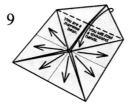

Think up two fortunes and write them as shown. Fold the flap back to the center.

10

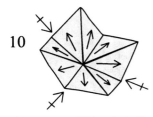

Repeat steps 8-9 on the remaining three flaps and you'll be ready to tell fortunes. Spin the model, and whichever arrow is pointing to your client, under that arrow will be their fortune. If your clients object to this simple approach to fortune telling, explain to them, **"Sorry, but crystal balls were recently banned for their lack of biodegradability, and were replaced by these paper fortune tellers, which are easily recycled, easier to store, and... <pause> ...easier to read."**

PERFORM IT!

Ask the audience, **"Who here has seen the origami Fortune Teller where you pick a number to get a fortune? Well, here you get to spin for your fortune. It's called 'Wheel-a-Fortune!' Spin the fortune teller and whichever arrow is pointing to you, under it will be your fortune. Who would like their fortune told?"** Choose a couple of volunteers to spin for their fortunes. Afterward, explain, **"I used to look deeply into my crystal ball to tell fortunes, but due to budget cuts I had to downsize to this paper fortune teller."**

Spinny Square

By Jeremy Shafer ©2009

Just as anything can be called a hat if you put it on your head, so can anything be called a spinner if you spin it! Well, actually, if YOU spin it, then you're the spinner! So that makes it the *spinnee*, or more namely, the "Spinny Square."

Inspired by Yami Yamauchi's Spinning Top and by the traditional two-piece spinning top that's spinning around the Internet.

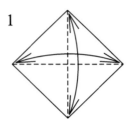

1

White side up, valley-fold diagonally and unfold in both directions.

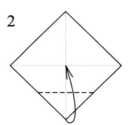

2

Valley-fold.

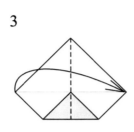

3

Valley-fold.

4

Valley-fold on both layers.

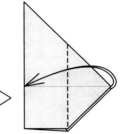

PERFORM IT!

Say to the audience, **"This is a Spinny Square. Ready, set, everyone yell, 'Spin!'"** [Audience yells, "Spin!"] Spin the model and say, **"Whoa, I'm feeling dizzy. I think I might throw up. Luckily, this model also works as a BARF bag."** Open the pocket (see step 7), show it to the audience and say, **"Quick everyone yell throw up!"** [Audience yells, "Throw up!"] Throw the model up in the air and say, **"I threw up and I feel much better now!"**

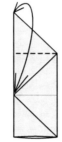

5

Valley-fold and unfold.

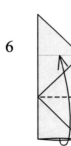

6

Valley-fold.

7

Valley-fold, tucking the flap into the pocket.

8

The Origami Square is complete, but to make it spinny...

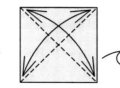

9

...valley-fold diagonally and unfold in both directions. **Turn over.**

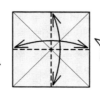

10

Valley-fold and unfold in both directions.

11

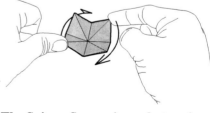

The Spinny Square is ready to spin. Holding as shown spin it clockwise. If you draw an even spiral around the center of the square, you will see the lines spiral inward or outward depending on which direction you spin it, and, if you look closely, you will get dizzy.

Tri-Color Spinner By Jeremy Shafer ©2009

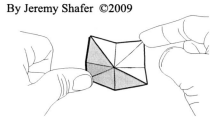

How can you make an origami model that is three colors from a paper that is just two colors? Well, you could fold so intricately that you rearrange the molecular structure and color of the paper, but there's a much easier way...

1

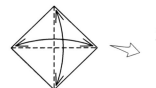

Begin with a sheet of paper whose front and back are of two different primary colors (e.g. blue and yellow). Valley-fold diagonally in half and unfold both ways.

2

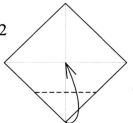

Valley-fold.

3

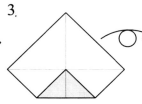

Turn over.

4

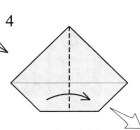

Valley-fold.

5

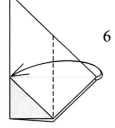

Valley-fold both layers.

6

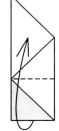

Valley-fold.

7

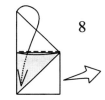

Valley-fold, tucking the flap into the pocket.

8

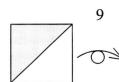

Turn over.

9

Valley-fold diagonally and unfold both ways.
Turn over.

10

Valley-fold and unfold both ways.

11

The Tri-Color Spinner is done. Holding as shown, flick your fingers to spin the model as fast as you can clockwise. The two colors will merge into a third color. Now you can call yourself an origami physicist, with a strong focus on visual perception.

12

The Three-Color Spinner spinning. There are hundreds of shades of colors if you take a picture at the right shutter speed as shown above!

PERFORM IT!

Say to the audience, **"This is an ordinary blue and yellow square, but in one single move, I will magically turn it green! Ready, set, everyone yell, 'Turn it green!'"** [Audience yells, "Turn it green"] Spin the model and declare, **"It's green! And it's also recyclable! How environmental! Shall I donate it to the Green Party?"**

Eight-Pointed Picture Frame Spinner

(Super Simple)

This model can really get you into origami! Well, maybe not you, but at least your picture!

8

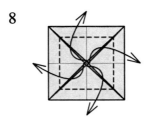

Begin with step 7 of Spin-a-Fortune (page 91). Valley-fold the four flaps to taste.

9

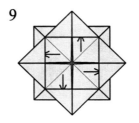

Insert a square picture into the frame.

10

If the model no longer spins, lightly refold the mountains and valleys being careful not to damage the picture.

11

The Eight-Pointed Picture Frame Spinner is ready for a picture-perfect spin!

PERFORM IT!

Prepare by inserting a square picture of yourself into the frame. Say to the audience, **"Before I show you the next model, I have a question: "What is the easiest way to get dizzy?"** [Audience says, "By spinning"] **"Correct! Do you want to see me get dizzy?"** [Audience says "Yes!"] **"OK, then, ready, set, everyone yell, 'SPIN!'"** [Audience yells, "SPIN!"] Hold up the model and say, **"This is me..."** Spin the model and say, **"...And look, I'm spinning!"** In the voice of a ventriloquist, make the picture say, **"Uh oh, I feel sick!"** Using nauseating sound effects and hand gestures, make the picture barf all over the audience.

PERFORM IT!

Prepare by inserting into the frame a portrait of you or someone the whole audience knows. Say to the audience, **"You've seen the star of David..."** Well this is the Star of "{person's name here}!"

Spinning Star of David

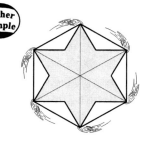

By Jeremy Shafer and thousands of others ©2009

Rather Simple

For origamists who have played with hexagonal paper, this model is probably a no-brainer, but since only a few thousand people have folded origami with hexagonal paper, that leaves nearly 7 billion people who might find this model interesting.

1

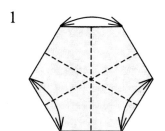

Begin with a hexagonal piece of origami paper. To cut out a hexagon, follow steps 1-11.666 of the Magical Transforming Polyhedron (page 171) . Valley-fold in half in three directions.

2

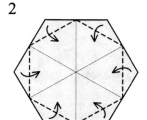

Valley-fold all six corners.

3

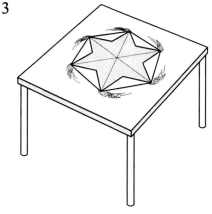

The completed Star of David. Place on a table and spin it like a top. For a better spinning AND better looking model, insert a picture of yourself (cut into a hexagon).

PERFORM IT!

Demonstrate to the audience as quickly as you can the different uses for the model: **"This star can be spun like a top, closed like a greeting card, transformed into picture frame, thrown like a frisbee, and magically viewed from behind when held up to the sun. And if that's not enough, it can also be used as a letter, or as a plate or be fashioned into a yarmulke"** (Jewish skullcap).

PERFORM IT!

Say to the audience, **"This is a star of David. Does anyone know why it's called the star of David?"** Turn it over and say, **"Because it has his name on it!"** You could go on to tell the real reason if you would actually like to be educational.

David

Star of David

By Lewis Simon   Diagrams by Jeremy Shafer ©2003

Here's a simple way to turn a triangle into a Star of David!
To turn a square sheet of paper into a triangle see page 248.

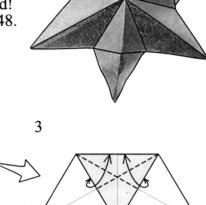

1

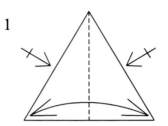

Valley-fold in half vertically and unfold. Do the same in the other two directions.

2

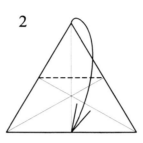

Valley-fold the top point to the bottom edge.

3

Valley-fold the shaded triangle in half both ways.

4

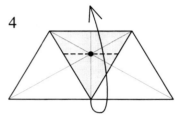

Valley-fold on the black dot.

5

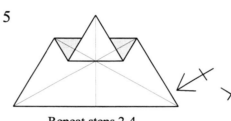

Repeat steps 2-4 on the right corner.

6

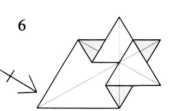

Repeat steps 2-4 on the left corner.

7

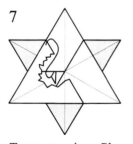

Tear-away view. Place the top flap under the indicated edge.

8

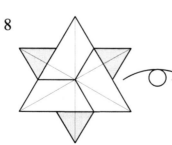

Turn over.

9

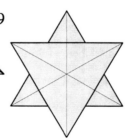

The completed Star of David.

10

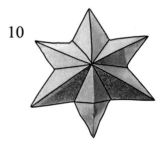

Variation: Fold the star in half in all directions, alternating mountains and valleys, so that the middle point sticks up 3-D as shown above. To turn it into a star that spins, flatten the model, turn it over and place on a smooth table. Flick a corner and it will spin like a top. This variation can also be called a Jewish Starfish.

PERFORM IT!

See the **PERFORM IT** boxes on the previous page.

Magic Dreidel By Jeremy Shafer ©2009

This model will be perfect to bring to any Hanukkah party, but might not be the best choice for a Christmas or Easter party.

1

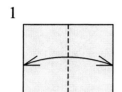

Colored side up, valley-fold in half and unfold.

2

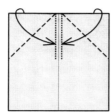

Valley-fold the two corners almost to the crease. The distance between them is the thickness of the dreidel handle.

3

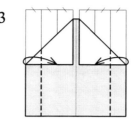

Valley-fold to taste. You could aim for thirds as a guide.

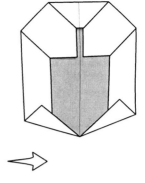

4

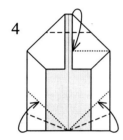

Valley-fold to taste. You could aim for the dotted lines as guides.

5

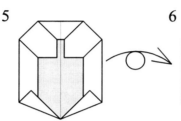

The Magic Dreidel is ready to play with. Turn it over...

6

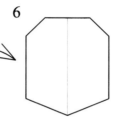

...and the dreidel will magically disappear!

7

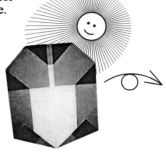

Hold it up to the sun and the dreidel will magically reappear! **Turn it over...**

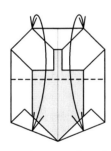

...and crease sharply as indicated...

...and now you and your friends can play a wild game of Spin the Dreidel!

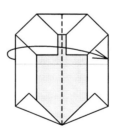

Close the Dreidel Card...

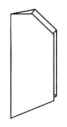

...and this Hanukkah story has come to an end!

PERFORM IT!

Say to the audience, **"This is a dreidel. It's even flatter than matzo, but it can still spin!"** Spin the model on a table or some other elevated surface. Then, hold the model up and say, **"Do you want to see it disappear?"** [Audience says, "Yes!"] Turn the model over showing the back side and say, **"The dreidel disappeared! Do you want to see it reappear?"** [Audience says, "Yes!"] Hold the model up to the light, so that the dreidel shape shows through, and say, **"The Dreidel has reappeared! A great miracle has happened here!"**

Dreidel By Jeremy Shafer ©2009

Here is an origami Hanukkah dreidel that actually can be used to play the Dreidel Game, and it even works better than traditional dreidels because it doesn't spin for as long, making the game move a lot faster.

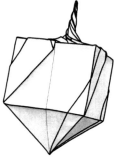

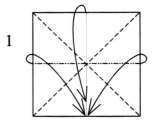

1

Begin by folding a Waterbomb Base (Basics, page 18).

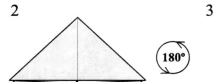

2

Rotate the model 180°.

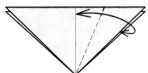

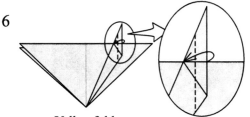

3

Valley-fold one flap edge-to-edge but only actually crease on the top edge.

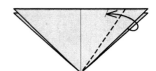

4

Valley-fold edge-to-creasemark.

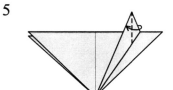

5

Valley-fold.

6

Valley-fold.

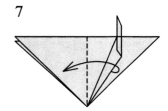

7

Valley-fold the flap to the left.

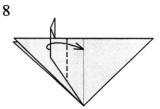

8

Valley-fold edge-to-crease.

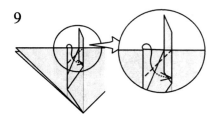

9

Valley-fold, inserting the flap behind the front layers.

10

Valley-fold the flap to the right.

11

Valley-fold.

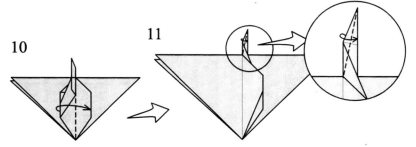

PERFORM IT!

Hold the completed model up and say to the audience, **"This is a Dreidel."** Spin it, and then ask, **"Does anyone know why it was named Dreidel? Because the name *spinning top* was already taken."**

12

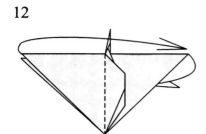

Valley-fold the front left flap to the right. Balance it out by folding the right flap behind to the left.

13

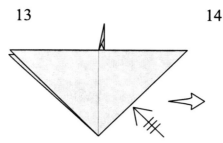

Repeat steps 3-12 three times. Follow the steps exactly; there is no orientation change.

14

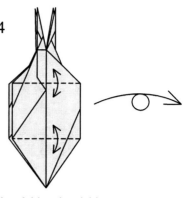

Valley-fold and unfold on all layers. **Turn over.**

15

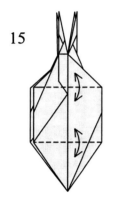

Valley-fold and unfold on all layers, exactly like you did on the other side.

16

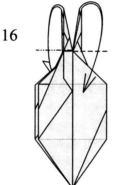

Valley-fold the two right flaps. Mountain-fold the two left flaps.

17

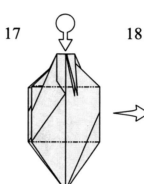

Inflate the model, and shape it by pinching on the existing creases.

18

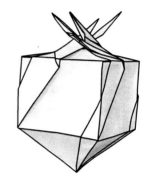

Like this. The four top flaps should overlap each other. The next view is from the top.

19

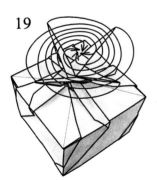

Top view. Now, twist the four flaps together clockwise to form the handle.

20

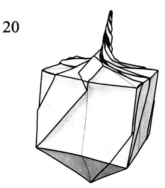

The Dreidel is folded and ready to spin.
If you would like to play the game, Dreidel, then you need to draw four Hebrew characters onto the dreidel, one on each face, as shown in step 21. On the next page is a template that when cut out and folded will result in a pre-printed, ready-to-play dreidel. Or, you could use the model, as is, to play the very popular and very simple game called, 'Spin the Top,' where you... um... spin the top!

21

Ready-to-Play Dreidel

The Four Dreidel Characters			
Shin	Hey	Gimmel	Nun
שׁ	ה	ג	נ
Put in Two	Take Half	Take All	Do Nothing

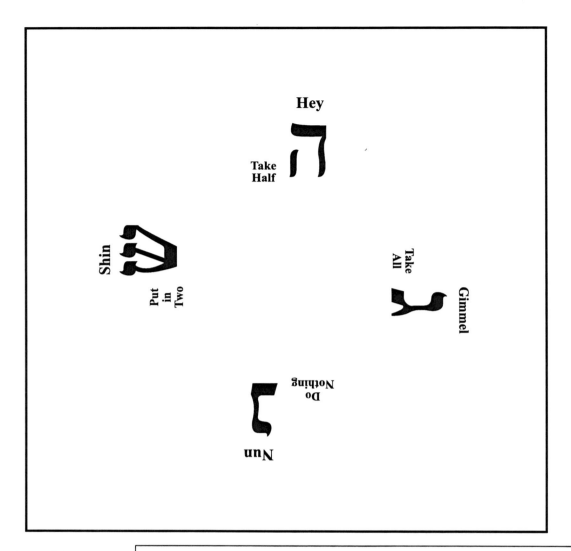

Dreidel Template

The above square template goes with the origami Dreidel diagrams and will result in a Dreidel that can actually be used to play Dreidel.

The template can be copied, cut out and folded as is, or it can be traced over onto the colored side of a six-inch square sheet of origami paper.

How to play Dreidel

Dreidel is a traditional Hanukkah game and rules vary.

How to Play
1. Any number of people (two or more) can take part in this game.
2. Each player begins the game with an equal number of game pieces (about 10-15) such as pennies, nuts, chocolate chips, raisins, matchsticks, etc.
3. At the beginning of each round, every participant puts one game piece into the center 'pot.' In addition, every time the pot is empty or has only one game piece left, every player puts one in the pot.
4. Every time it's your turn, spin the dreidel once. Depending on the outcome, you give or get game pieces from the pot:
a) *Nun* means '*nisht*' or 'nothing' [in Yiddish]. The player does nothing.
b) *Gimmel* means '*gantz*' or 'everything' [in Yiddish]. The player gets everything in the pot.
c) *Hey* means '*halb*' or 'half' [in Yiddish]. The player gets half of the pot. (If there is an odd number of pieces in the pot, the player takes half of the total plus one).
d) *Shin* (outside of Israel) means '*shtel*' or 'put in' [in Yiddish]. The player adds two game pieces to the pot.
5. If you find that you have no game pieces left, you are 'out.'
6. When one person has won everything, that round of the game is over.

Reference: www.myjewishlearning.com

Greeting Card Spinner Super Simple

By Jeremy Shafer ©2009

This design, which sprouted out of the Square Base Spinner (see next page), is easier to fold and spins just as well.

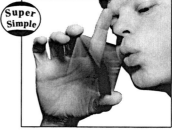

1

For a model that can be held in one hand, begin with a paper no bigger than 4-inches square. White side up, valley-fold in half.

2

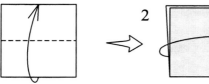

Valley-fold in half.

3

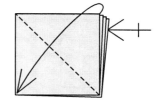

Fold the front flap and **repeat behind.**

4

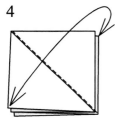

Valley-fold on all layers and unfold.

5

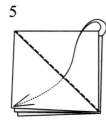

Valley-fold, tucking both flaps into the pocket.

6

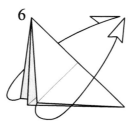

Unfold the front and rear flaps.

7

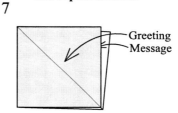

Greeting Message

Optional: Turn the model into a greeting card. Since the greeting card is locked (thanks to step 5), it's only half-openable but it still functions. You could also completely unfold it, write a secret message in the middle and refold it. Hey, you could do that with any origami model, but probably no one would read it, unless it were folded out of a dollar!

8

Happy B-day to Sunny
Spinfully yours, Windy

45°

Separate the two flaps so that the three black dots are spaced evenly. The model should not lie flat. Rotate 45° clockwise.

9

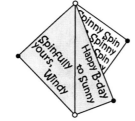

Spinny Spin Spinny Spin
Happy B-day to Sunny
Spinfully yours, Windy

The Greeting Card Spinner is ready to take for a spin. Hold the model at the two white dots between your thumb and index finger as shown to the right. Blow onto it, making it spin as shown in the picture at the top of this page. Notice that the greeting card is harder to read when it's spinning!

10

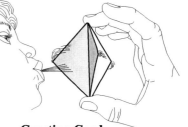

Greeting Card Spinner Spinning!

PERFORM IT!

Say to the audience, **"This is a three-blade rotary origami engine specially designed to run off my powerful breath, which is so powerful it will blow you away! Ready, set, everyone say 'blow!'"** [Audience says, "Blow!"] Blow, making the model spin and then blow so hard that the model flies out of your hands and into the audience. Recover the model and say, **"See? I told you I'd blow you away. Not you guys! I'm talking to this origami engine!"**

Square Base Spinner

Super Simple

By Jeremy Shafer ©2009

This model was inspired by Annie Pidel's Two-Color Spinner which she says was based on my Strobe Light (*Origami to Astonish and Amuse,* page 219).

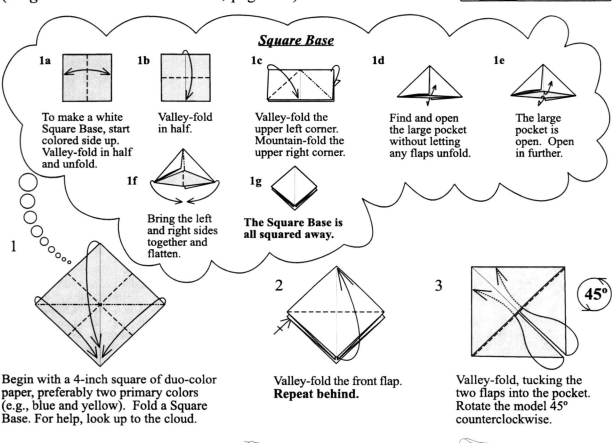

Square Base

1a To make a white Square Base, start colored side up. Valley-fold in half and unfold.

1b Valley-fold in half.

1c Valley-fold the upper left corner. Mountain-fold the upper right corner.

1d Find and open the large pocket without letting any flaps unfold.

1e The large pocket is open. Open in further.

1f Bring the left and right sides together and flatten.

1g **The Square Base is all squared away.**

1 Begin with a 4-inch square of duo-color paper, preferably two primary colors (e.g., blue and yellow). Fold a Square Base. For help, look up to the cloud.

2 Valley-fold the front flap. **Repeat behind.**

3 Valley-fold, tucking the two flaps into the pocket. Rotate the model 45° counterclockwise.

45°

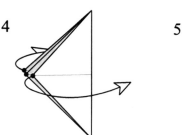

4 Unfold the two flaps so that the three black dots are spaced evenly (like the points of a regular triangle). The model will not lie flat.

5

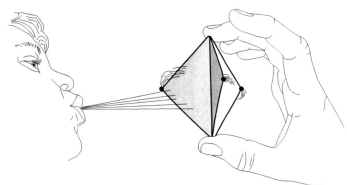

The Square Base Spinner is ready to spin. Hold the model between your thumb and index finger as shown. Blow onto it, making it spin. Notice that it makes the sound of a motor and spins about as fast as one too.

Heart Carousel By Jeremy Shafer ©2009

Here's a model with four hearts that balances on top of a pen or pencil, and if you blow onto it, 'round and 'round it will go, just like the carousel at the carnival, but free!

1

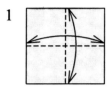

Colored side up, valley-fold and unfold. **Turn over.**

2

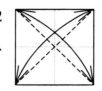

Valley-fold and unfold diagonally both ways.

3

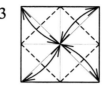

Valley-fold all four corners to the center and unfold.

4

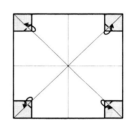

Valley-fold to the intersections of the creases.

5

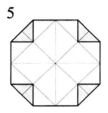

Turn over.

6

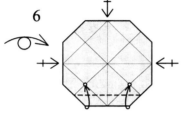

Valley-fold the bottom edge to the white dots. Repeat on the other three sides.

7

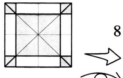

Turn over.

8

Valley-fold to form an abstract heart. A more shapely heart can be formed but that is beyond the scope of these diagrams.

9

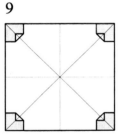

Turn over.

10

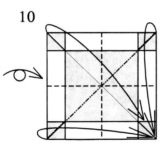

Fold on the existing creases to form a Square Base. (Look into the cloud on the previous page to learn how to fold the Square Base.)

11

Separate the four corners and insert a pointed object such as a pencil or pen, as shown to the right.

12

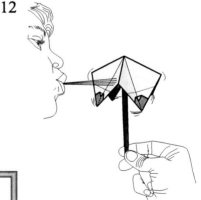

The Heart Carousel is fully constructed. Blow onto it as shown to make it spin. For a happier model, call it a Heart Merry-Go-Round.

PERFORM IT!

Say to the audience, **"This is a Heart Merry-Go-Round. It's powered by love! Ready, set, let's all blow it kisses!"** Blow it a kiss, but keep blowing, making the model spin. Say, **"Look at those hearts go round and round! It's so touching! It makes me want to cry of happiness! Let's all cry of happiness!"**

Balancing Heart

By Jeremy Shafer
©2010

This is an origami heart specially designed to balance on your finger and do spinning tricks. **Warning:** Playing with this model is addictive, so avoid folding it unless you have hours of free-time to kill. With practice, you too can master the art of Heart Balancing, but please do so at your own risk. Balance responsibly!

1

The larger the paper, the easier the heart will be to balance. I recommend using a 10-inch square of paper. White side up, valley-fold in half and unfold.

2

Valley-fold edge-to-edge and unfold.

3

Valley-fold edge-to-crease.

4

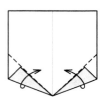

Valley-fold on the existing crease.

5

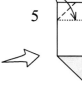 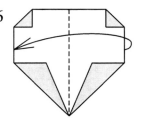

Valley-fold to the dotted line. These folds do not need to be exact. It's better to estimate than to put extra horizontal creases on the finished model.

6

Valley-fold.

7

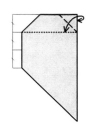

Valley-fold to the dotted line.

8

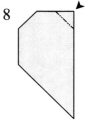

Reverse-fold on the existing creases.

9

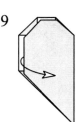

Open, the flap so that it sticks straight up. The model will not lie flat. **Turn over.**

10

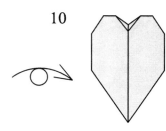

The Balancing Heart is ready to balance on a finger. As you try to keep it from falling, it will naturally spin one way or the other, and with practice, you can control which way it spins. If you can't manage to balance it, try using larger paper, and if that doesn't work, please accept my heart-felt sympathy.

Heart Combat

Every player starts balancing a heart on their finger and whoever balances it the longest wins. You are allowed to blow air or wave your other hand around to try to knock another player's heart down, but if you actually touch the player or their heart, you lose.

Spin the Bottle By Jeremy Shafer ©2009

Now, you and your friends can play Spin the Bottle without having to worry about broken glass!

1

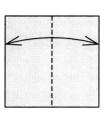

Colored side up, valley-fold in half and unfold.

2

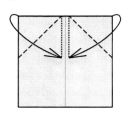

Valley-fold the two corners almost to the crease. The distance between them is the thickness of the bottle neck.

3

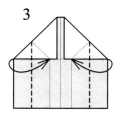

Valley-fold to taste.

4

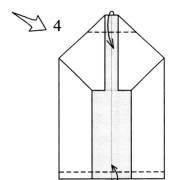

Valley-fold the top and bottom flaps to taste.

5

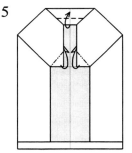

Valley-fold the top flap to form the bottle cap and mountain-fold the middle flaps to taste.

6

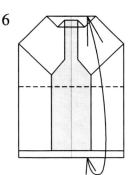

Valley-fold in half, creasing sharply, and unfold...

7

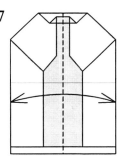

...and crease sharply the other way too.

8

Note: There is an almost identical game called "Spin the Model," which can be played with any origami model provided that a front end can be established.

Spin the Bottle is ready to play!
Spin the Bottle is a game where players take turns spinning the bottle. Each time it stops, whoever it is pointing to has to either kiss it or take an imaginary drink from it. For a break in the action, **turn the model over**, hold it up to the sun or light...

9

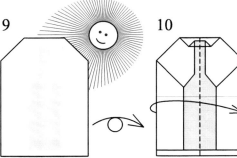

...and you can call it, 'Light Beer.' **Turn the model over** again and continue playing.

10

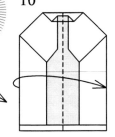

When you are done playing, call it a 'Bottle of Wine Card,' close it...

11

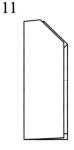

...and age to taste.

Spin the Bottle **105**

Magic Cross

 Super Simple · By Jeremy Shafer ©2009

This Cross is widely accepted as the symbol of Christianity, the most prevalent religion in the world, but, in order to appeal to an even wider audience, it can also be called an intersection, a telephone pole or a lower case letter 't.'

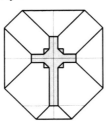 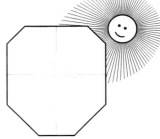

1

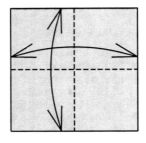

Colored side up, valley-fold in half and unfold in both directions. **Turn over.**

2

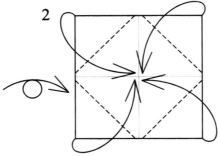

Valley-fold the four corners not quite to the center.

3

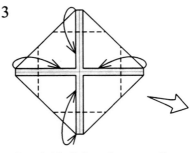

Valley-fold all four flaps equally (to taste). Unfold the bottom flap.

4

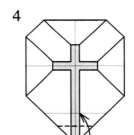

Valley-fold.

5

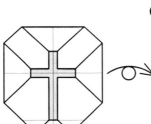

The Magic Cross is created. To create a miracle, **turn the model over.**

6

The cross has miraculously disappeared! For another miracle, hold the model up to the sun.

7

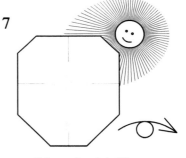

It's a miracle! The cross has returned! **Turn it over.**

8

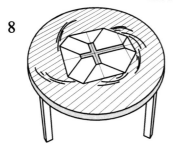

The Magic Cross is also a spinner...

9

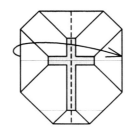

...or fold a lot of them and they can be used as greeting cards or as invitations to baptisms, first communions, Easter parties and other Christian events. The model can also be decorated and displayed as a medieval shield. To close the card, valley-fold it in half.

10

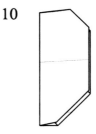

The Magic Cross Card is closed. **WARNING: BAD PUN ALERT!** Store the card in your dresser and you can call it a 'Cross Dresser.'

Spinning Octahedron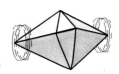

By Jeremy Shafer ©2009

This is an Octahedron, but, mind you, it is not a regular octahedron, as the faces are not equilateral triangles. To make it even more irregular and cool, try to spin the model by holding it in front of your mouth and blowing as shown in step 15.

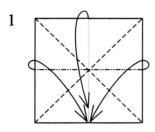

1

Begin by folding a
Waterbomb Base
(Basics, page 18).

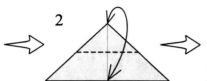

2

Valley-fold and unfold.

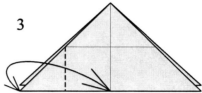

3

Valley-fold and unfold.

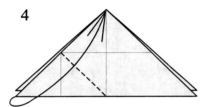

4

Valley-fold.

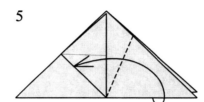

5

Valley-fold edge-to-crease.

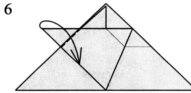

6

Valley-fold.

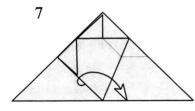

7

Unfold the fold
made in step 5.

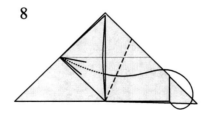

8

Refold, inserting the flap
into the pocket.

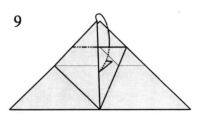

9

Mountain-fold, inserting
the flap into the pocket.

PERFORM IT!

Spin the model (step 15) and then say to the audience, **"This spinner is a polyhedron with eight triangular faces. Does anyone know what it's called?"** [Audience says, "Octahedron"] Reply, **"No, it's called Popeye..."** Spin the model again and say, **"...Because of all the spin-ach."**

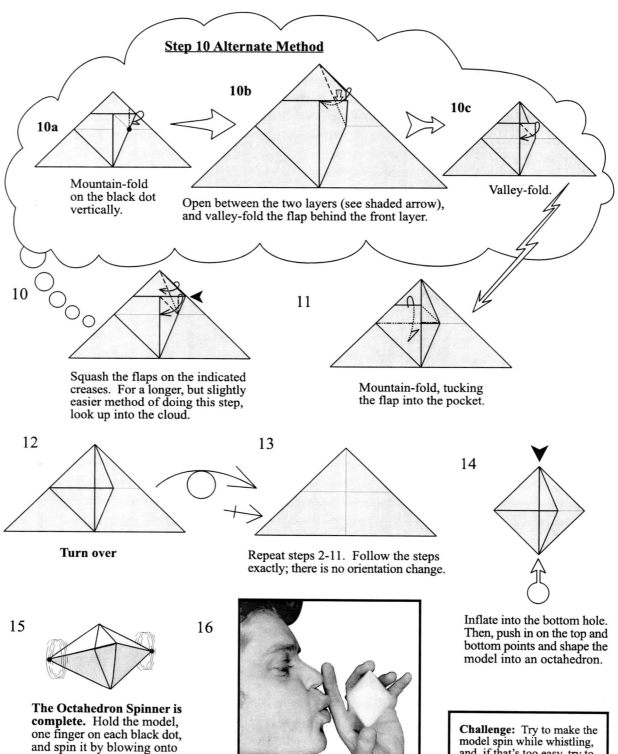

Step 10 Alternate Method

10a

Mountain-fold
on the black dot
vertically.

10b

Open between the two layers (see shaded arrow),
and valley-fold the flap behind the front layer.

10c

Valley-fold.

10

Squash the flaps on the indicated
creases. For a longer, but slightly
easier method of doing this step,
look up into the cloud.

11

Mountain-fold, tucking
the flap into the pocket.

12

Turn over

13

Repeat steps 2-11. Follow the steps
exactly; there is no orientation change.

14

Inflate into the bottom hole.
Then, push in on the top and
bottom points and shape the
model into an octahedron.

15

**The Octahedron Spinner is
complete.** Hold the model,
one finger on each black dot,
and spin it by blowing onto
it as shown to the right.

16

Octahedron Spinner Spinning

Challenge: Try to make the
model spin while whistling,
and, if that's too easy, try to
do it while unicycling too!

Acid Lemon (Rather Simple)

by Jack Skillman

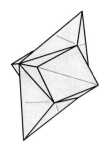

I diagrammed this model designed by Jack Skillman from sketches by Earle Oakes which were given to me by Samuel Randlett. Why is it called 'Acid Lemon?' I'm not sure, but it is somewhat shaped like a lemon and lemons are acidic. Nevertheless, I would not recommend it be used to make lemonade!

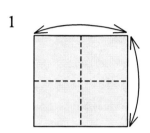

1 Begin colored side up. Valley-fold and unfold both ways in half. **Turn the model over.**

2 Valley-fold and unfold in half diagonally in both directions.

3 Valley-fold and unfold each edge to the center.

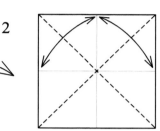

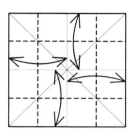

4 Valley-fold and unfold. Repeat on the other 3 corners.

5 Collapse to a Waterbomb Base (Basics, page 18).

6 Valley-fold.

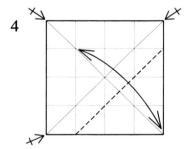

7 Valley-fold.

8 Unfold.

9 Mountain-fold the interior flap.

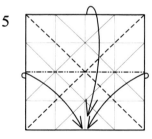

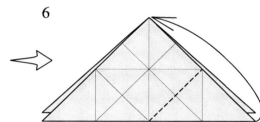

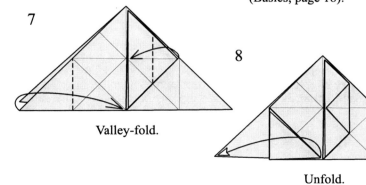

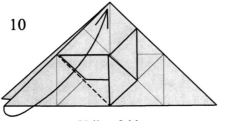

10

Valley-fold.

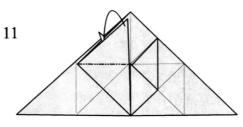

11

Mountain-fold, tucking the flap
inside the pocket.

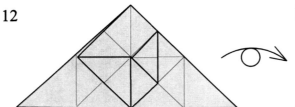

12

Turn the model over.

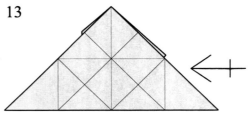

13

Repeat steps 6-11 on this side.
Follow the steps exactly; there
is no orientation change.

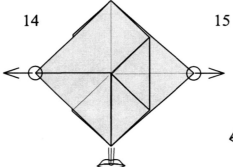

14

Inflate the model by blowing
in at the bottom while pulling
out at the sides...

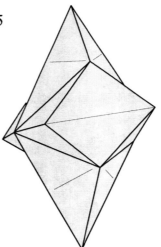

15

...and voila!
Here it is, the
Acid Lemon!

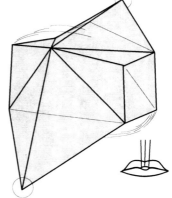

16

And, voila, here it is from another
view. To make the acid lemon twirl
like crazy, hold it lightly between
your thumb and index finger at its
sharpest points (indicated by the
circles), and blow on the model as
hard as you can, directing the air
slightly off center.

PERFORM IT!

Spin the model and say to the
audience, **"This is a another
spinner. "Do you know what
it's called, yes or no?"**
[Audience says, "No."] **"Wrong!
It's called 'Yes!' Everyone say,
'Yes sir!'"** [Audience says, "Yes
sir!"] **"And, in case you were
wondering, 'sir' is its surname."**

Magic Star*

By Jeremy Shafer ©2009

This star is only magical because it is based on the origami troublewit techniques popularized by magician, Harry Houdini. What makes it even better is that it spins too!

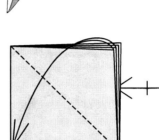

1

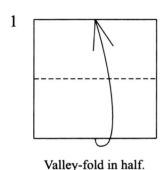

Valley-fold in half.

2

Valley-fold.

3

Valley-fold two layers.
Repeat behind.

4

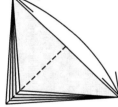

Valley-fold on all layers and unfold.

5

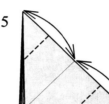

Valley-fold and unfold.

6

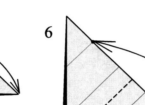

Valley-fold and unfold.

7

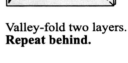

Valley-fold and unfold.

PERFORM IT!

Say to the audience, **"This is a Spinning Starfish. Everyone say, 'Spin it!'"** [Audience says, "Spin it!"] Spin the model and then let go, blowing the model into the audience. Recover the model and say, **"Oh, no! I think it might be injured! But don't worry, I am a Spin Doctor. I will put a good spin on this spinfully bad situation."** Attach a smiley face sticker to the model and say, **"Look, all better! It's happy! Now, we must return you to your natural habitat. Back to the tide pool you go!"** Place the model back in the box.

8

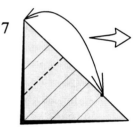

Valley-fold and unfold.
Turn over.

9

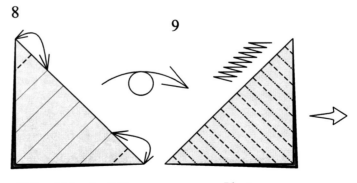

Pleat.

*This model also goes by the name "Magic Asterisk."

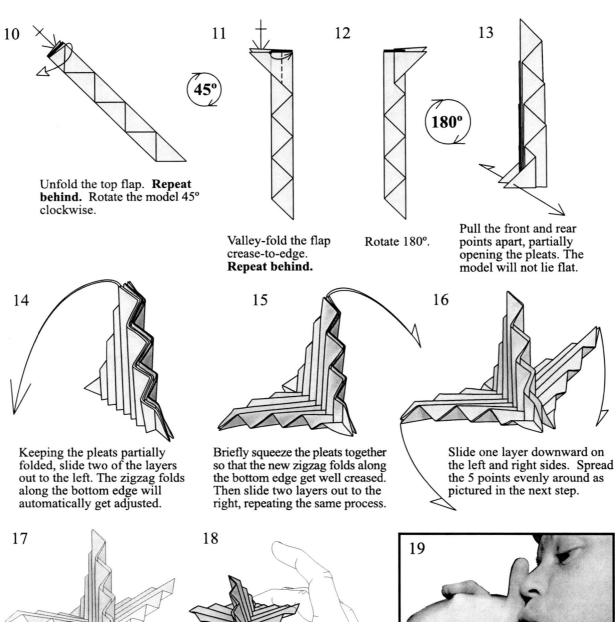

10

Unfold the top flap. **Repeat behind.** Rotate the model 45° clockwise.

11

45°

Valley-fold the flap crease-to-edge. **Repeat behind.**

12

Rotate 180°.

13

180°

Pull the front and rear points apart, partially opening the pleats. The model will not lie flat.

14

Keeping the pleats partially folded, slide two of the layers out to the left. The zigzag folds along the bottom edge will automatically get adjusted.

15

Briefly squeeze the pleats together so that the new zigzag folds along the bottom edge get well creased. Then slide two layers out to the right, repeating the same process.

16

Slide one layer downward on the left and right sides. Spread the 5 points evenly around as pictured in the next step.

17

The Magic Spinning Star is complete. The model is fine as is – a pleated star sculpture! But if you would like it to spin too, go to the next step.

18

Holding as shown, blow onto the model to make it spin. When spinning, it looks somewhat like a UFO. Since this is a relatively unknown model, for most people this really is an Unidentified Flying Object, or at least it's a USO... Unidentified Spinning Object. And, to make it a UFO, just let go!

19

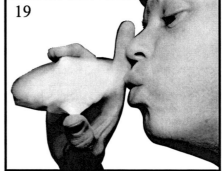

The Magic Spinning Star, twirling in the wind!

112 *Origami Ooh La La!*

Eight-Pointed Spiral Star (Intermediate)

So, what's the point of this model? Well, there's at least eight good points and that's more than some politicians can come up with!

By Jeremy Shafer
©2007

I am the star of this book!

1 Colored side up, valley-fold and unfold diagonally in half. **Turn over**.

2 Valley-fold.

3 Valley-fold and unfold.

4 Valley-fold the black dots to the bottom edge.

5 Repeat steps 2-4 on the other three corners.

6 Valley-fold in half.

7 Valley-fold on the right, and mountain-fold on the left.

8 Inserting your hand into the indicated pocket, squash the left and right corners together.

9 In progress.

10 Lift and squash the right front flap.

11 Valley-fold one flap to the right.

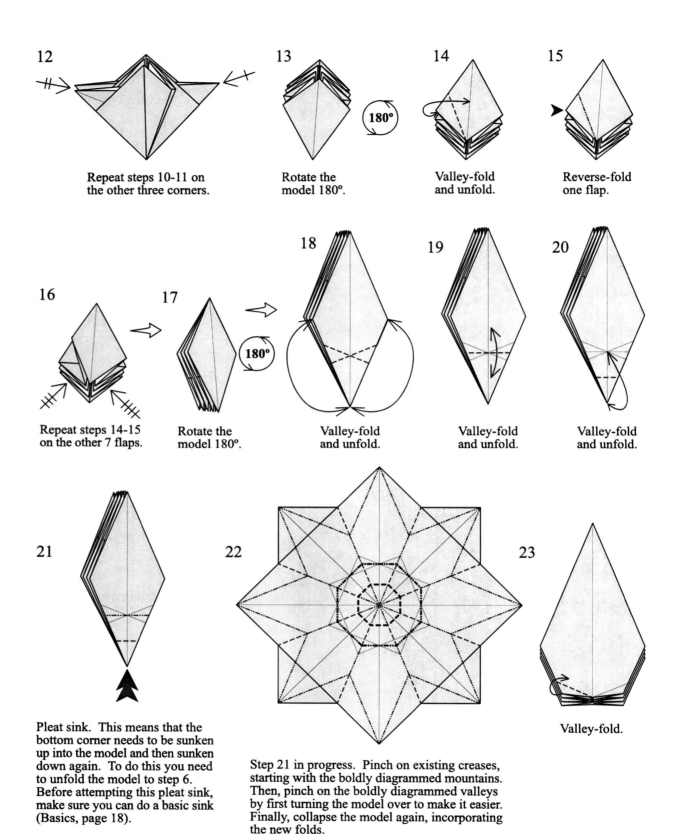

12

Repeat steps 10-11 on
the other three corners.

13

Rotate the
model 180°.

14

Valley-fold
and unfold.

15

Reverse-fold
one flap.

16

Repeat steps 14-15
on the other 7 flaps.

17

Rotate the
model 180°.

18

Valley-fold
and unfold.

19

Valley-fold
and unfold.

20

Valley-fold
and unfold.

21

Pleat sink. This means that the
bottom corner needs to be sunken
up into the model and then sunken
down again. To do this you need
to unfold the model to step 6.
Before attempting this pleat sink,
make sure you can do a basic sink
(Basics, page 18).

22

Step 21 in progress. Pinch on existing creases,
starting with the boldly diagrammed mountains.
Then, pinch on the boldly diagrammed valleys
by first turning the model over to make it easier.
Finally, collapse the model again, incorporating
the new folds.

23

Valley-fold.

24

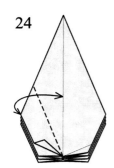

Valley-fold and unfold.

25

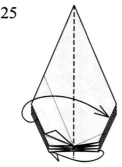

Valley-fold the left front flap to the right. Balance it out by folding the right rear flap to the left.

26

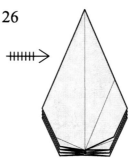

Repeat steps 23-25 seven more times, so that all eight flaps get folded.

27

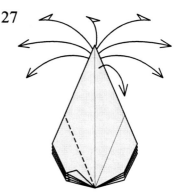

Pull the eight flaps apart and flatten on the existing creases.

28

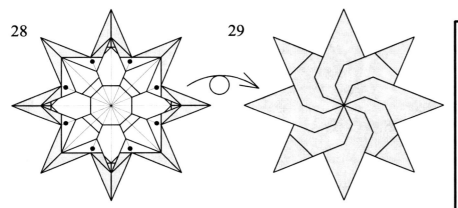

Fully flatten the model, especially at the black dots. **Turn over.**

29

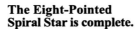

The Eight-Pointed Spiral Star is complete.

Note: This model could be called 'Deluxe Ninja Star,' but since we really don't need any more violence in world, you could just call it a 'Star Frisbee.' It could also be used as a yarmulke (or kippah). To make the more appropriate six pointed yarmulke, begin by folding steps 1-9 of the Star of David (page 96), and then fold steps 6-29 of this model.

PERFORM IT!

Before showing the model say, **"And now for the star of the show. Knee patter patter clap clap! Make some noise! It's...It's..."** Hold up the model and exclaim, **"...It's an origami star! Does anyone know how many points this star has?"** Move the model around just enough so that the audience can't count the points. Say, **"Trust me, you'll know when I spin it. Ready, set, everyone yell, 'Spin it!'"** [Audience yells, "Spin it!"] Spin the model, and, while it's spinning, call out, **"It has Eight Points!"** Pick up the model and say, **"I'm now going to ask you again, How many points does this star have? [Audience says, "Eight!"] "Correct! I'm sure glad I spun it!"** [Audience calls out, "You told us!"] Answer, **"Yes, I told you you'd know."**

30

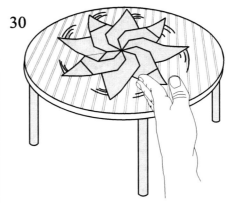

To make the star spin, place it on a table and hit one of the corners as shown above. Spinning this model over and over, will help soothe fidgety fingers. (I didn't say it would make them any less fidgety!)

Tip: Make sure the center point is pressed down so that it is concave, or else the star won't spin.

Objects
in Action

Here are some more action models. These particular models could be displayed on a wall or in a box, but then they wouldn't be action models! So, instead, they should be displayed in your hands in front of an audience, even if that audience is just you!

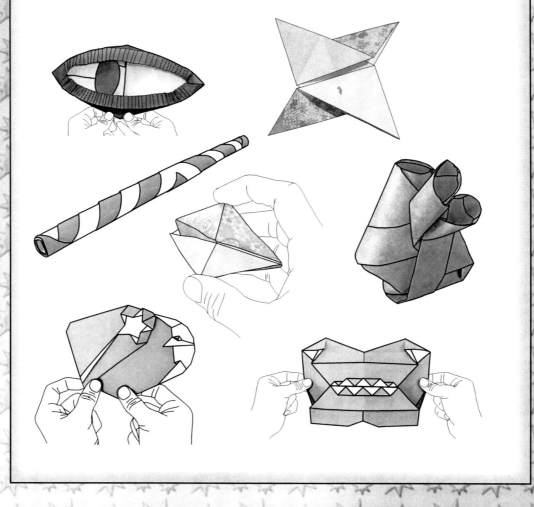

Striped Straw

By Jeremy Shafer
©2010

Here's an easy-to-fold, decorative straw that can even be used to sip hot apple cider. But that's not all! Slide them onto the ends of Christmas tree branches and you'll have the most unusual candy cane ornaments, throw them into the air and you'll have deluxe high-speed Flying Candy Canes (see page 81), or stick them into any berries and you'll have yummy 'Strawberries!'

1

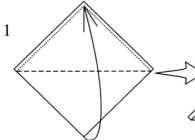

Valley-fold almost, but not quite, in half. The thickness of the resulting white line will determine the width of the straw's white stripe.

2

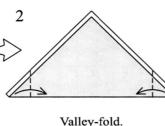

Valley-fold.

3

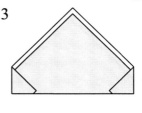

Turn over.

4

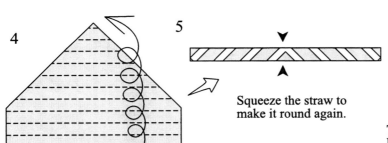

Valley-fold over and over rolling the paper up completely. Completely flatten the model so that it stays rolled up.

5

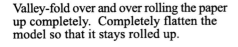

Squeeze the straw to make it round again.

6

The straw is ready sip some juice with. Use like an ordinary straw, and get ready for extraordinary results – it even sparkles the juice for you! At each sip, air bubbles will abound in your mouth.
Wetfolding Approach: For water that is less sparkling, completely submerge the model in water prior to using.

PERFORM IT!

Say to the audience, **"This is a miniature replica of the famous NORTH POLE! You know, the one Santa uses to mark his underground mansion where he lives with thousands of elves. It can also be used as a Christmas straw to sip hot apple cider..."** Take a sip from the straw and continue, **"...or it can be used to play poker. Who wants to get poked?"** Pretend to poke the kids. Say, **"I'm Pokeyman! I do the Hokey Pokey and turn myself around. That's what it's all about!"**

Glancing Eye

This eye glances left and right by secretly moving the rear flap. And, if you rotate it 90°, it can also glance up and down.

By Jeremy Shafer
©2002

What did the Australian optometrist say to the eagle? Good eye, mate!

1

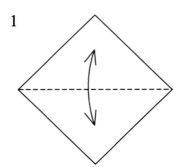

White side up, valley-fold diagonally in half and unfold.

2

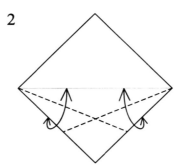

Valley-fold and unfold edge-to-crease.

3

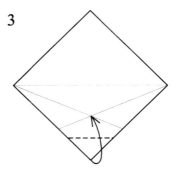

Valley-fold.

4

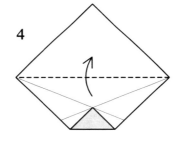

Valley-fold.

5

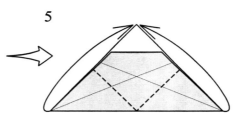

Valley-fold.

6

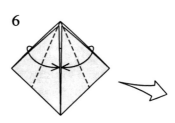

Valley-fold.

7

Valley-fold.

8

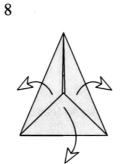

Unfold to step 6.

9

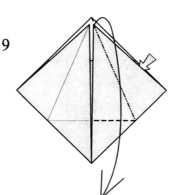

Petal-fold one flap. (For help, see Petal Fold, page 17.)

10

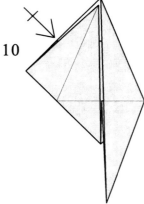

Repeat step 9 on the left side.

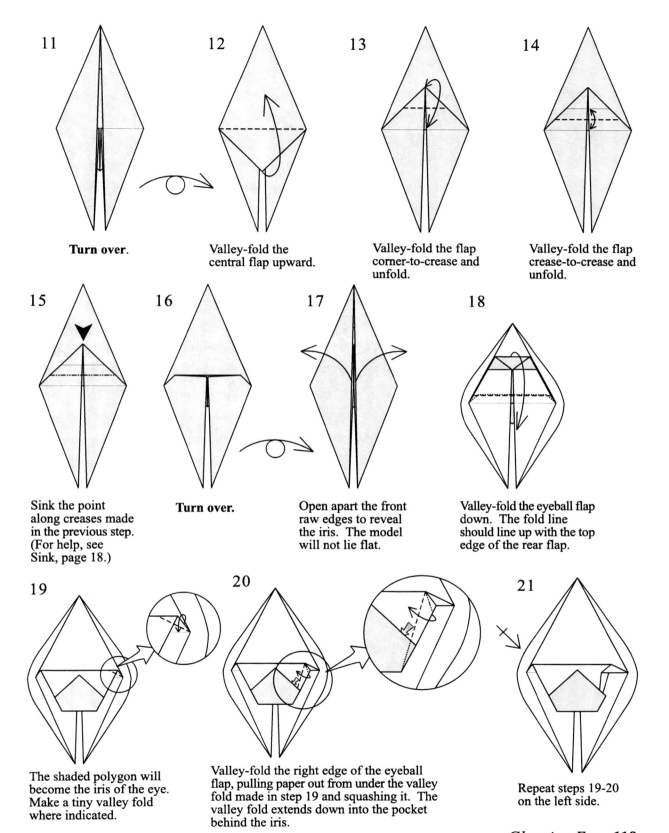

11

Turn over.

12

Valley-fold the central flap upward.

13

Valley-fold the flap corner-to-crease and unfold.

14

Valley-fold the flap crease-to-crease and unfold.

15

Sink the point along creases made in the previous step. (For help, see Sink, page 18.)

16

Turn over.

17

Open apart the front raw edges to reveal the iris. The model will not lie flat.

18

Valley-fold the eyeball flap down. The fold line should line up with the top edge of the rear flap.

19

The shaded polygon will become the iris of the eye. Make a tiny valley fold where indicated.

20

Valley-fold the right edge of the eyeball flap, pulling paper out from under the valley fold made in step 19 and squashing it. The valley fold extends down into the pocket behind the iris.

21

Repeat steps 19-20 on the left side.

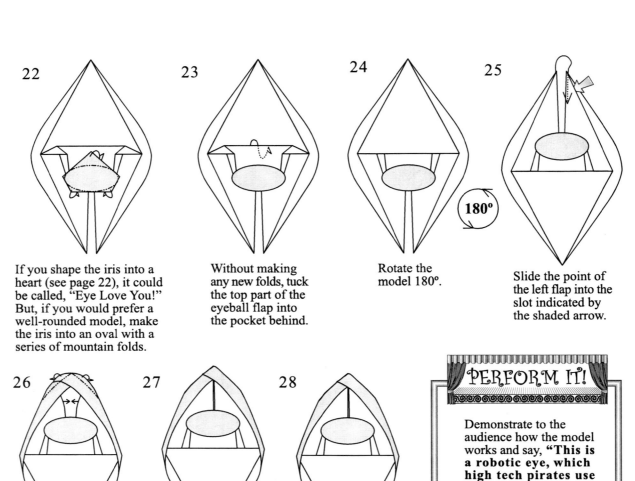

22

If you shape the iris into a heart (see page 22), it could be called, "Eye Love You!" But, if you would prefer a well-rounded model, make the iris into an oval with a series of mountain folds.

23

Without making any new folds, tuck the top part of the eyeball flap into the pocket behind.

24

Rotate the model 180º.

25

180º

Slide the point of the left flap into the slot indicated by the shaded arrow.

26

Squash the top, pulling the rear raw edges together.

27

Valley-fold.

28

Valley-fold.

PERFORM IT!

Demonstrate to the audience how the model works and say, **"This is a robotic eye, which high tech pirates use instead of a patch. Pirates and sailors love them! That's why they always say, 'Eye eye Captain!' Ready, set, everyone cover an eye and say, 'Eye eye Captain!'"**

29

90º

Valley-fold. Rotate the model 90º counterclockwise.

30

Bend the iris oval to the left. Pinch mountains to form the eyelashes and shape the model to taste, in other words, eyeball it!

31

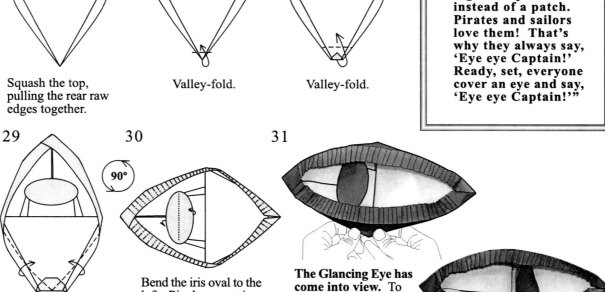

The Glancing Eye has come into view. To make it glance, move the rear flap left and right. To make it blink pull the left and right corners of the model away from each other.

Man in the Moon
Watching a Shooting Star

Rather Complex

Become a star gazer without even having to go outside.

By Jeremy Shafer ©2005

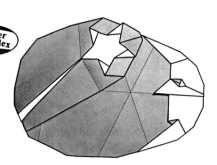

PERFORM IT!

Hold up the model as shown in step 43, and say to the audience, **"This is the Man in the Moon."** Hold it up high and say, **"Everyone say, 'Hi Moon.'"** [Audience says, "Hi Moon."] Hold it low and say, **"Everyone say, 'HelLOW Moon'"** Hold it regular and say, **"But, you know, the Man in the Moon is not the star of the show. Guess who is? Ready, set, everyone say, "Shooting star!"** [Audience says, "Shooting Star!"] Show the shooting star and say, **"Ouch! It just shot me twice on the nose! Look, I have two holes to prove it!"** Flare your nostrils.

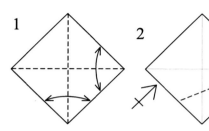

1. White side up, valley-fold and unfold.

2. Valley-fold edge-to-crease and unfold. Repeat on the left side.

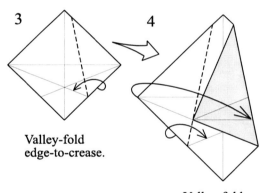

3. Valley-fold edge-to-crease.

4. Valley-fold.

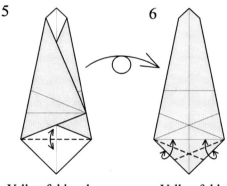

5. Valley-fold and unfold. **Turn over.**

6. Valley-fold and unfold.

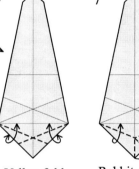

7. Rabbit-ear. (For help, see Rabbit Ear, page 17.)

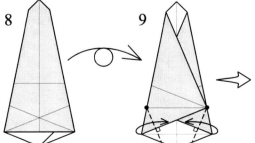

8. **Turn over.**

9. Valley-fold. The folds originate at the black dots and are perpendicular to the raw edges.

10. Squash. Repeat on the left side. (For help, see Squash Fold, page 16)

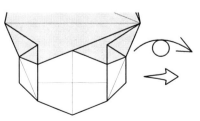

11. **Turn over.**

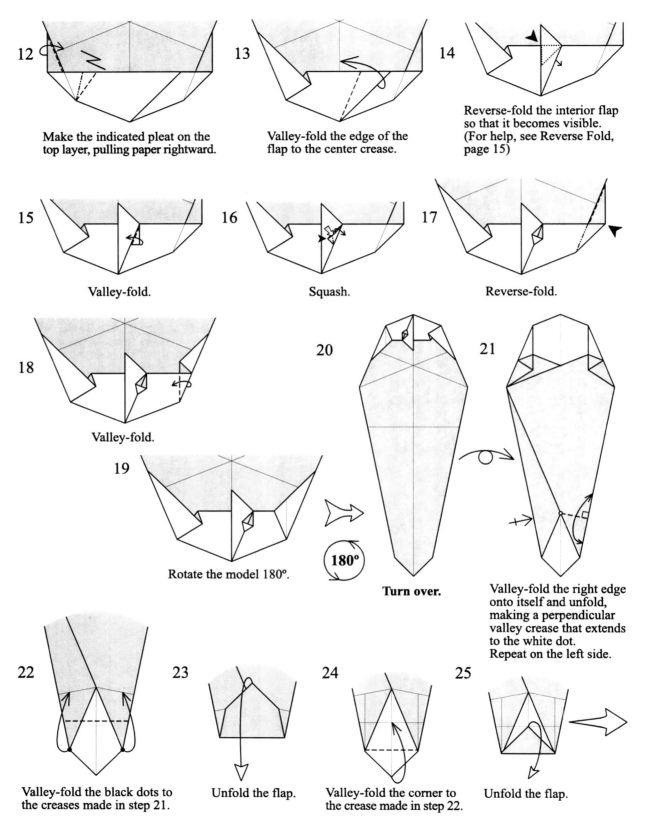

12 Make the indicated pleat on the top layer, pulling paper rightward.

13 Valley-fold the edge of the flap to the center crease.

14 Reverse-fold the interior flap so that it becomes visible. (For help, see Reverse Fold, page 15)

15 Valley-fold.

16 Squash.

17 Reverse-fold.

18 Valley-fold.

19 Rotate the model 180°.

180°

20

Turn over.

21 Valley-fold the right edge onto itself and unfold, making a perpendicular valley crease that extends to the white dot. Repeat on the left side.

22 Valley-fold the black dots to the creases made in step 21.

23 Unfold the flap.

24 Valley-fold the corner to the crease made in step 22.

25 Unfold the flap.

122 *Origami Ooh La La!*

26

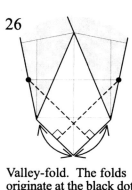

Valley-fold. The folds originate at the black dots and are perpendicular to the raw edges.

27

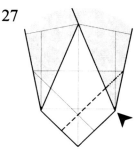

Valley-fold again, this time reverse-folding the right side.

28

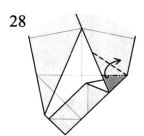

On the top layer, pinch to form a horizontal mountain, and pull it upward and flatten. Watch the shaded triangle.

29

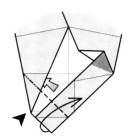

Two points of the star are complete. Valley-fold, reverse-folding the left side.

30

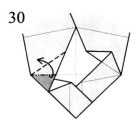

On the top layer, pinch to form a horizontal mountain, and pull it upward and flatten. Watch the shaded triangle.

31

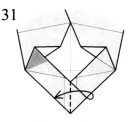

Three points of the star are complete. Valley-fold.

31

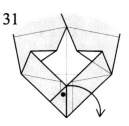

Pull out the paper. Watch the black dot.

32

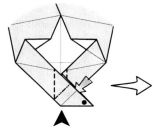

Open and squash the bottom flap upward. The vertical valley folds (on existing creases) should be made first. The rest of the folds get formed as the flap is flattened.

33

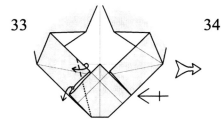

Make the indicated valley fold behind the front layer while pulling the white dot, which forms the forth point of the star. Repeat on the right side, forming the fifth point.

34

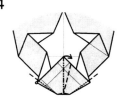

Make the fourth and fifth points of the star shorter by forming a pleat on the middle of the front layer.

35

Fold the flap to the left.

36

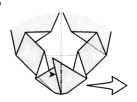

Reverse-fold the flap.

Thoughts Behind the Folds

I first designed The Man in the Moon Watching a Shooting Star in 1994. It started as a challenge Mark Turner gave me to design a man in the moon. I discovered that a rabbit-ear on the corner of the paper practically did the trick. In experimenting with what else could be done with the rest of the square, I happened upon the shooting star. The resulting model was almost identical to the model diagrammed here, but it took me more than 10 years to diagram it because I wanted to make the points of the star mathematically even all around. At one point, I thought I had a perfect 8-pointed star, but in trying to prove it was perfect (the most I've ever used my math degree!) I instead proved that it was not perfect, and that in order to make it perfect would require making an awkward microscopic pleat. So, finally, in lieu of shelving the model forever, I settled for a 5-pointed star that is not perfect. In order to find guidelines to make it as even as possible, I printed and cut out a 5-pointed star of the right size. I literally placed it onto the origami model and tried to make the edges line up, and this is the result! And that's the story of 'How the Moon and Stars Came to Be!'

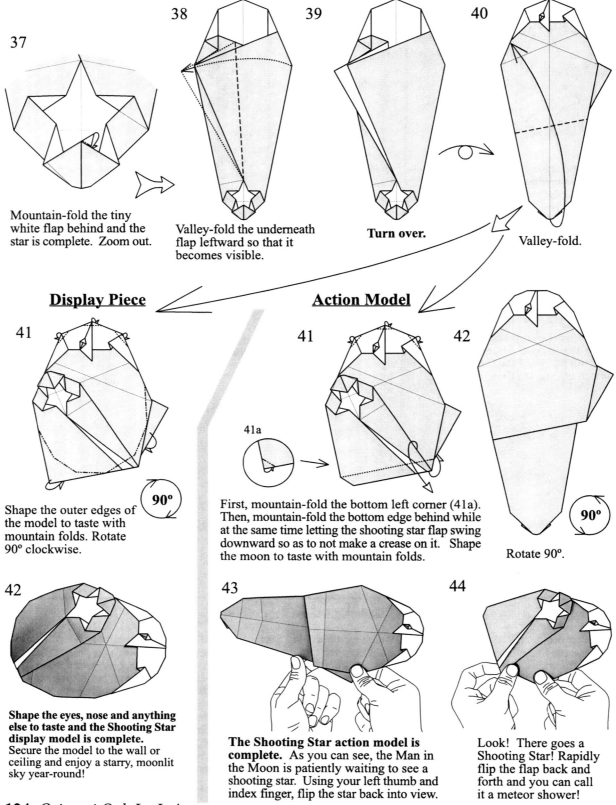

37

Mountain-fold the tiny
white flap behind and the
star is complete. Zoom out.

38

Valley-fold the underneath
flap leftward so that it
becomes visible.

39

Turn over.

40

Valley-fold.

Display Piece

41

Shape the outer edges of
the model to taste with
mountain folds. Rotate
90° clockwise.

90°

42

**Shape the eyes, nose and anything
else to taste and the Shooting Star
display model is complete.**
Secure the model to the wall or
ceiling and enjoy a starry, moonlit
sky year-round!

124 *Origami Ooh La La!*

Action Model

41

41a

First, mountain-fold the bottom left corner (41a).
Then, mountain-fold the bottom edge behind while
at the same time letting the shooting star flap swing
downward so as to not make a crease on it. Shape
the moon to taste with mountain folds.

42

90°

Rotate 90°.

43

**The Shooting Star action model is
complete.** As you can see, the Man in
the Moon is patiently waiting to see a
shooting star. Using your left thumb and
index finger, flip the star back into view.

44

Look! There goes a
Shooting Star! Rapidly
flip the flap back and
forth and you can call
it a meteor shower!

Pureland Iso-Area Pinwheel Puzzle

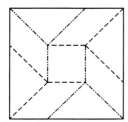

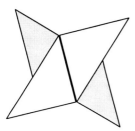

Can you construct the above model using only mountains and valleys?

Unfolding and folding on multiple layers are permitted as long as the folded edges do not separate. In other words, reverse folds, squash folds, and sinks, etc., are not permitted.

Pureland Iso-Area Pinwheel

By Jeremy Shafer ©2001

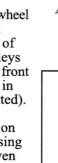

Here's a solution to the Pureland Iso-Area Pinwheel Puzzle shown to the left. Pureland is a term borrowed from Buddhism by John S. Smith of England to describe models folded with valleys and mountains only. Iso-area means that the front and back are identical in shape but opposite in color and often orientation (rotated or reflected). The solution to the puzzle, not counting the precreasing, requires eight folds and begins on step 10. The precreasing involves first creasing the square in thirds both ways. The first seven steps show a mathematically sound Pureland method for doing this, but the non-Pureland method shown to the right I find is faster and even more accurate.

Thirds Anyone?

Alternate method of folding a square of paper into thirds: Holding as shown, fiddle with the folds until they line up.

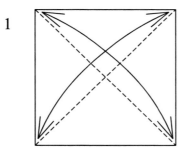

1

Begin white side up. Valley-fold and unfold in half diagonally in both directions.

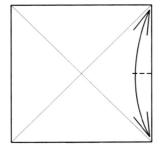

2

Valley-pinch on the right side and unfold.

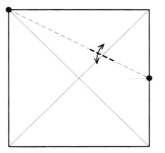

3

Make a very light valley crease between the two black dots, but crease it sharply where it crosses the diagonal.

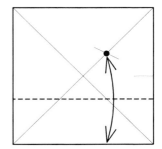

4

Valley-fold the bottom edge to the black dot and unfold.

5

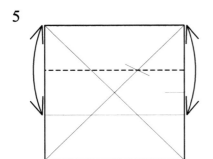

Valley-fold the top edge to the horizontal crease and unfold.

6

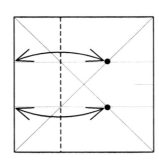

Valley-fold the left edge to the black dots and unfold.

7

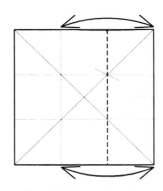

Valley-fold the right edge to the vertical crease and unfold.

8

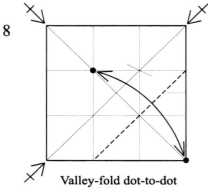

Valley-fold dot-to-dot and unfold. Repeat on the other three corners.

9

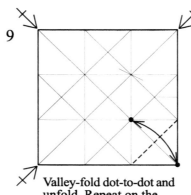

Valley-fold dot-to-dot and unfold. Repeat on the other three corners.

10

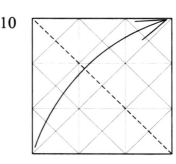

All of the creases are complete. Now, exactly eight folds must be made in order to complete the Pureland Iso-area Pinwheel. **Fold 1**: Valley-fold.

11

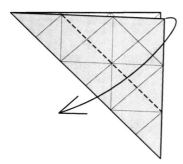

Fold 2: Valley-fold.

Thoughts Behind the Folds

The Pureland Iso-Area Pinwheel Puzzle is part of the larger question, "What can be folded using only mountains and valleys?" Or, more to the point, "What **can't** be folded using only mountains and valleys?" I haven't been able to answer that question yet (perhaps it's a topic for serious origami mathematicians such as Erik Demaine or Robert Lang), but I have explored many examples. The approach I take for any given folded example is to first fold it in the traditional way (with reverse folds, rabbit ears, squash folds, etc.) and then try to completely unfold it using just pureland moves: mountain-folding, valley-folding and "un-mountain-folding" and "un-valley-folding." Besides the Iso-Area Pinwheel, other models that I've managed to break up into pureland moves include, the Square Base, Waterbomb Base, Pinwheel Base and Fish Base. A particularly fun challenge is the Traditional Flapping Bird. A particularly difficult challenge is a sunken Waterbomb Base as pictured below. I came up with a solution (unpublished), but it requires 100 moves, so it obviously won't make sinking any easier for beginning folders! I haven't even begun to explore the pureland foldability of origami tessellations, but I expect that most are not pureland foldable!

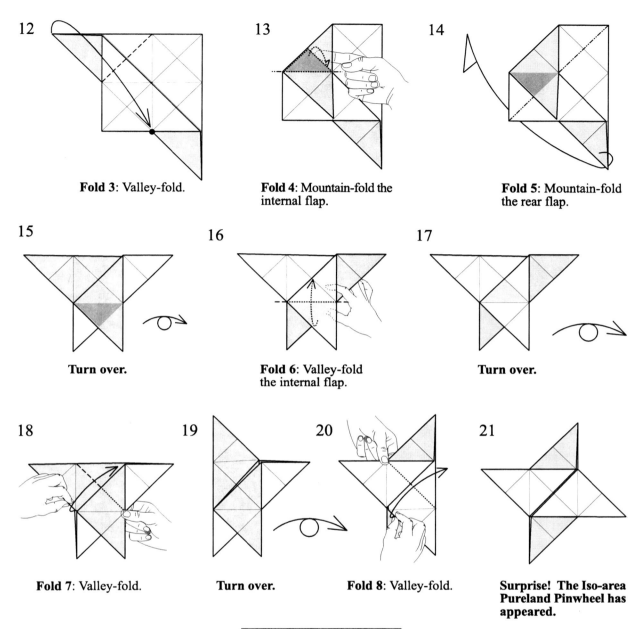

12

Fold 3: Valley-fold.

13

Fold 4: Mountain-fold the internal flap.

14

Fold 5: Mountain-fold the rear flap.

15

Turn over.

16

Fold 6: Valley-fold the internal flap.

17

Turn over.

18

Fold 7: Valley-fold.

19

Turn over.

20

Fold 8: Valley-fold.

21

Surprise! The Iso-area Pureland Pinwheel has appeared.

PERFORM IT!

This model isn't really a performance piece, but rather a stepping stone to the Imperfect Polyhedron (page 128), but if you really need to use it as a performance piece (because you haven't yet found enough in this book) it can be easily transformed into a spinning pinwheel. Say to the audience, **"I will now perform acupuncture on this origami patient."** Stick a pin through the middle of the model and blow onto the side of the model making it spin. Say, **"It's spinning like crazy! As you can see, I am a genuine spin doctor. OK, next patient. Would anyone else like to spin on a pin?"** Pretend to attack the audience with the pin. This routine will also work with other models, since, surprisingly, most origami models will spin on a pin. Prince Charming (page 71) is an excellent model to experiment on, just don't tell PETA!

Imperfect Polyhedron

By Jeremy Shafer ©2001

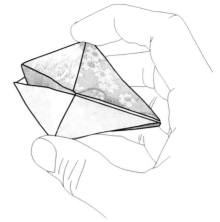

This is a model for all you imperfectionists out there, which really includes all honest people for nobody's perfect. But philosophy aside, this model makes great fidgeting material during long boring lectures or staff meetings.

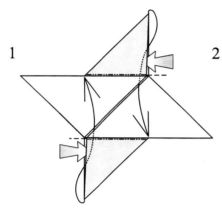

1

2

Valley-fold the front flap.

3

Valley-fold the raw corner.

The ideal paper to use is a six-inch square of Washi, but Kami works too. Begin by folding the Iso-area Pureland Pinwheel (page 125). Reverse-fold the colored flaps.

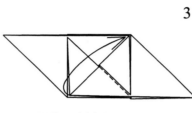

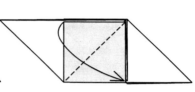

4

Insert the corner into the pocket.

5

Valley fold the flap.

6

Valley-fold the raw corner.

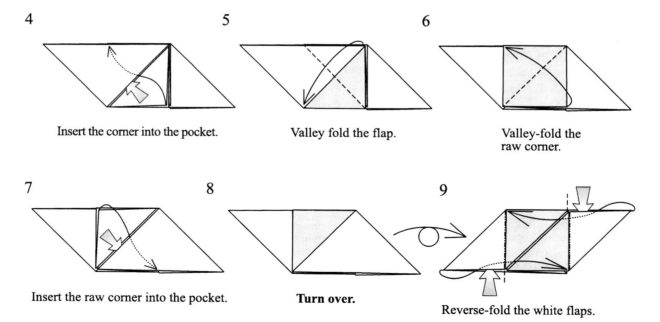

7

Insert the raw corner into the pocket.

8

Turn over.

9

Reverse-fold the white flaps.

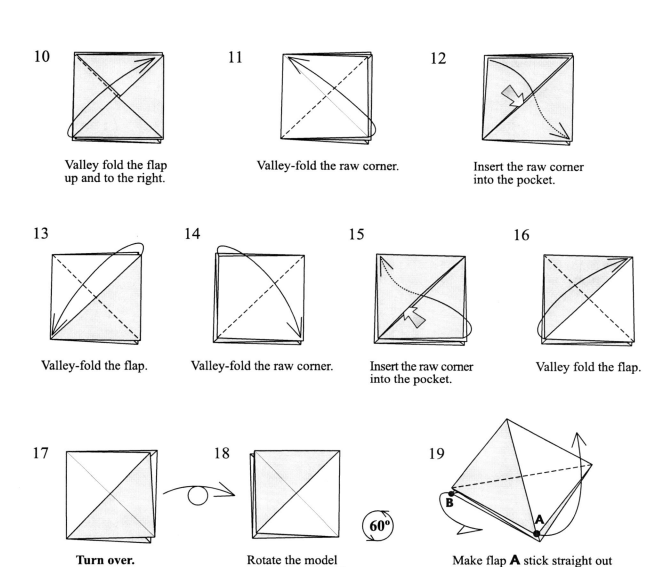

10 Valley fold the flap up and to the right.

11 Valley-fold the raw corner.

12 Insert the raw corner into the pocket.

13 Valley-fold the flap.

14 Valley-fold the raw corner.

15 Insert the raw corner into the pocket.

16 Valley fold the flap.

17 **Turn over.**

18 Rotate the model approximately 60° counterclockwise.

19 Make flap **A** stick straight out in front and flap **B** stick straight out in back. The next drawing is in 3-D.

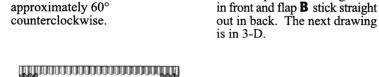

PERFORM IT!

Hold the completed model up and say to the audience, **"This is my pet polyhedron. Her name is..."** <pause> **"Polly."** Show them the separated corners and say, **"But, look, she's broken. I need someone to push these two corners together."** Have a volunteer push the two corners together and then say, **"Thanks. Wait, you didn't fix it!"** Show them the newly separated corners and say, **"Look, it's still broken!"** Repeat the shtick one or two more times, and finally say, **"I give up!"** Say to the origami model, **"I hereby demote you from polyhedron..."** Flatten the model so that it looks like step 18 and continue, **"...to a polygon! Ha Ha! Back in the box, you little polygoon!"**

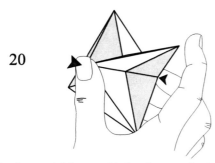

20

As is, the model is two thirds of an octahedron skeleton – an interesting shape in its own right. To go on, hold the model firmly between your thumb and middle finger as shown. Squeeze the two opposite corners until the model puffs out into a polyhedron. Try to do this cleanly, i.e., crisply define the new edges with mountain folds. You may need to reach inside the model to offer support.

21

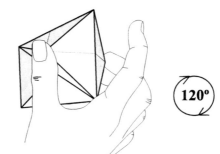

Rotate the model approximately 120° clockwise.

22

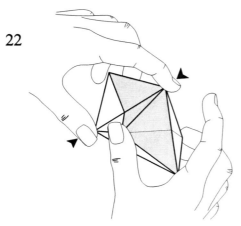

With the other hand, squeeze the other two opposite corners making the model puff out more. The other end should naturally come apart as shown in the next step.

23

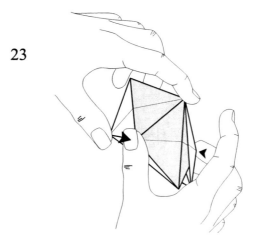

But when you try to push that end back together the opposite end will come apart (as shown in the next step), hence the Imperfect Polyhedron.

24

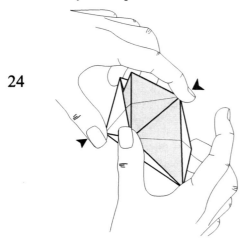

The Imperfect Polyhedron is done! Click the model back and forth to your heart's content – a fine toy for fidgety fingers!

Attaining the 'Perfect Imperfect Polyhedron'

The 'Perfect Imperfect Polyhedron' will stay by itself in the each of the two positions. In other words, when you push the open end together it will stay together even when you let go. This property gives the model a much more satisfying action. So, how does one achieve the Perfect Imperfect Polyhedron?

Collapse the model and swing flaps **A** and **B** (refer to step 19) back and forth, flattening several times in each direction. Re-puff the model.
If it still hasn't gained 'Perfect' status, repeat the procedure, but this time put several extra creases anywhere on flaps **A** and **B**. If that doesn't work try using smaller paper and re-puff the model.
If that doesn't work try folding out of Washi paper – the ultimate paper for this model. But if that still doesn't work, try reinstalling Windows!

Human Heart By Jeremy Shafer ©2007

For Valentine's Day people exchange millions of those silly supposedly heart-like shapes that, in fact, look very little like a real human heart. With so many 'heart' chocolates, 'heart' greeting cards, and origami 'hearts,' people can't grasp the true nature of the heart. So, in that same vein, or at least attached to it, here is a model that is so much more realistic than other origami hearts, that I declare it the heart to fold! Besides, it's not so **heart**-to-fold as you might think!

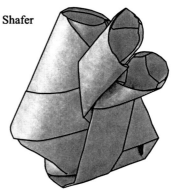

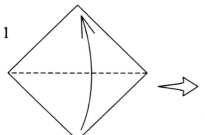

1 White side up, valley-fold in half diagonally.

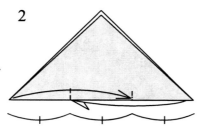

2 Divide the base of the model into thirds by folding the left side in front and the right side behind. These are pinches, not folds.

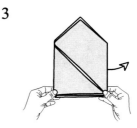

3 Fiddle with the folds until the thirds are exact. Then completely unfold the model.

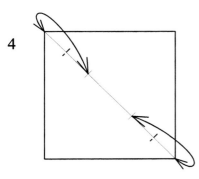

4 Make two new creasemarks.

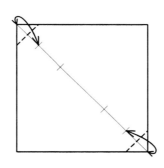

5 Valley-fold and unfold.

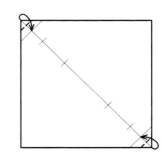

6 Valley-fold.

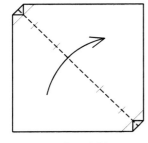

7 Valley-fold.

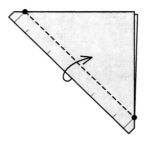

8 Valley-fold on the black dots.

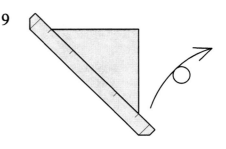

9 **Turn over.**

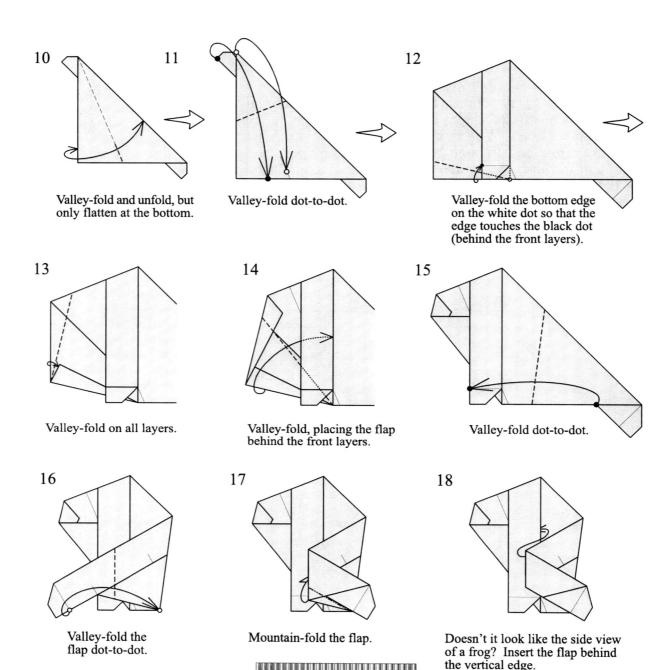

10

Valley-fold and unfold, but only flatten at the bottom.

11

Valley-fold dot-to-dot.

12

Valley-fold the bottom edge on the white dot so that the edge touches the black dot (behind the front layers).

13

Valley-fold on all layers.

14

Valley-fold, placing the flap behind the front layers.

15

Valley-fold dot-to-dot.

16

Valley-fold the flap dot-to-dot.

17

Mountain-fold the flap.

18

Doesn't it look like the side view of a frog? Insert the flap behind the vertical edge.

PERFORM IT!

Hold the completed model up and ask the audience, **"Who knows what this is?"** [Audience says, "It's a heart"] **"But it's not just a heart, it's a HUMAN heart! And look, it's stopped beating! I must perform CPR. Ready, set, everyone say, 'resuscitate!'"** [Audience says, "Resuscitate!"] Blow into the heart making it beat like a heart and say, **"Look it's beating again! That was a close one! It almost died! I better put it back in the box quickly before it stops beating again!"** [Audience says, "It stopped beating!"] **"Well, I tried. I guess it is dead. Time to bury it back in the box."**

19

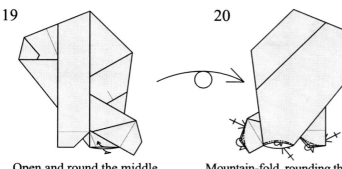

Open and round the middle pocket. **Turn over.**

20

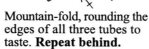

Mountain-fold, rounding the edges of all three tubes to taste. **Repeat behind.**

21

Turn the model over top-to-bottom.

22

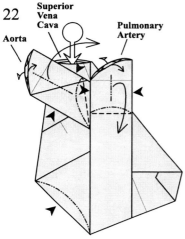

Inflate the heart by blowing into the Superior Vena Cava. Open and round the Aorta and Pulmonary Artery and bend them so that they protrude. Shape the model to taste – if you fold it out of thin baloney, you can then eat your heart out (unless you're vegetarian)!

23

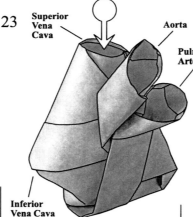

The Human Heart is done.
Blow repeatedly into the Superior Vena Cava and the heart will beat. An Inferior Vena Cava could be suggested by closed-sinking the leftmost corner, but since it's 'inferior,' it really doesn't matter.

24

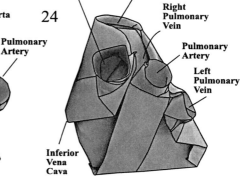

In the variation pictured above, I shortened the Aorta and Pulmonary Artery and pulled out the flap folded in step 14 and fashioned it into a Left Pulmonary Vein. A Right Pulmonary Vein can also be seen hiding behind the Pulmonary Artery. **Challenge:** Design an origami heart that contains all the tubes, valves, and interior chambers, and pumps blood as illustrated below.

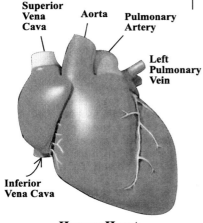

Human Heart

(Tilted so that all of the veins and arteries are pointing away. How discreet!)

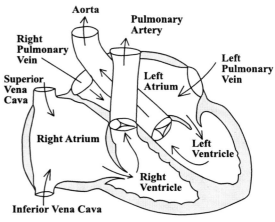

Human Heart

Monster Mouth (Rather Simple)

By Jeremy Shafer ©2007

This is a Monster Mouth in all senses of the word Monster. It opens huge and is so scary it'll even make origami police run in fear.

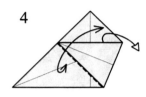

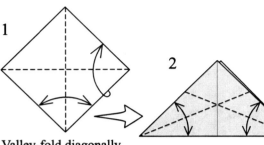

1

Valley-fold diagonally left-to-right and unfold. Valley-fold diagonally bottom-to-top.

2

Valley-fold and unfold through both layers.

3

Valley-fold to the black dot.

4

Valley-fold and unfold. Then unfold the flap.

5

Valley-fold to the black dot.

6

Valley-fold and unfold. Then unfold the flap.

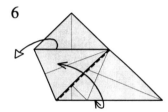

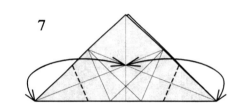

7

Valley-fold and unfold.

PERFORM IT!

Here's a routine I regularly perform using a giant Venus Flytrap (*Origami to Astonish and Amuse*, page 87), but it works with this model too. Take the model out of the box, say, **"Oh no, this one's too scary!"** and quickly put it back in the box and go on to your next model. [Audience says, "No, we want to see the scary one!"] Repeat the **"No, it's too scary!"** line a few more times until the audience is demanding to see it. Finally, pull it out and say, **"OK, I'll show it to you. Everyone hold up your hands like you're in a horror movie, and on the count of three, everyone SCREAM!!!"** [Audience screams] **"I said on the count of three! One, two, three!"** [Audience screams] Run toward the audience with the model's mouth open, acting as ferocious as possible. Exclaim, **"Wasn't that so scary?!"** [Entire Audience responds, NO!!] **"Wait, I thought I heard someone say, 'NO!' Who was it?"** Pick someone with their hand up and ask, **"Why didn't you think it was scary?"** [Volunteer says, "Because it's just paper!" or "Because it's not real!"] Answer, **"No, the real reason it's not scary is because, it's just a hat!"** Place the model on the volunteer's head and say, **"Everyone give a hand to the fearless monster warrior!"**

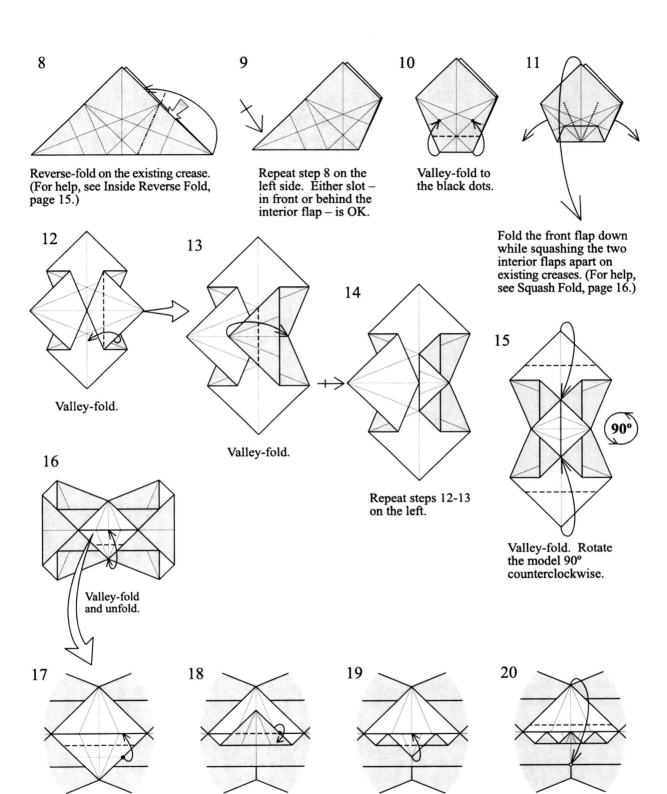

8

Reverse-fold on the existing crease. (For help, see Inside Reverse Fold, page 15.)

9

Repeat step 8 on the left side. Either slot – in front or behind the interior flap – is OK.

10

Valley-fold to the black dots.

11

Fold the front flap down while squashing the two interior flaps apart on existing creases. (For help, see Squash Fold, page 16.)

12

Valley-fold.

13

Valley-fold.

14

Repeat steps 12-13 on the left.

15

90°

Valley-fold. Rotate the model 90° counterclockwise.

16

Valley-fold and unfold.

17

Valley-fold the flap so that the black dot touches the folded edge.

18

Valley-fold the flap on the black dot.

19

Valley-fold.

20

Valley-fold the flap to the white dot.

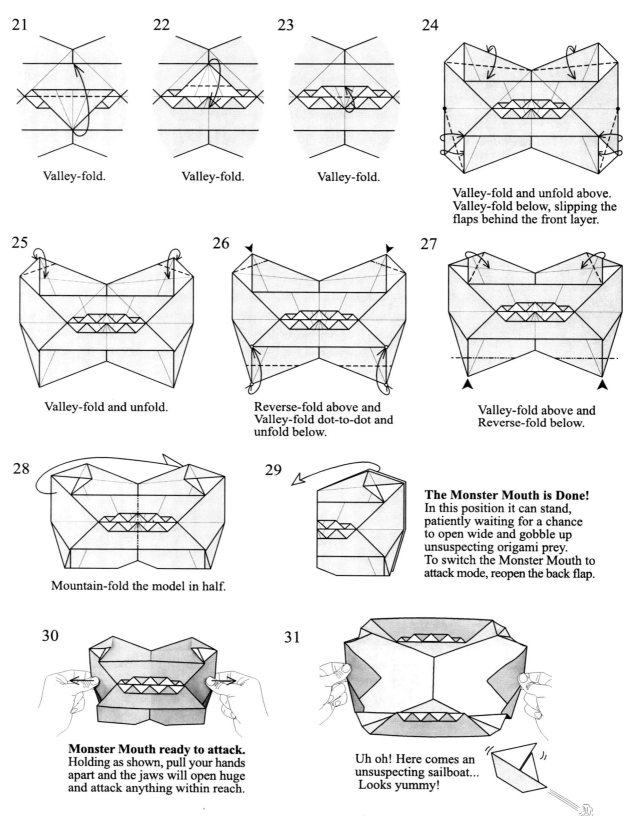

21 Valley-fold.

22 Valley-fold.

23 Valley-fold.

24 Valley-fold and unfold above. Valley-fold below, slipping the flaps behind the front layer.

25 Valley-fold and unfold.

26 Reverse-fold above and Valley-fold dot-to-dot and unfold below.

27 Valley-fold above and Reverse-fold below.

28 Mountain-fold the model in half.

29 **The Monster Mouth is Done!** In this position it can stand, patiently waiting for a chance to open wide and gobble up unsuspecting origami prey. To switch the Monster Mouth to attack mode, reopen the back flap.

30 **Monster Mouth ready to attack.** Holding as shown, pull your hands apart and the jaws will open huge and attack anything within reach.

31 Uh oh! Here comes an unsuspecting sailboat... Looks yummy!

Tricks
and
Puzzles

This chapter includes models that surprise or challenge the audience. Most of them are best shown close-up to small audiences... though large people will also enjoy them!

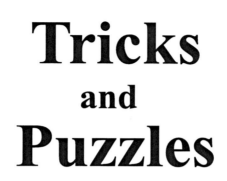

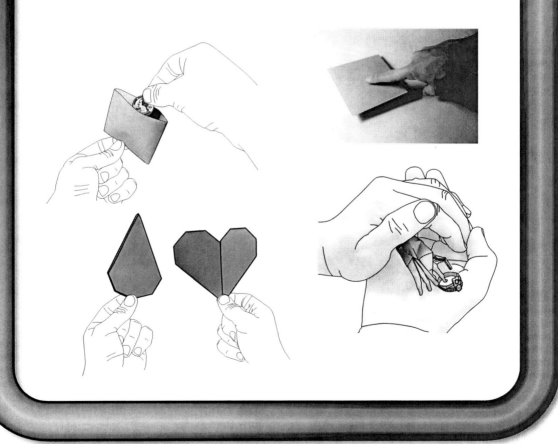

Magic Teardrop

Turn sadness into happiness with this magical transforming origami teardrop.

By Jeremy Shafer
©2009

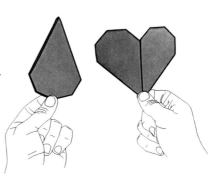

1

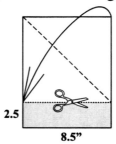

2.5

8.5"

Begin with a 8.5-inch by 2.5-inch rectangle. A sheet of this dimension can be cut off from an 8.5-inch by 11-inch sheet of paper as illustrated above.

2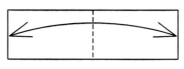

Valley-fold and unfold.

3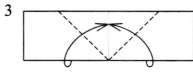

Valley-fold.

4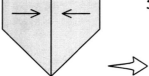

Slide the two flaps together so that they overlap (left flap in front). The model will not lie flat.

5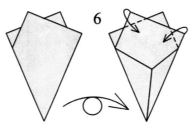

Turn over!

6

Valley-fold.

7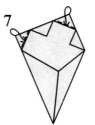

Valley-fold the other two flaps, tucking them behind the front layer.

8

Turn the model over top to bottom and hold as shown.

9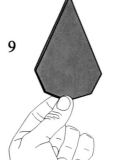

The Magic Teardrop is complete, and ready to transform. Say to your audience, "Once upon a time, there lived a lonely raindrop that was sad and all alone. One day, it looked up to the sky..." Rotate the model 180° and continue, "...and it cried out, 'How I wish I had a friend?'" Hold as shown in the next step.

10

180°

11

"And all of a sudden, the wish came true..." Release your top hand while pressing your other two fingers together.

"...and it was instant love! And that is how the heart came to be."

Blinky the Magic Elf (Super Simple)

By Jeremy Shafer ©2007

Here's a Four-fold hyper action model. If you prefer not to draw on origami, skip steps 4 and 5, and instead call it an **'Oscillator.'**

1

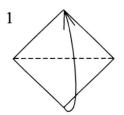

Begin with a 6-inch square of paper. White side up, valley-fold in half diagonally. **Note:** This model even works better folded from an equilateral triangle (begin at step 2).

2

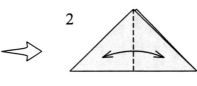

Valley-fold and unfold. **Turn over.**

Don't forget to turn over!

3

Valley-fold.

4

The Magic Elf's hat is done. Draw a feather and band to decorate the hat. **Turn over top-to-bottom.**

5

Draw the elf's face. **Turn over top-to-bottom.**

6

Hold as shown. Pull your hands apart and the hat will turn into an elf's face.

7

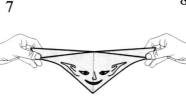

Blinky the Magic Elf has appeared. Relax your hands and the elf will turn back into a hat.

8

Rapidly pull your hands apart and together and you will see why this little elf is called, "Blinky."

PERFORM IT!

Take the model out of the box and say to the audience, **"This is an elf hat. It belongs to Blinky the Magic Elf. Sometimes Blinky just appears out of nowhere."** Make Blinky flash into view and quickly hide him again. Exclaim, **"Wait, did you see him? Let's see if he comes back. Everyone say, 'Here Blinky!'"** [Audience says, "Here Blinky!"] Make Blinky appear repeatedly and then say, **"Now everyone say 'Bye Blinky'"** [Audience says, "Bye Blinky!"] Put Blinky back in the box.

PERFORM IT!

Here's a close-up magic routine to perform using the Oscillator (Blinky minus the drawing). Hold the model as shown in step 6. Say to your audience, **"This is a cool trick that I learned in Physics Class. It's really freaky!"** Pick a volunteer and instruct them to blow softly on the point. As they blow, secretly pull your hands apart repeatedly, making the point oscillate. Try to do it moving your hands as little as possible so that it appears the blowing is making the point oscillate. When they stop blowing, stop oscillating and say, **"Almost, but you have to blow just right. Try again."** As they blow, oscillate again, but this time keep oscillating even after they stop blowing. Exclaim, **"Check it out! Isn't that amazing!"**

Magic Cup (Super Simple)

By Jeremy Shafer ©2009

This cup holds water, but money just falls through!

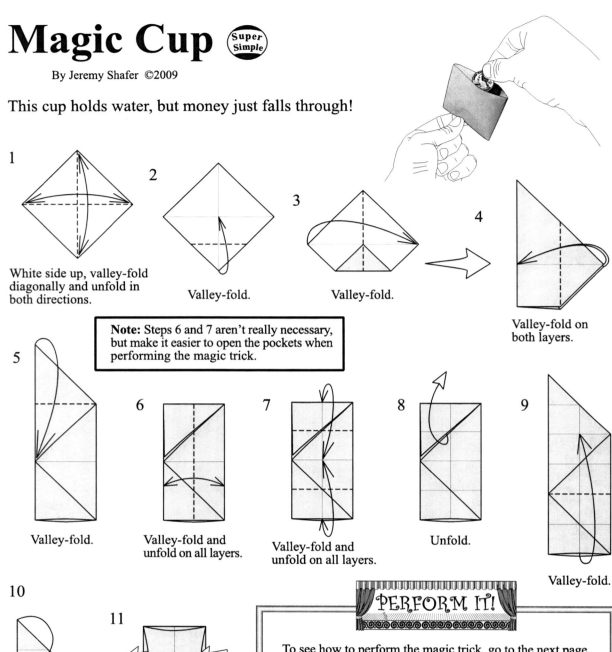

1
White side up, valley-fold diagonally and unfold in both directions.

2
Valley-fold.

3
Valley-fold.

4
Valley-fold on both layers.

Note: Steps 6 and 7 aren't really necessary, but make it easier to open the pockets when performing the magic trick.

5
Valley-fold.

6
Valley-fold and unfold on all layers.

7
Valley-fold and unfold on all layers.

8
Unfold.

9
Valley-fold.

10
Valley-fold, tucking the flap into the pocket.

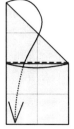

11
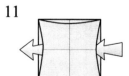

The Magic Cup is prepared and ready to serve. If you pour water into the top pocket you can fill up the cup, but if you pour into a side pocket it will go right through and get your hand all wet!

PERFORM IT!

To see how to perform the magic trick, go to the next page, but here's the 'silly gag' version: Fill the top pocket with water to "prove" to the audience that there are no holes. Drink the water and then ask, **"Now, does anyone have a quarter... dime... or nickel!?"** Ask the volunteer with the coin to place it into the cup, but secretly turn the model 90-degrees, so that they put it into the pocket and it falls out the other end (see step 11). Blatantly catch the coin, and with a big smile put it in your pocket and say, **"Thanks!"** and holding the model out, say, **"Does anyone else have any spare change for me?"** or, **"I am accepting donations for the Bernie Madoff Charity Foundation."**

Magic Cup Magic Trick

The Effect: The magician introduces the model as just an ordinary origami cup and shows it to be empty and even fills it with water and drinks from it to prove that it is just a plain cup! A volunteer is given a coin on to which s/he is instructed to draw a face so as to make it undeniably unique. S/he then places it into the Magic Pocket, which the magician places onto the volunteer's head. Then the magician pulls out of his/her pocket another Magic Cup and places it onto his/her own head. S/he tells the volunteer to harness the power of the mind to teleport the coin from one cup to the other. The magic words are said by all and the magician reveals that the coin is now in his/her own cup!

Figure 1

Figure 2

Figure 3

The Trick: Introduce the model by saying to the audience, **"Origami is like magic, but magic that is real! Take for instance this traditional origami cup."** Show the audience the empty pocket {Figure 1}, and turn it upside down to show that it is indeed empty. (Optional: fill the cup with water and drink it or splash it on the audience.) Say, **"Now, I need a volunteer to help bring out the profound magic that's contained in this simple model."** Hand the volunteer a coin (or get a coin from the audience) and say, **"Here's an ordinary coin. Please check to make sure it's an ordinary coin."** While the attention of the volunteer and audience is on the coin, rotate the cup 90° so that side pocket is pointing up; this pocket has an open bottom!

Instruct the volunteer to make the coin special and unique by drawing a face on it, and then instruct her/him to drop it into the cup, making sure that s/he drops it into the pocket with the open bottom {Figure 2}.

Make sure to catch the coin as it comes out the other end and hide it in your hand. {Figure 3} Place the cup on the volunteer's head and say, **"Hold still!"** In one motion, reach into your coat pocket, place the hidden coin into a preset second cup, take the cup out of your pocket and place it on your own head. Tell the volunteer to harness the power of the mind to teleport the coin from one cup to the other. Have the audience say the magic words and reveal that the coin is now in your own cup! Say, **"Origami is magic! May the folds be with you!"**

Illusion Cube By Jeremy Shafer ©2009

This model is an origami optical illusion! From the top view it looks like a 3-D cube, but it's really just a flat piece of paper!

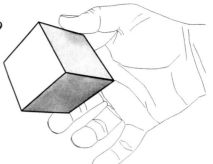

1

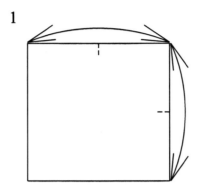

Begin with a dark-colored 6-inch or smaller square of origami paper or foil. White side up, valley-fold and unfold in half making crease marks on the top and right edges.

2

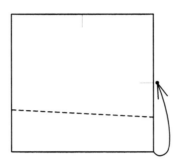

Valley-fold the corner to the point three millimeters to the right of the crease mark.

3

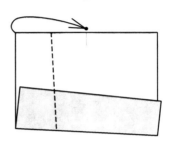

Valley-fold the corner to the point three millimeters above the crease mark.

4

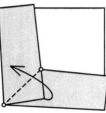

Valley-fold the flap on the white dots.

5

Unfold to step 3.

6

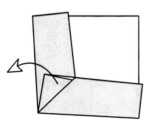

Valley-fold on the existing crease.

7

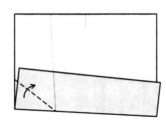

Valley-fold the flap and unfold.

8

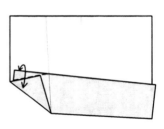

Valley-fold on the existing crease.

9

Like this. The next view is a tear-away view. Do not really tear the paper!

10

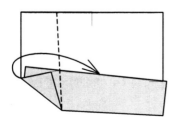

Mountain-fold the flap on the existing crease, tucking it into the rear-most slot.

11

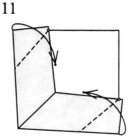

Valley-folding on the white dots, fold the corners to the black dots (about two millimeters from the raw edges).

142 *Origami Ooh La La!*

12

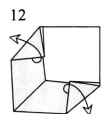

Unfold the flaps.

13

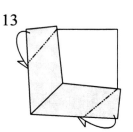

Mountain-fold the flaps on existing creases.

14

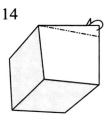

Mountain-fold.

15

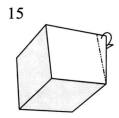

Mountain-fold.

16

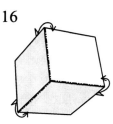

Mountain-fold and unfold on the indicated edges.

17

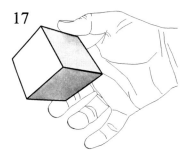

The Illusion Cube is ready to trick the eyes.

PERFORM IT!

This illusion works best in a dimly-lit room. Hold the model sideways as shown to the left, with the white part pointing in the direction of the room's light source. The model must be in this position when the audience first sees it, so, while picking it up, make sure you are facing away from the audience, so they can't see it. Then, when the model is in position, simply move your body away, so the audience can now see it. Say, **"This is a very special origami cube..."** To re-enforce that it is 3-D, wave your other hand around it, as a fortune teller does with a crystal ball. Continue, **"...because it's really NOT a cube!"** Slowly rotate your hand, so the audience can see that the model it is really flat.

Red Cross Table Glider

With just four folds you can create a red cross that slides across the table like an air hockey puck. So, support your local Red Cross and fold this model today!

By Jeremy Shafer ©2009

1

Begin with a 6-inch sheet of red paper, red side up. For a blue cross, use blue paper. Valley-fold the four corners.

2

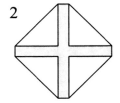

The Red Cross Table Glider is complete. Play catch with it by sliding it back and forth on a smooth table.

Bad Pun Alert: Why does this model have a cross on it? Obviously, because it slides **across** the table.

PERFORM IT!

This isn't a performance routine, but rather an idea for how to play with the model, which can provide many minutes of entertainment! Place on a smooth table, and, with a flick of the fingers, slide it across the table. The act of skillfully flicking the model back and forth can be developed into various origami versions of popular sports, which will promise far more exercise than watching real sports on TV. Even better, any games invented using this model can be called 'The Origami X-games!'

Levitating Square

Super Simple

We all know that origami is in-creasing.
But did you know that it is also on the rise?

By Jeremy
Shafer
©2004

Materials: One 6-inch square of dark origami paper.
Effect: By softly blowing, a seemingly normal piece of paper gets levitated almost one inch above the table and stays there!

1

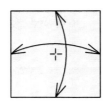

Colored side up, valley-fold in half and unfold in both directions, but flatten the folds only in the very center of the paper.

2

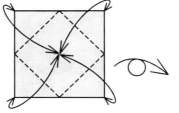

Valley-fold the four corners to the exact center and unfold. Folding them perfectly to the center will create an almost airtight pocket which will result in a good slow-rising levitation. **Turn over.**

3

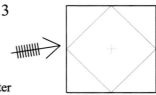

Repeat step 2 nine times reversing the creases over and over again.

4

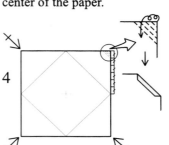

Role up the tips of the four corners equally and flatten. The more of the corner you roll up, the less likely the floating square will tip over, but, also, the lower it will rise.

5

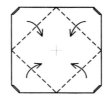

Fold the flaps to the center again, but do not flatten; leave them partially sticking up.

6

Done! The model should be stored like this, but in a box out of sight of the audience until the trick is ready to perform.

PERFORM IT!

To perform the trick, take the model out of the box, and hold it making sure the four flaps are held down by your four fingers and hidden from the audience, as shown to the right. Say, **"Here we have just an ordinary piece of paper."** Pretend to show the other side by briefly and casually lifting it up and back down as shown above right. You are in fact only showing one side of the paper. Say, **"You know how airplane wings lift an airplane? Well I'm going to demonstrate a similar principle."** Making sure the audience is viewing from well above the model, place it on the floor, holding it down with your index finger. Blow gently onto an edge of the model while slowly lifting your finger, letting it rise. When the model reaches its maximum height, stop blowing, let go, and the model will look like it is magically suspended almost an inch above the table! Exclaim, **"Isn't science amazing?!"** and quickly put it back in the box being careful not to reveal the four flaps.

Magical Levitating Star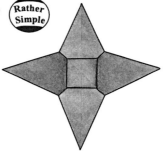

By Jeremy Shafer ©2003

This model uses the same mystical energy to
levitate as the Levitating Square (previous page),
but it significantly differs in shape!

1

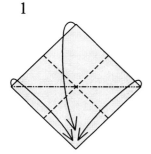

Start by folding a
white Square Base.
(For help, see cloud on
page 102.)

2

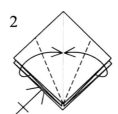

Valley-fold the raw edges of
the near flaps to the center
crease. **Repeat behind.**

3

Valley-fold.
Rotate 180°.

180°

4

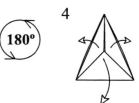

Unfold.

5

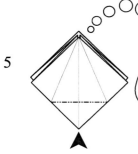

Open-sink. (For help,
look into the cloud or
see Sink, page 18)

Sink Fold

5a

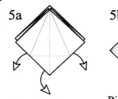

Completely
unfold the
model and place
it white side up.

5b

Pinch mountain
folds around the
center square of
existing creases.

5c

Start reforming
the Square Base,
making sure that
the folds inside
the center square
get pushed
inward.

5d

In progress.

5e

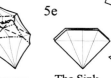

The Sink
has been
excavated.

6

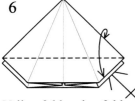

Valley-fold and unfold
on the front layer.
Repeat behind.

7

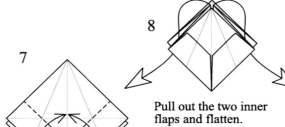

Valley-fold edge-to-crease.
Repeat behind.

8

Pull out the two inner
flaps and flatten.

9

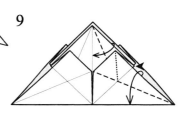

Follow the arrows, flattening
on existing creases.

10

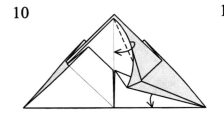

In progress.

11

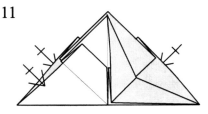

Repeat steps 9-10 on the three remaining areas.

12

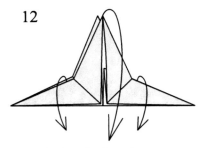

Swing the front layers downward.

13

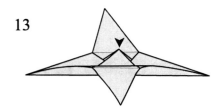

Now the fun part! Squash the center point squarely, allowing the model to flatten.

14

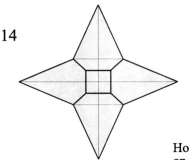

The Levitating Star is ready.

15

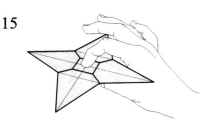

Hold the model as shown. The four flaps on the bottom should be held together by your thumb and index finger. Say, **"This is a Magical Star!"** and show the audience both sides of the model showing that the model is flat.

16

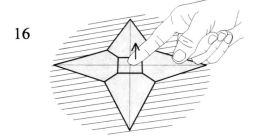

Softly press the model against a hard surface. Lift your finger about an inch from the surface and the model will appear to rise off the surface. The middle flaps will still be touching, but you don't see that if you are looking from the top of the model. For a higher levitating model, fold and unfold model several times or try reversing all the creases. For an even higher levitating model, consult a magician.

PERFORM IT!

Before showing the model, say to the audience, **"My next model is a rising star in the origami community."** Show the model (see step 15) and ask, **"Do you want to see it rise?"** [Audience says "Yes!"] Place the paper on the floor (to ensure the audience is viewing from well above the paper) and press firmly on top with your index finger and say, **"Now, with just a slight breath the star will magically levitate."** Blow gently on the paper and slowly lift your finger. **"Amazing!"** Quickly press the model back against the floor and ask, **"Do you want to see the model rise higher?"** [Audience says "Yes!"] Pick the model up and throw it up as high as you can, and say, **"Did you see how high it rose?"** [Audience says "You threw it!"] Reply, **"No, I just helped it rise, and now I will help it disappear."** Put the model back in the box.

Thoughts Behind the Folds

This star, which I designed in high school, is the first model I ever diagrammed. I designed it while playing with a Bird Base. I taught it at an OrigamiUSA convention, but I didn't have a name for it. People at the convention started calling it 'Jeremy's Star,' but, you know, I don't really need a star named after me, and, besides, 'Magical Levitating Star' sounds way more mystical!

Bermuda Triangle

By Jeremy Shafer ©2008

Challenge your friends to unfold this model without tearing, and watch as they haplessly struggle to navigate their ship out of the Bermuda Triangle unscathed.

1
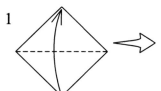
White side up, valley-fold in half diagonally.

2
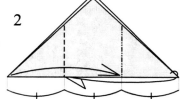
Divide the base of the model into thirds by folding the left side in front and the right side behind.

3
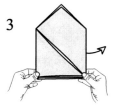
Fiddle with the folds until the thirds are exact. Then unfold the back flap.

4
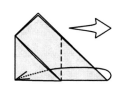
Valley-fold on the existing crease, inserting the point into the pocket.

5

Valley-fold the single layer.

6
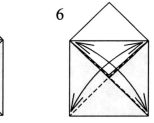
Valley-fold and unfold diagonally on all layers.

7

Valley-fold the interior flap inserting it into the white pocket.

8
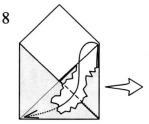
Cut-away view: Valley-fold the interior white flap.

9
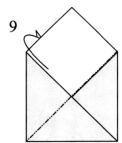
Mountain-fold.

10
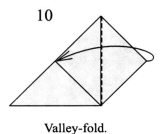
Valley-fold.

11
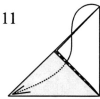
Valley-fold the model in half, inserting the entire white flap into the pocket. Be careful not to tear the model.

12

The Bermuda Triangle is ready to be embarked upon. It can be a disposable unfolding puzzle as described above, or, if you would rather not kiss the model goodbye, it can be used as an origami football.

Design inspected and approved by the commissioner of the WPFA. (World Paper Football Association).

PERFORM IT!

This model really works best as a party puzzle, not as a performance piece, but if you really want to incorporate it into a kids show, say to the audience, **"This triangle is virtually impossible to unfold. Who wants to try?"** Instead of choosing a kid, choose an adult, and say, **"Here, you try."** Continue with the rest of your show, but every few minutes refer back to the adult, **"And now, back to our big story still unfolding, or at least trying to! How's it going? Remember, don't tear the paper or you'll have to fold me another one! Don't give up! All your fans are cheering for you! Let's all cheer!..."**

Bermuda Sailboat

13 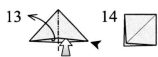 14

Squash and then fold steps 21-24 on page 149 to make the Bermuda Sailboat, which will besiege the unfortunate unfolder with yet another torrent of tearbulent waters.

Unopenable Greeting Card

Keeps your
Greeting Cards
Safe and Private!

Intermediate

By Jeremy Shafer ©2003

Here's a greeting card that is not nearly as inviting as it looks.
The card is locked in the closed position so firmly that the challenge
of trying to open it will likely stump even the most avid unfolders.

1

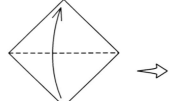

White side up, valley-fold
in half diagonally.

2

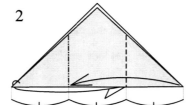

Divide the base of the model into
thirds by folding the right side in
front and the left side to the back.

3

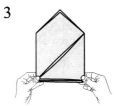

Fiddle with the
folds until the
thirds are exact.

4

Unfold the
rear flap.

5

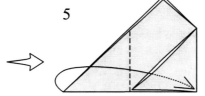

Valley-fold, inserting the
flap into the pocket.

6

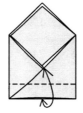

Valley-fold
and unfold.

7

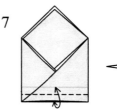

Valley-fold
and unfold.

8

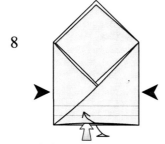

Push the left and right
sides inward and sculpt
the model to form a tube.

9

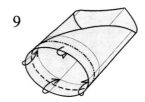

On existing creases, fold
the rim of the tube inside.

10

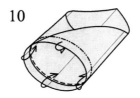

Fold the rim of the
tube inside again...

11

...and again.

PERFORM IT!

See **PERFORM IT!** box on previous page.

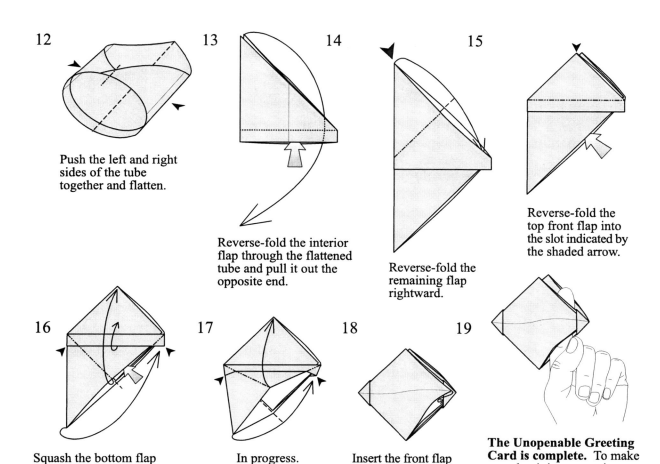

12

Push the left and right sides of the tube together and flatten.

13

14

Reverse-fold the interior flap through the flattened tube and pull it out the opposite end.

15

Reverse-fold the remaining flap rightward.

Reverse-fold the top front flap into the slot indicated by the shaded arrow.

16

Squash the bottom flap rightward. The thick layer also gets squashed upward.

17

In progress.

18

Insert the front flap into the pocket.

19

The Unopenable Greeting Card is complete. To make sure that it is correct, insert your finger as indicated above. Now it's time to test the model on a willing victim. Say, **"Here's a greeting card with just an origami lock – no tape or glue. Try to open it without tearing it."**

Ununfoldable Boat (Intermediate)

This model floats about as good as an anchor, but in unfolding competitions, it holds up like a battleship!

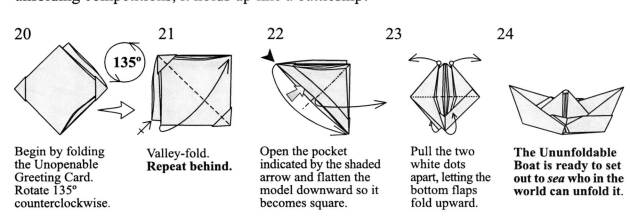

20

Begin by folding the Unopenable Greeting Card. Rotate 135° counterclockwise.

135°

21

Valley-fold. **Repeat behind.**

22

Open the pocket indicated by the shaded arrow and flatten the model downward so it becomes square.

23

Pull the two white dots apart, letting the bottom flaps fold upward.

24

The Ununfoldable Boat is ready to set out to *sea* who in the world can unfold it.

Unopenable Greeting Card (Consolation Version)

 Super Simple

By Jeremy Shafer ©2004

This unopenable greeting card is a real self-esteem booster, for the recipient should have no problem opening the model and should therefore feel very good about themselves. But beware, if they can't unfold it, they could suffer severe psychological damage.

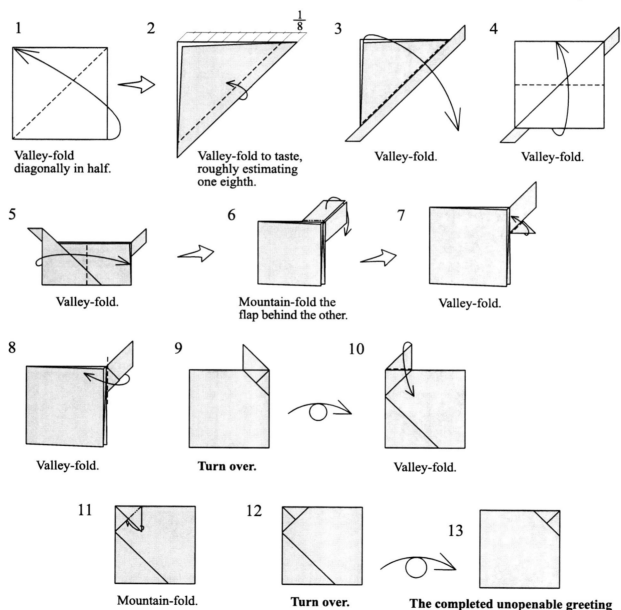

1

Valley-fold diagonally in half.

2

$\frac{1}{8}$

Valley-fold to taste, roughly estimating one eighth.

3

Valley-fold.

4

Valley-fold.

5

Valley-fold.

6

Mountain-fold the flap behind the other.

7

Valley-fold.

8

Valley-fold.

9

Turn over.

10

Valley-fold.

11

Mountain-fold.

12

Turn over.

13

The completed unopenable greeting card, ready to give a self-esteem boost to anyone origamically challenged.

Flying Color Mixer (Super Simple)

By Jose Arley Moreno ©1997

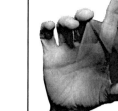

WARNING: This model is the one model in this book that requires two sheets of paper! Fold at your own risk of being classified as a 'Modular Folder.'

Here's a model that demonstrates how two colors can combine to form a third color. So, if you just can't find that purple sheet of paper, here's your chance... just use red and blue!

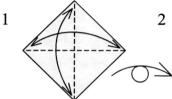

1

Requires two 3" squares of different colors. Colored side up, valley-fold and unfold. **Turn over.**

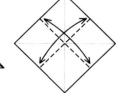

2

Valley-fold and unfold.

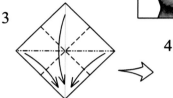

3

Fold a Square Base. (For help, see Square Base, page 17.)

4

As thus. Now fold the other sheet the same way and face the two together as shown in the next step.

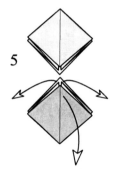

5

Unfold one of the Square Bases.

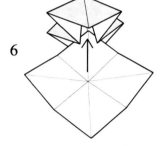

6

Insert one corner in the rear pocket of the other Square Base.

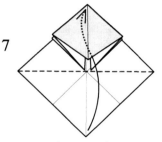

7

Insert the opposite corner into the front pocket.

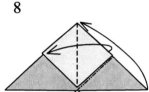

8

Squash-fold, following the arrows. (For help, see Squash Fold, page 16.)

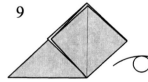

9

Turn the model over.

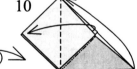

10

Make another squash fold.

11

Make one corner stick out forward and the other stick out behind.

12

The Flying Color mixer has been assembled. Hold the model either between two fingers or between two hands. Blow on the top part and the model will spin, thereby mixing the colors. It's called a '**Flying** Color Mixer' because when spun fast, it tends too **FLY** out of your hands.

PERFORM IT!

This model can be used to perform the same PERFORM IT routine that accompanies the Greeting Card Spinner (page 101), only this model will work even better because it has four flaps instead of three. However, since it's a modular model, the puns need to be twice as bad, so, if you're at home and the model flies out of your hands, make sure to call it a 'house fly.'

Undoable Slide By Unknown Creator

This is a brain teaser that will surely frustrate your friends. It looks easy and is, once you learn how, but, at first try, it's a real doozie of a puzzle!

1
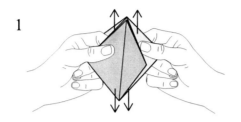

Begin with step 12 of the Flying Color Mixer. Holding the model with two hands as shown, try to slide the two square bases apart.

2
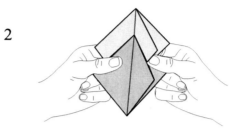

Like this. Now slide them back together. Once you get it, it's time to go befuddle your friends. If you are having trouble, rotate this page 180° and read the tips below (¿ǝʌoqɐ).

PERFORM IT!

Choose a volunteer, show them how it works, and say, **"Now, you try!"**

(180°)

˙lǝpoɯ ǝɥʇ qɐɹɓ ɹǝʇʇǝq uɐɔ ʎǝɥʇ ʇɐɥʇ os sdiʇ ɹǝɓuıɟ ɹnoʎ ʇǝʍ oʇ sdlǝɥ ʇI ˙uoıʇɔıɹɟ ɥɔnɯ ooʇ pıoʌɐ oʇ ʎlǝsool lǝpoɯ ǝɥʇ ploɥ oʇ ǝɹns ǝʞɐɯ 'osl∀ ˙puɐɥ ɹǝɥʇo ǝɥʇ ɟo ɹǝɓuıɟ xǝpuı ǝɥʇ dn ɓuıpıls ǝlıɥʍ puɐɥ ǝuo ɟo qɯnɥʇ ǝɥʇ dn ǝpıls oʇ sı ʞɔıɹʇ sıɥʇ oʇ ʞɔıɹʇ ǝɥ┴

Open Space*

*Complies with City of Berkeley 1977 Master Plan Open Space zoning ordinance 3.17, which states goal to establish a standard of at least 30 square inches of open space per 1000 steps of origami diagrams.

Finger Eater By Jeremy Shafer ©2008

Warning: Do NOT fold this model from an 8-inch square of 5-mil stainless steel sheet metal, or else it may literally eat your finger!

1

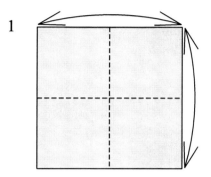

This model is best folded from a 6-inch square of stiff, strong paper. Kami paper is too light, but if you put two sheets together it works alright. Colored side up, valley-fold in half and unfold in both directions. **Turn over.**

2

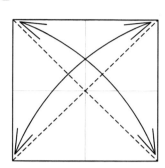

Colored side up, valley-fold diagonally in half and unfold in both directions.

3

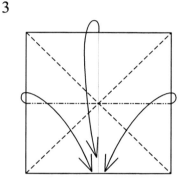

Collapse on existing creases following the arrows to form a Waterbomb Base. (For help, see Waterbomb Base, page 18.)

4

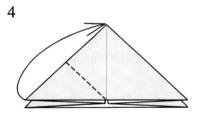

Valley-fold one flap.

5

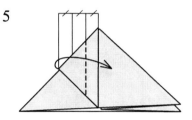

Valley-fold the flap.

6

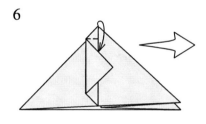

Valley-fold.

7

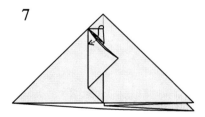

Valley-fold, tucking the flap into the pocket.

8

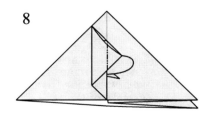

Mountain-fold the flap, tucking the flap into the pocket. One flap is locked.

9

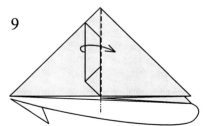

Valley-fold the front flap to the right. Balance it out by folding the rear flap to the left.

Finger Eater **153**

10

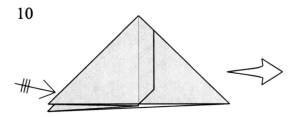

Repeat steps 4-9 three times so that all of the flaps get folded up and locked.

11

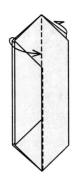

Make the left front flap stick out in front and make the right rear flap stick out behind. The model will not lie flat.

12

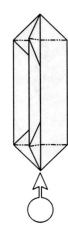

Inflate the model through the hole in the bottom, and shape it into a rectangular box.

13

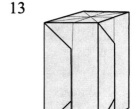

Like this. The next view is from the underside.

PERFORM IT!

Choose a volunteer and say, **"I'm going to put this on your finger and you have to shake it off."** Place on the volunteer's finger and continue, **"Ready, set, everyone yell, 'Shake!'"** [Audience yells, "shake!"] If the volunteer manages to shake off the model, congratulate him saying, **"Wow, you sure know how to shake!"** If he gives up say, **"Well, good effort. Oh, my! How your finger is swollen! Let's see if we can bring down the swelling."** Remove the model and say, **"All better!"**

14

The infamous Finger Eater is ready to devour its prey – your finger! Slip your finger into the hole, trying not tear the paper. You will notice it is much easier to push your finger into the hole than it is to pull your finger back out!

> The newest trend in fashion is to wear Finger Eaters on all of your fingers. Hand models in particular wear them, not just for the stylish look, but also for the added protection.

15

The finger is trapped in the jaws of the Finger Eater. To make the scene even more dramatic, frantically shake your finger in the air while screaming, **"It's got me! Help!!!"** After successfully pulling your finger out a couple times, the model will lose it's grabbing effect. Next, you can try inserting your thumb. After the model loses all grabbing effect, it can still be called a swollen finger.

The Finger Eater can also be used to play Finger Jousting: Each player wears a Finger Eater on the their index finger and uses it to try to knock off the other players' Finger Eaters. The last person still wearing their Finger Eater wins. Finger Jousting can also be played as a two-player game by wearing the Finger Eaters on thumbs and locking hands in the position of Thumb War.

Freaky Fingers Finger Puppet

By Jeremy Shafer

This model can make finger-pointing much more dramatic. You can also use it if you have a question in class – raise your hand by just lifting one finger!

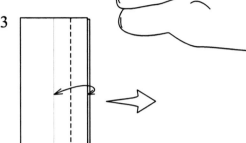

1

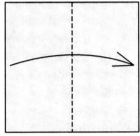

Begin with a 6-inch square of paper colored side up (for small fingered folk, use a 5" square). Valley-fold in half.

2

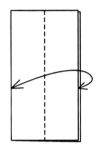

Valley-fold and unfold.

3

Valley-fold and unfold.

4

Valley-fold the front layer.

5

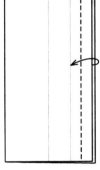

Valley-fold all layers.

6

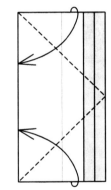

Turn over.

7

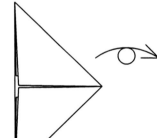

Valley-fold.

8

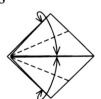

Valley-fold.

9

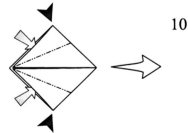

Reverse-fold.

10

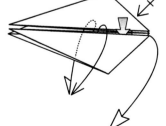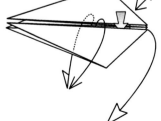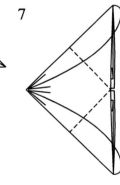

Pull out the single-layer flap. Partially unfolding makes this easier. Repeat above.

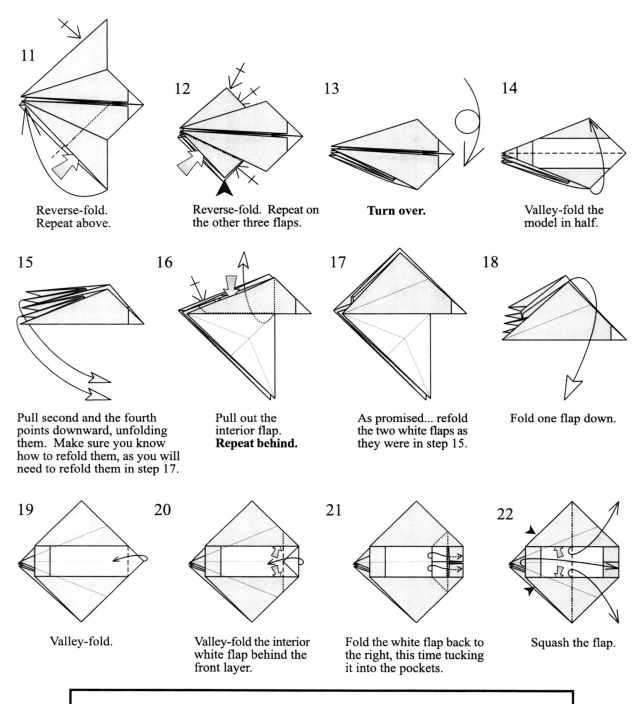

11 Reverse-fold.
Repeat above.

12 Reverse-fold. Repeat on
the other three flaps.

13 Turn over.

14 Valley-fold the
model in half.

15 Pull second and the fourth
points downward, unfolding
them. Make sure you know
how to refold them, as you will
need to refold them in step 17.

16 Pull out the
interior flap.
Repeat behind.

17 As promised... refold
the two white flaps as
they were in step 15.

18 Fold one flap down.

19 Valley-fold.

20 Valley-fold the interior
white flap behind the
front layer.

21 Fold the white flap back to
the right, this time tucking
it into the pockets.

22 Squash the flap.

Note: This model is ideal for Halloween. While trick-or-treating, or at a party, when somebody asks you why you aren't wearing a costume, you can answer, **"Oh, but I am!"** as you hold up your one origami-adorned finger. For a more elaborate costume, fold one for each finger. For an extreme costume, add one for each toe, one for your nose, a giant one for your head, and one for your tongue too! You can call yourself a handyman/handywoman.

23

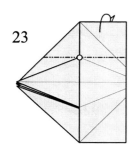

Mountain-fold on
the white dot.

24

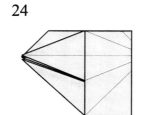

Turn over.

25

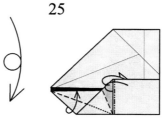

Valley-fold on the existing
crease, while mountain-
folding the shaded triangle
behind the front layer.

26

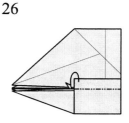

Mountain-fold the
flap into the
rearmost pocket.

27

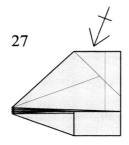

Repeat steps
23-26 on the top.

28

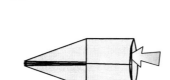

Check to see if your ring finger
(fourth finger) fits comfortably
into the pocket. If the pocket is
just the right size go directly to
step 29 on the next page. If the
pocket is, too big, unfold to step
23 and follow steps 23a-28a.
If the pocket is too small, then,
WOW, you've got big fingers!
You could either wear it on
your pinky or begin again with
a square of paper larger than
6 inches.

23a

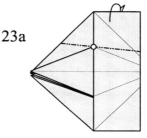

Mountain-fold on the
white dot, this time
making the fold angled
slightly. The smaller
the target finger is, the
more angled this fold
needs to be.

24a

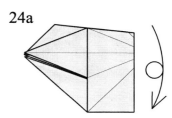

Turn over.

25a

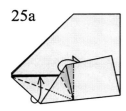

Valley-fold on the
existing crease, while
mountain-folding the
shaded region behind
the front layer. The
mountain fold should
be vertical.

26a

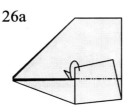

Mountain-fold the
flap into the
rearmost pocket.

27a

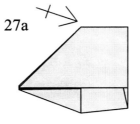

Repeat steps
23a-26a on
the top

28a

Now try to insert your finger
again. If it still isn't the
right size, go back and
adjust the mountain fold in
step 23a. Continue redoing
steps 23a-28a until the
resulting step 28 fits
comfortably on your finger.

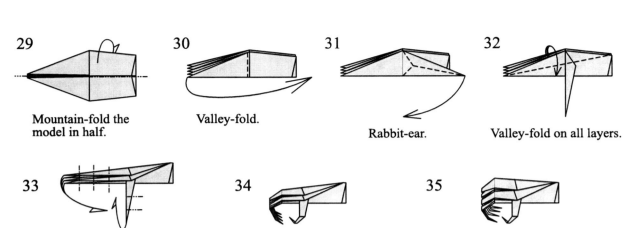

29 Mountain-fold the model in half.

30 Valley-fold.

31 Rabbit-ear.

32 Valley-fold on all layers.

33 Bend the appendages to taste forming knuckle joints.

34 Spread out the fingers so that they are distinct and shape hand to taste.

35 Open the pocket as in step 28 and insert one of your fingers. Sculpt the hand to taste, making sure the pocket remains open.

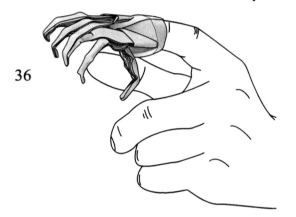

36

The Freaky Fingers Finger Puppet is ready to lend a hand! Whether you use it as the evil character in a finger puppet show or just as a stage hand, or choose from one of the many ideas presented on this page, you'll find there are dozens of ways in which this model can come in handy. However, if you really want to make the most of it, use it to perform the **Freaky Fingers Magic Trick,** as diagrammed on the next page.

Here's a handful of additional uses for this hand:

- If you wiggle it around, it can be called a **"Hand Shake"**

- If you fold two of them, you can play **"Freaky Finger Jousting,"** where each person tries to knock the hand off his opponent's finger.

- Fold one for each finger, and you will have a **"Handful of Hands!"**

- Fold it from giant paper, and you will have a **"Handy Hat"** or, if you turn it to the side, a **"Spiky Mohawk."**

- Fold it out of a giant sheet of cardboard (wetfolded) or metal and you will have a **"Hand Chair."**

- Wear it on your finger while proposing to your partner: **"Will you accept my hand in marriage?"**

- Wear several of them on your fingers to a job interview and you can claim you have **hands-on** job experience.

PERFORM IT!

On the next page are instructions for how use this model to perform the Freaky Fingers Magic Trick, but here's a simpler way to present it to an audience: Before showing the model, say, **"Now I need a volunteer to lend me a hand."** Choose a volunteer and ask them, **"Alright, which hand are you going to give me, your right or your left?"** Pull on one of the hands and say, **"Hmmm, I can't seem to get it off! You'd better keep it. No, actually, I'm going to lend YOU a hand!"** Slip the model onto one of their fingers and say, **"OK, now, raise your hand. Wave to the audience. Scratch your head. Pick your nose. Let's all give this handyman/handylady a big hand! OK, I need the hand back now. Please, HAND it over."**

Freaky Fingers Magic Trick

By Jeremy Shafer ©2007

The following is a method of turning the Freaky Fingers Finger Puppet into a freaky close-up magic trick, which, with a little practice, can really freak out your friends and give them a good laugh.

Materials: All you need is to fold the origami Freaky Fingers Finger Puppet and then find some decoy object – a ring, pebble, woodchip or any pea-sized object that won't roll. Practice the trick in front of a mirror to ensure that the origami hand stays hidden from the audience until the right moment.

1

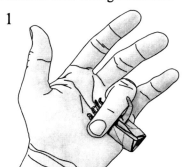

2

Pocket

3

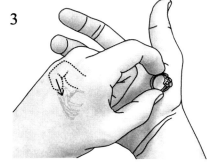

Set-up: First, make the origami hand grab your left ring finger (fourth finger), as shown above.

Now, curl up your ring finger, middle finger and little finger, hiding the origami hand inside as shown above. The thumb and index finger are in position to grab the "Magic Ring" (or pebble, woodchip, etc...). With practice, the set-up can be done all with your left hand hidden inside a pants pocket.

Now for the Trick: Tell your audience that you're going to perform a very weird, freaky magic trick with this Magic Ring. You can have them inspect the ring. Make sure the origami hand stays hidden from audience view! With your left index finger and thumb grab the ring and press it into your right palm near the thumb and tell the audience to watch the ring very carefully. **While pressing it, secretly insert your right ring finger (fourth finger) into the pocket of the origami model.**

4

5

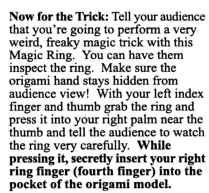

Cup your hands as shown above, again, being careful not to accidentally flash the origami model, which should remain on your ring finger hidden at the roof of the space in your cupped hands. Now, completely cover the magic ring by cupping your hands together. Say to your audience, **"I will now turn this ring into an ugly green alien!"** (or any other ridiculous claim). **"Abracadabra!"** Open your hands once again to the position shown above and exclaim, **"Wait, something went wrong. Well, actually, it kinda looks like a green alien... No, really! Look at the ring up close! Look carefully at its reflection."**

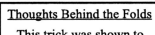

Thoughts Behind the Folds

This trick was shown to me by "Magic Steve" (Steve Ringel) who used a plastic hand. A half-hour later I came back to him with this origami version of the magic trick.

Now for the freaky part! As the audience looks up close at the ring, slowly grab the ring with the origami hand and drag it deep into the space in your cupped hands and cup your hands together again. If done correctly this will startle the audience and then cause a big laugh. While they are laughing, dump the origami hand and Magic Ring back into your pocket. When the ring's owner requests the ring back, say, **"Didn't you see? The ugly green alien took it! Just kidding, here it is."**

Transforming Designs

All action models transform from one position to
another. The flapping bird for instance transforms from
a bird with it's wings up, to a bird with its wings down,
but it's still a bird. The following models transform
so much that they their different positions can each be
viewed as a separate model two subjects for the price
of one paper!

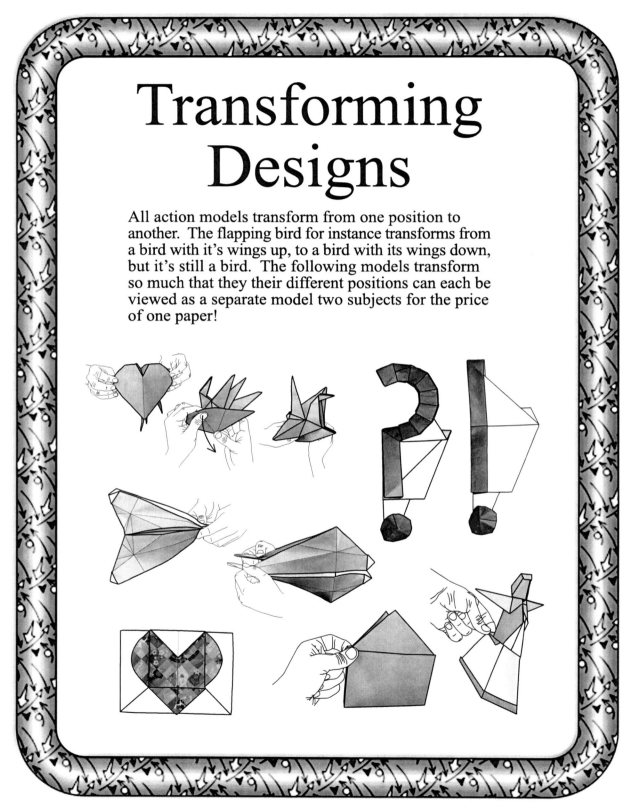

Super Heart

By Alicia Shafer
©2002

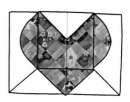

It's a Card! It's a Frame! No, it's.... **Super Heart!!** Easy-to-fold and full of possibilities, Super Heart, you're my hero!

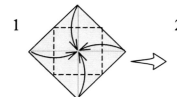

1

Colored side up, Valley-fold and unfold diagonally both ways. Blintz!

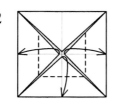

2

Valley-fold three points.

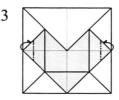

3

Mountain-fold to

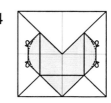

4

Round to taste and behold...

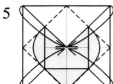

5

...**Super Heart is ready for action!** Blintz!

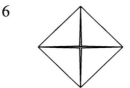

6

Put a sticker on the center and Super Heart is ready to be flung into the mail! Unblintz to uncover Super Heart.

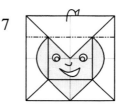

7

Mountain-fold to taste. If you don't like Super Heart's pointy ears, make the mountain fold lower.

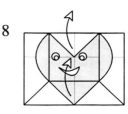

8

Now it's time for a magic trick. Super Heart is going to turn upside down without rotating the paper!

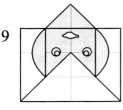

9

Incredible! In case you didn't see it the first time, watch Super Heart do it again!

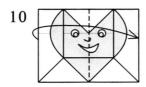

10

Wow! Super Heart is ready for another adventure. Fold in half.

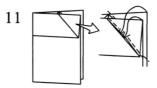

11

Super Heart is trapped between two walls of paper! To make the escape even harder, tuck both corners into the pocket.

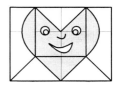

12

Super Heart escapes! For more escapades let your imagination fly! Tune in next time for more adventures of **Super Heart!**

PERFORM IT!

Say to the audience, **"This is not just an origami model! It's a superhero! Is it a bird? Is it a plane? No, it's Super Heart! This superhero will come to the rescue in any delicate situation. Like, say you hurt someone's feelings or you're worried about losing a friend, simply send Super Heart out and they will surely forgive you! Let's try it..."** Choose an adult and say **"You're a dumb dumb. Oops, I'm sorry for hurting your feelings."** Give the model to them and ask, **"Will you accept my apology?"** If the Adult accepts the apology, exclaim, **"And once again, Super Heart saves the day! Let's hear some thunderous applause for Super Heart! And for the apology-accepting grown-up too!"** (If the adult doesn't accept the apology, grab the model back and say to it sadly, **"It's OK, Super Heart, even superheroes aren't perfect."**)

Can Love be Squashed?

This is a heart that transforms into another heart! ©2000
Sy Chen

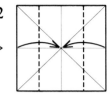

1 White side up,
valley-fold in half
every which way.

2 Valley-fold.

3 **Turn over.**

4 Valley-fold and
unfold on the
existing diagonal
creases. **Turn over.**

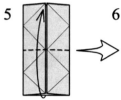

5 Valley-fold
in half.

6 Fold down the
front layers.

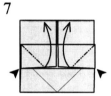

7 Squash.

8 Inside-reverse-fold.

9 Inside-reverse-fold.

10 Tuck the flaps
into the pockets.

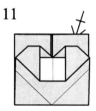

11 **Repeat steps
6-10 behind.**

12 Unfold the rear
flap downward.

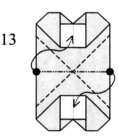

13 Fold a Waterbomb Base;
hide the collapsed
middle corners beneath
the white rectangles.

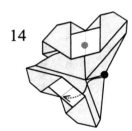

14 In progress. The
left corner is safely
hidden. Hide the
right corner.

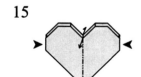

15 **The model is finished.**
Say to your audience,
**"This model is a question:
Can love be squashed?"**
Squash the left and right
sides together, resulting in
an almost identical heart!

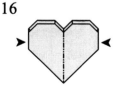

16 **"The answer is
yes, but as you
can see, it is
very resilient!**

PERFORM IT!

Ask the audience, **"What is this?"** [Audience says
"It's a Heart."] Reply, **"No it's not. It's a question.
The question is, 'Can love be squashed?' Let's
find out. Ready, set, everyone say, 'Squash!'"**
[Audience says, "Squash!"] Squash the model and
say, **"Again, everyone say, 'Squash!'"** Repeat once
or twice more and conclude by saying, **"There you
have it! The answer is yes, love can be squashed,
but it is very resilient; it heals very quickly!"**

Pregnant Heart

 Rather Simple — By Jeremy Shafer ©2003

Here's a heart that is so big that it's actually pregnant and ready to give birth... to another heart that will someday, no doubt, grow to be just as large and loving.

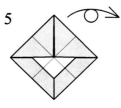

1

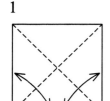

Valley-fold diagonally in half and unfold, in both directions.

2

Valley-fold and unfold.

3

Valley-fold to the intersections of the creases.

4

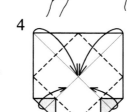

Valley-fold.

5

Turn over.

6

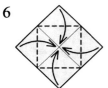

Valley-fold the corners to the center.

7

Turn over.

8

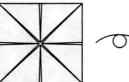

Form a Waterbomb Base.

9

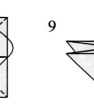

Unfold the rear flap.

10

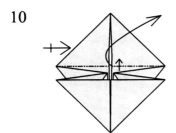

Pull the edge rightward, releasing the trapped paper. Repeat on the left side.

11

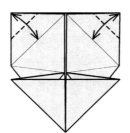

Valley-fold and unfold.

12

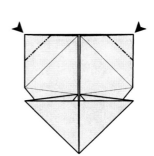

Reverse-fold.

PERFORM IT!

Set-up: Fold steps 1-22 and then fold the model in half. Pull the model out of the box, and very slowly open it (like opening a book) while saying to the audience, **"This is a heart, but do you know why it's getting bigger? Because it's pregnant. In fact I thinks it's going into labor right now! Do we have a doctor or nurse in the audience that can help deliver the baby? We're out of time; here it comes! Everyone, yell, 'Push!'"** [Audience yells, "Push!"] **"It's a... It's a..."** Pull out the heart and declare, **"...It's a baby! Everyone take a picture of the newborn baby heart!"**

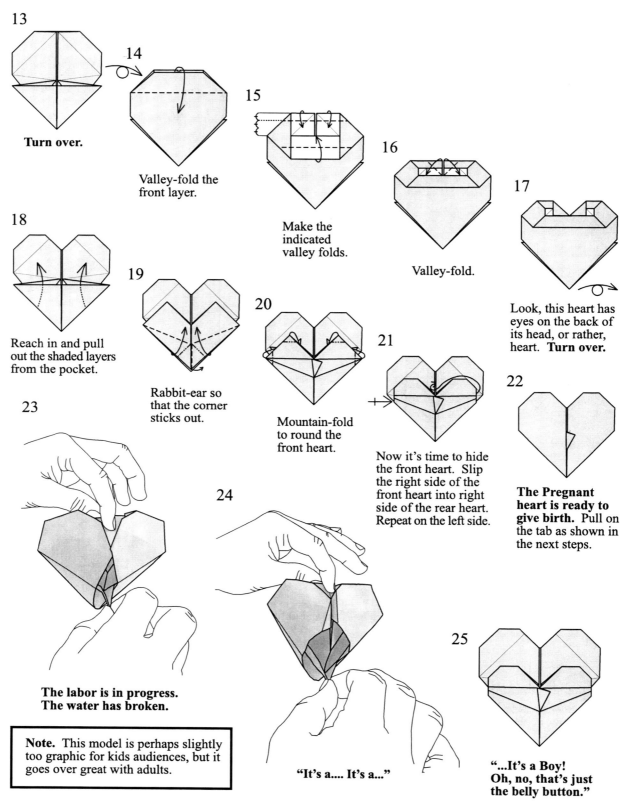

13

Turn over.

14

Valley-fold the
front layer.

15

Make the
indicated
valley folds.

16

Valley-fold.

17

Look, this heart has
eyes on the back of
its head, or rather,
heart. **Turn over.**

18

Reach in and pull
out the shaded layers
from the pocket.

19

Rabbit-ear so
that the corner
sticks out.

20

Mountain-fold
to round the
front heart.

21

Now it's time to hide
the front heart. Slip
the right side of the
front heart into right
side of the rear heart.
Repeat on the left side.

22

**The Pregnant
heart is ready to
give birth.** Pull on
the tab as shown in
the next steps.

23

**The labor is in progress.
The water has broken.**

Note. This model is perhaps slightly
too graphic for kids audiences, but it
goes over great with adults.

24

"It's a.... It's a..."

25

"...It's a Boy!
Oh, no, that's just
the belly button."

164 *Origami Ooh La La!*

Canoe (Rather Simple)

with Convertible Canopy

By Jeremy Shafer ©2010

The next time you are stranded on a desert isle with nothing but a 30-foot square of heavyduty waterproof cardboard, you can rest assured that you will be able to fold the most stylish escape canoe of all the Origami Survivor contestants.

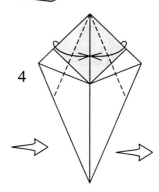

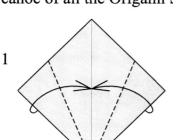

1

2

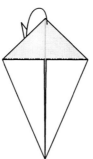

3

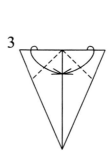

4

Colored side up, fold a Kite Base.

Mountain-fold.

Valley-fold.

Valley-fold.

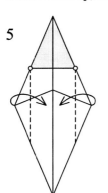

5

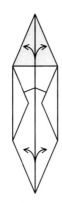

6

90°

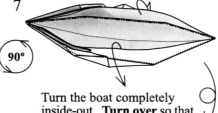

7

Valley-fold on the white dots.

Spread open the middle edges and rotate 90° counterclockwise so that it looks like a boat.

Turn the boat completely inside-out. **Turn over** so that it still looks like a boat.

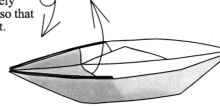

8

The Canoe is built and is ready for its maiden voyage, perhaps in the gutter on a rainy day? And, in case it is a rainy day, be sure to pull out the bimini canopy to provide the passengers with shelter from the wind and rain.

Note. Incorporating this model into a performance might be difficult, but it is a great model to teach at parties. The bimini top makes it a good boat for racing in a swimming pool, pond or large puddle, because the wind will really carry it, and, if there's no wind, you can propel it by blowing on it.

It is also a good model to hang from a string attached to the tip of the bimini top (Wow, that's fun to say!). The boat will hang almost level, because the center of balance is near the tip of the flap.

9

Canoe with bimini top. This top also serves as a sail in the wind. You can pull the sail out even higher, but good luck trying to change its direction!

Searching for Pajama Joe

Model and original story by Sy Chen ©2002 (Story embellished by Jeremy Shafer)

Super Simple

This is a model that can be performed as a story while you fold it! Begin with a red sheet of paper, red side up.

1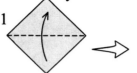

One day, my dog and I decided to climb to the top of Mt. Everest, in search of the famous bird god, Pajama Joe.

2

Looking at the map, we saw there were two ways up the mountain: The Black Blizzard Trail...

3

...or the Sunny Snow Trail. We chose the Sunny Snow Trail.

4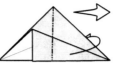

When we came to the middle of the mountain...

5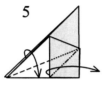

...something jumped out at us!

6

It was just a friendly fox...

7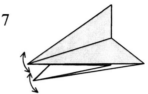

...who said to us, Let me guess, you're looking for the famous bird god, Pajama Joe."

8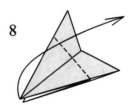

"Why yes!" I replied, "Do you know where we might find him?" The fox looked up...

9 **10**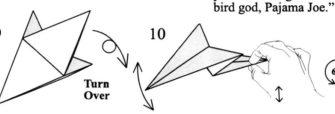

Turn Over

...and nodded his head. "You must climb to the top of the mountain, stand on the South Ledge, and call out: "EE KNEE, ME KNEE, MY KNEE MOE, PLEASE COME OUT, PAJAMA JOE!"

11

60°

We thanked him and continued hiking up the mountain. Suddenly, the sky grew dark and we realized we were hiking up the Black Blizzard Trail by mistake!

PERFORM IT!

Flapping Blue Jay/Cardinal Story

By Sy Chen inspired by Michael LaFosse's Crane Watching Story

To Perform with this model, You can use my variation (see above diagrams), make up your own version, or use Sy Chen's original story as told in this box. Steps are numbered to match above diagrams. Use mono colored paper, red for Cardinal and blue for Blue Jay.

1. My dog and I went mountain hiking one time.

2. There were two trails to the middle of the mountain. One from this end...

3. But I chose the other end.

4. On the way to the middle of the mountain,

6. I saw a fox.

7. The fox opened its mouth

10. And another one nodded it's head.

12. My dog began barking.

13. I had to grab his mouth and pull one ear backward to stop his barking. (I know my dog!)

16. We reached the top of the mountain after a long hike and rested on the extruded cliff there.

15. I saw a blue jay's head.

19. I showed what I saw to my resting dog.

20. He lay on the grass and his ears flopped downward.

22. Suddenly my dog stood up to bark at the bird and even kicked up his hind leg and jumped.

24. The bird got scared and flew away.

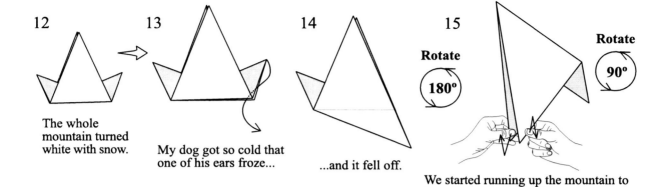

12

13

The whole
mountain turned
white with snow.

My dog got so cold that
one of his ears froze...

14

...and it fell off.

15

Rotate

180°

Rotate

90°

We started running up the mountain to
keep from freezing AND to make the story
move faster. Before we knew it, we
had reached the top of the mountain!

16

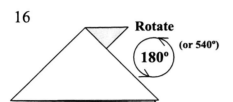

Rotate

(or 540°)

180°

We stood out on the rocky red ledge
and called out the fox's magic words,
"EE KNEE, ME KNEE, MY KNEE
MOE, PLEASE COME OUT,
PAJAMA JOE!" All of a sudden, a
huge wind came out of nowhere and
blew the whole mountain – with us
on it – up into the air, and it started
turning. It turned and turned...

17

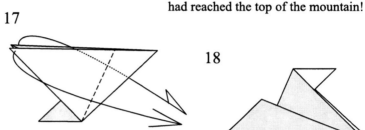

...and it magically turned...

18

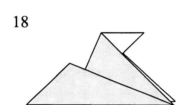

...all red, all except for the rocky red
ledge which turned WHITE! But,
still, there was no sign of Pajama Joe.

19

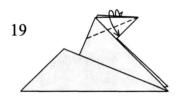

We called out again even louder
the magic words, "EE KNEE,
ME KNEE, MY KNEE MOE,
PLEASE COME OUT,
PAJAMA JOE!" and magically...

20

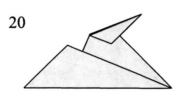

...the ledge turned red again.
But there was still no Pajama Joe.

21

We went up to the very tip
of the ledge, stood up tall...

22

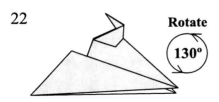

Rotate

130°

...and called out one last time as loud as we could,
"EE KNEE, ME KNEE, MY KNEE MOE,
PLEASE COME OUT, PAJAMA JOE!"

23

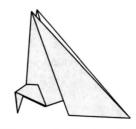

Then magically, the whole
mountain turned over...

24

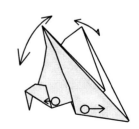

...and we flew away
with Pajama Joe.

The END

Searching for Pajama Joe **167**

Heart Hand Crane (Intermediate) By Jeremy Shafer ©2003

Have a change of heart,
Lend a helping hand
Help spread peace
Throughout the land.

1

If you were to fold this model from a sheet of pink/white paper you could call the fifth finger a "pinky," but, in my opinion, the model is more convincing folded from paper that is the same color on both sides. Begin by folding a Square Base.

2

Valley-fold and unfold on all layers.

3

Valley-fold. **Repeat behind.**

4

Squash. **Repeat behind.**

5

Valley-fold the left front flap rightward.

6

Turn over.

7

Valley-fold the left front flap rightward.

8

Valley-fold. **Repeat behind.**

9

Valley-fold and unfold. **Turn over.**

10

Valley-fold and unfold.

11

Sink. 180°

<u>Thoughts Behind the Folds</u>

In March of 2003 I was a contestant on the origami episode of "TV Champion," a Japanese reality game show. The first round of the competition was to fold a model that completely transforms and changes color in one move. A month after the competition, with transformation still on my mind, I came up with this model. It started out as a folding exercise to make a pop-up crane card. Then I asked myself what else did the folded-up model look like. I saw a four-fingered hand. The heart came out of an attempt to make the fifth finger. **Challenge:** Can you come up with a story to tie together a Heart, Hand, and Crane?

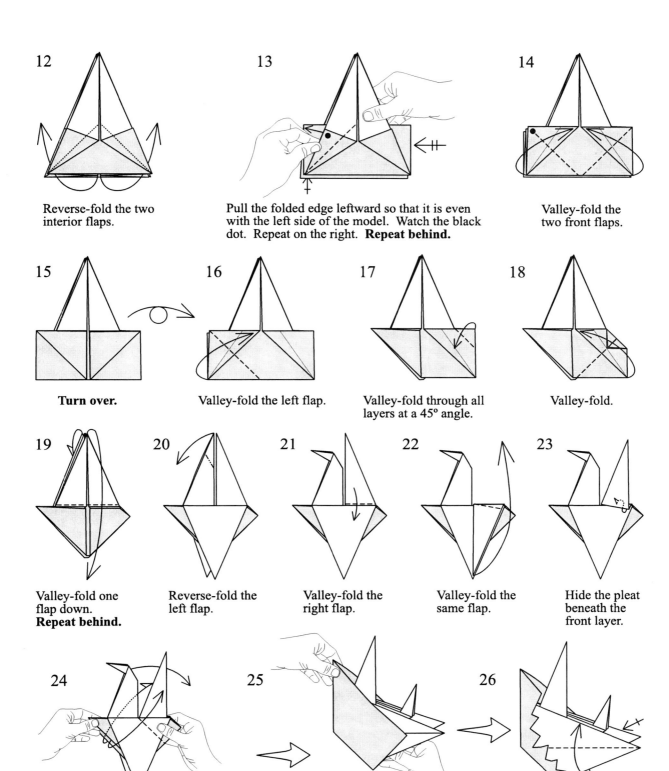

12 Reverse-fold the two interior flaps.

13 Pull the folded edge leftward so that it is even with the left side of the model. Watch the black dot. Repeat on the right. **Repeat behind.**

14 Valley-fold the two front flaps.

15 **Turn over.**

16 Valley-fold the left flap.

17 Valley-fold through all layers at a 45° angle.

18 Valley-fold.

19 Valley-fold one flap down. **Repeat behind.**

20 Reverse-fold the left flap.

21 Valley-fold the right flap.

22 Valley-fold the same flap.

23 Hide the pleat beneath the front layer.

24 Outside-reverse-fold the whole left half of the model, letting the head swing behind the tail.

25 Like this. Imagine tearing off the front flap. The next step is what it would look like. But don't really tear the paper! Just imagine.

26 Valley-fold the white flap. **Repeat behind.**

Heart Hand Crane **169**

27

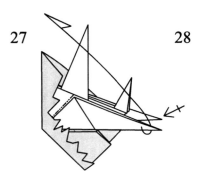

Mountain-fold the flap upward. **Repeat behind.**

28

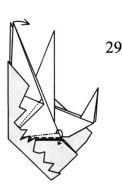

Rotate the frontmost white flap about 10° clockwise.

29

Rotate the rearmost white flap about 35° clockwise. Stop imagining that the front flap is torn off.

30

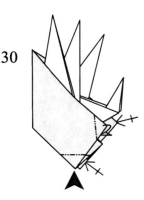

Reverse-fold below. Mountain fold on the right. **Repeat behind.**

31

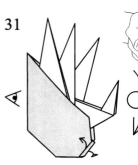

The hand is ready for transformation. Turn the model over top-to-bottom, open it slightly and view the model from the left side.

32

It's a Heart! Show the Heart to the audience and say, **"Now let's all give this model a big hand!"** Rotate the model 90°.

33

"Thanks for giving the model such a big hand!..." Point to someone who wasn't clapping and say, **"...except for you. Why didn't you clap? What, do you think this model is for the birds?"** Holding as shown, swing the front and rear flaps down, letting the head and tail swing into place.

34

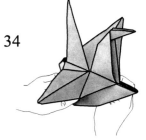

"Well, you're right! Ok, let's give this bird a big hand." Go back to step 33, wave the hand and say, **"Thank you!"** Finish by going back to step 32, holding up the heart and exclaiming, **"I love you all!"**

PERFORM IT!

Say to the audience, **"This is a magic heart, but it's scared of being in front of people. It was nervous about coming here, but it came anyway, so lets all give it a hand!** [Audience applauds.] Turn it into a hand and say, **"Wow! You really did give it a hand! I told you it was magic! And now for its big finish... Abracadabra, broccoli brain, Turn yourself into a Japanese...everyone say...CRANE!"** [Audience says "CRANE!"] Turn it into a crane and exclaim **"Amazing! How about another hand for this magical model?!"** [Audience applauds.] Turn it back into a hand and wave it to the audience saying, **"Thank you, thank you! It's waving good-bye..."** Switch it back to a heart and say, **"...and it's saying, 'I love you all!' And look...no more stage fright!"**

Magical Transforming Polyhedron

By Jeremy Shafer ©2009

(Intermediate)

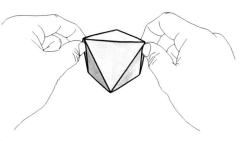

New sides seemingly pop out of nowhere, as this magical model transforms from hexahedron to octahedron to decahedron, and finally into a simple hexagon, which makes a fine coaster for a glass of fine wine.

1

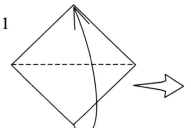

White side up, valley-fold in half diagonally.

2

Valley-fold in half and unfold.

3

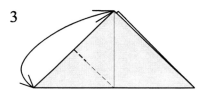

Valley-fold and unfold the flap, creasing only where boldly diagramed.

4

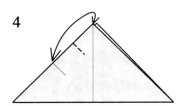

Valley-fold and unfold, creasing only near the edge.

5

Valley-fold the flap on the white dot so that the black dot touches the crease mark.

6

Valley-fold.

7

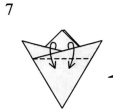

Valley-fold.

8

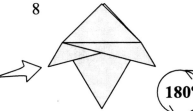

Rotate 180°.

180°

9

Valley-fold.
Repeat behind...

10

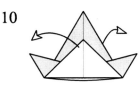

... and the Elf's Hat is done! What, we're not making an Elf's hat? Oops, my mistake. Well then, completely unfold the model.

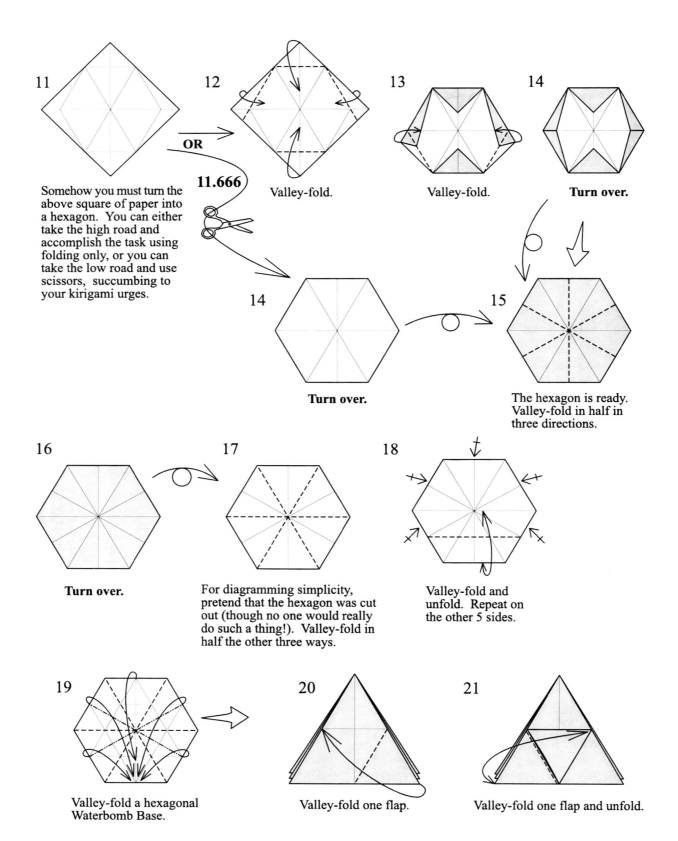

11

Somehow you must turn the above square of paper into a hexagon. You can either take the high road and accomplish the task using folding only, or you can take the low road and use scissors, succumbing to your kirigami urges.

OR

11.666

12

Valley-fold.

13

Valley-fold.

14

Turn over.

14

Turn over.

15

The hexagon is ready. Valley-fold in half in three directions.

16

Turn over.

17

For diagramming simplicity, pretend that the hexagon was cut out (though no one would really do such a thing!). Valley-fold in half the other three ways.

18

Valley-fold and unfold. Repeat on the other 5 sides.

19

Valley-fold a hexagonal Waterbomb Base.

20

Valley-fold one flap.

21

Valley-fold one flap and unfold.

22

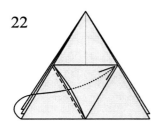

Refold the flap inserting it into the pocket.

23

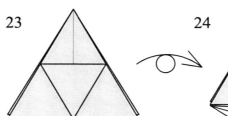

Turn over.

24

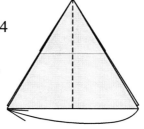

Valley-fold one flap to the left.

25

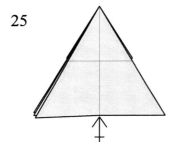

Repeat steps 20-22.

26

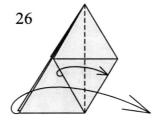

Valley fold the two flaps to the right.

27

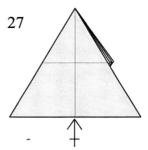

Repeat steps 20-22.

28

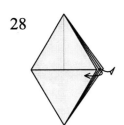

Separate the middle-layer flaps as indicated. The model will no longer lie flat.

29

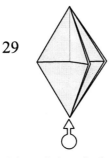

Blow air into the hole to inflate the model, forming a hexahedron. Pinch along the horizontal edges of the hexahedron to better define its shape.

30

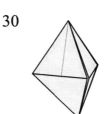

The Hexahedron is complete, but the performance has just begun. Rotate the model slightly so that one point is facing you.

31

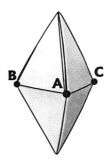

Like this. Name the three middle corners, **A**, **B** and **C** as indicated.

32

Holding the model as shown, pull your hands apart, turning point **A** into two separate points.

33

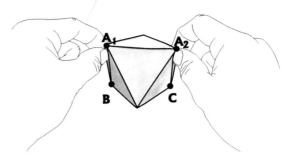

The Octahedron! Now turn the model so that point **B** is facing you.

34

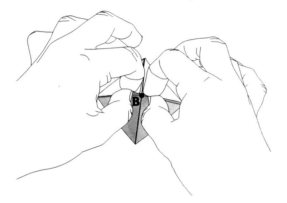

Holding the model as shown, pull your hands apart, turning point **B** into two separate points.

35

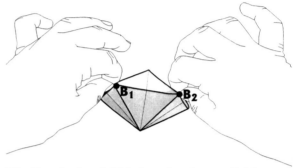

The Decahedron! This is a nice place to finish, as it is still not too difficult to return the model to step 31.

If you would like to turn model into a 2-D hexagon coaster then pull apart the final point **C**, but beware, if you do this, it will make it rather difficult to turn the model into a polyhedron again.

36

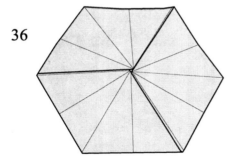

The Hexagon Coaster is done. For a strolling magician at a banquet table, a nice way to finish the trick would be to put the coaster under someone's wine glass and offer it to them as a present. If you would like to transform the Hexagon back into the Hexahedron, completely unfold it and refold steps 1-31!

PERFORM IT!

Start with the Hexahedron (step 31) and say, **"This is an origami polyhedron. Can anyone guess how many faces it has?"** Choose a volunteer to count the number of faces. [Volunteer counts six faces.] Secretly turn it into the octahedron (step 33) and ask, **"Are you sure? Here, count again."** [Volunteer counts eight faces.] Secretly turn it into a decagon (step 35) and ask, **"Is that your final answer? Here, count one more time!"** [Volunteer counts ten faces.] Put the model back in the box and say, **"It seems to me you're having trouble counting; maybe you should stick with reading and writing."**

Fish's Tail / Fish's Head

Rather Simple

By Jeremy Shafer ©2002

Three models in one!... Alligator Head, Fish Head, and Fish Tail. This transforming model brings new light to the famous question, "Heads or Tails?," and works great for story-telling, especially at libraries and schools of fish.

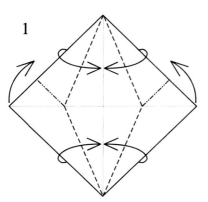

1

White side up, fold a Fish Base. (For help, see Fish Base, page 17)

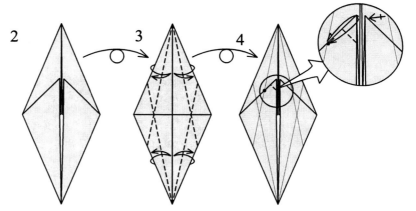

2

Turn over.

3

Valley-fold and unfold. **Turn over.**

4

Outside-reverse-fold the corner to the black dot.

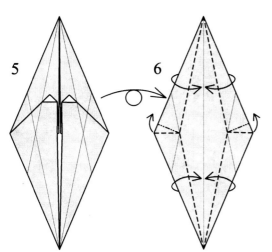

5

Turn over.

6

Rabbit-ear the side flaps.

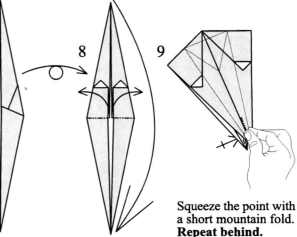

7

Turn over.

8

Fold the top down while opening apart and squashing the front layers.

9

Squeeze the point with a short mountain fold. **Repeat behind.**

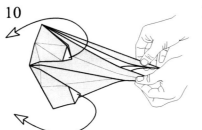

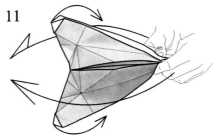

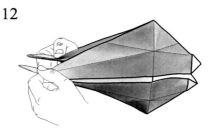

Here we have the Alligator Mouth. Unfold the eye flaps. Then hold the two pinched flaps as shown.

The Fish's Tail has appeared. To turn it into the Fish's Head, swing the pinched flaps leftward, the front flap going in front and rear flap going behind. The little white triangles should swing to the right and come together, forming the fish's mouth.

The Fish's Head has appeared. Swing the pinched flaps back to the right to bring back the Fish's Tail.

Wiggling Fish's Tail / Fish's Head

This variation features a tail that actually wiggles, which from the audience might get some giggles.

Rather Simple

By Jeremy Shafer
©2010

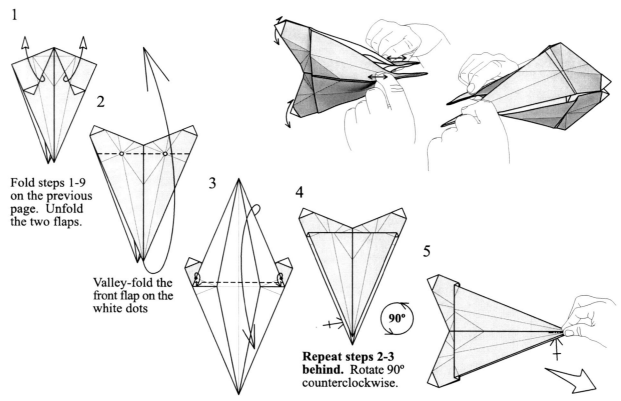

1

Fold steps 1-9 on the previous page. Unfold the two flaps.

2

Valley-fold the front flap on the white dots

3

Valley-fold the black dots to the folded edge.

4

Repeat steps 2-3 behind. Rotate 90° counterclockwise.

90°

5

Squeeze the point of the front flap with a short mountain fold. **Repeat behind.** Partially unfold the pleats made in steps 2-4.

6

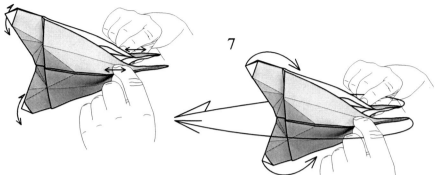

7

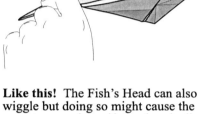

8

The Wiggling Fish's Tail is ready to wiggle! Holding as shown move your near hand to the left and your far hand to the right, and the tail flaps will bend away. To make the tail bend toward you, move your near hand to the right and the far hand to the left, and you will have completed one wiggle. Make 7 wiggles and you will have completed one waggle.

To turn it into the Fish's Head, swing the pinched flaps all the way to the left, the front flap going in front and rear flap going behind. The little white triangles will swing to the right and come together, forming the fish's mouth.

Like this! The Fish's Head can also wiggle but doing so might cause the paper to crumple, and harm the wiggling action of the tail. So, wiggle the head at your own risk!

PERFORM IT!

Ask the audience, **"Do you know what this is? This is a fish's head. Would you like to see the fish's tail?"** [Audience says, "Yes."] **"Well I can't show you the fish's tail..."** Keeping your eyes glued to the audience, switch to the fish's tail and wiggle it, while saying, **"...because I just have the fish's head"** [Audience: "There's the fish's tail!"] While still looking at the audience, flip it back to the fish's head. Look at it and say, **"No, you guys are going crazy! It's just a fish's head. I can't show you the fish's tail because I've only got the fish's head!"** Repeat the patter, but make sure to stop before the joke gets old. Finish by saying, **"Maybe I'm the one whose going crazy!"**

Unfortunate Fisherman

By Jeremy Shafer ©2001

Intermediate

Here is a fish that got the bait and a whole lot more!

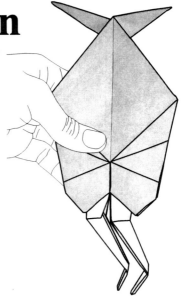

1

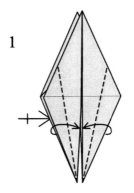

Begin by folding a Bird Base. Valley-fold the sides to the center. **Repeat behind.**

2

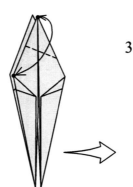

Valley-fold point-to-point and unfold.

3

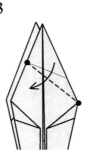

Valley-fold between the black dots.

4

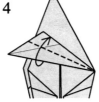

Valley-fold.

5

Unfold the pleat.

6

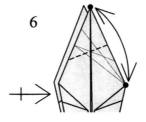

Repeat steps 2-5 on the right side.

7

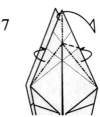

Mountain-fold the sides of the flap behind while pinching the tip and collapsing to the right. This is a rabbit ear from the other side.

8

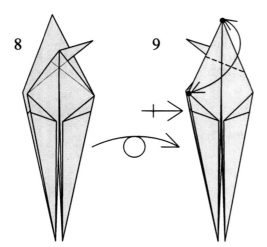

Turn over.

9

Repeat steps 2-7.

10

The tail is complete. Valley-fold the two bottom points to the end of the tail and unfold.

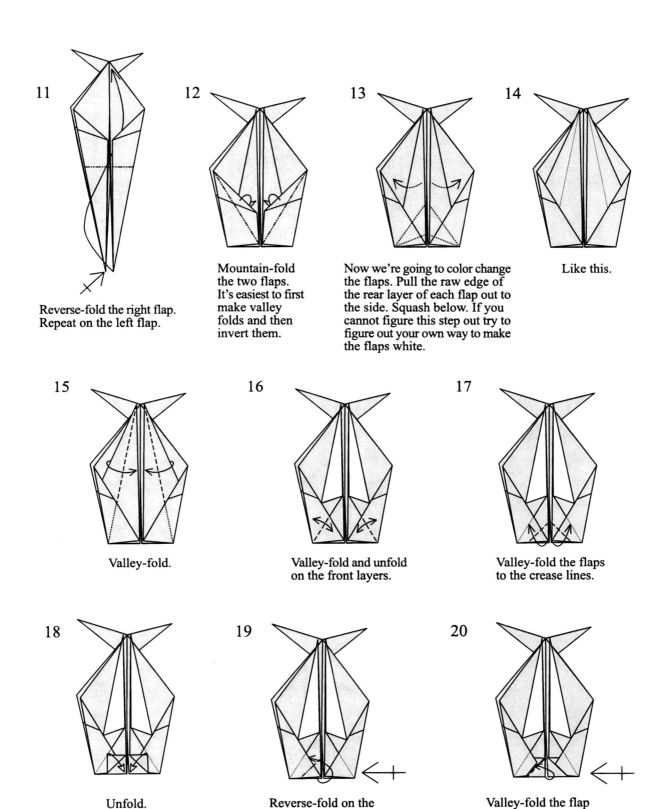

11

Reverse-fold the right flap.
Repeat on the left flap.

12

Mountain-fold
the two flaps.
It's easiest to first
make valley
folds and then
invert them.

13

Now we're going to color change
the flaps. Pull the raw edge of
the rear layer of each flap out to
the side. Squash below. If you
cannot figure this step out try to
figure out your own way to make
the flaps white.

14

Like this.

15

Valley-fold.

16

Valley-fold and unfold
on the front layers.

17

Valley-fold the flaps
to the crease lines.

18

Unfold.

19

Reverse-fold on the
left side. Repeat on
the right side.

20

Valley-fold the flap
into the pocket. Repeat
on the right side.

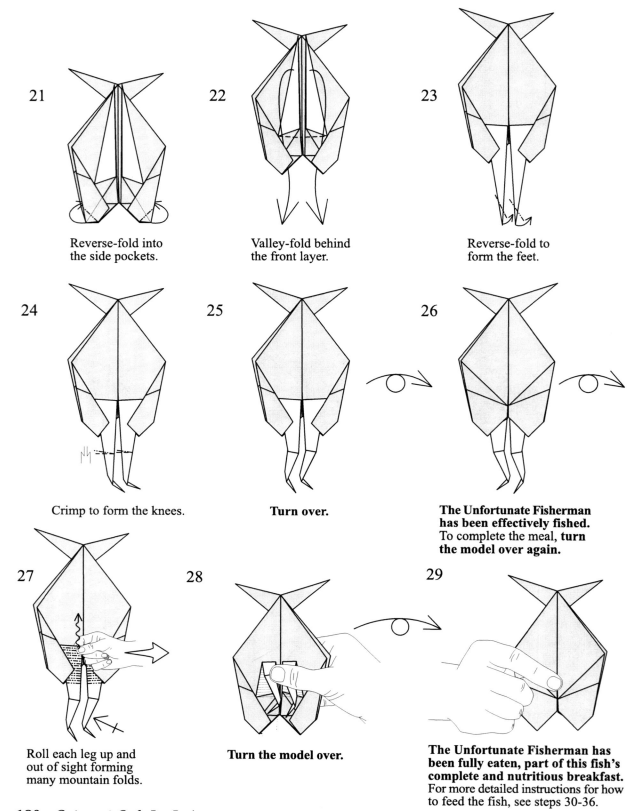

21

Reverse-fold into the side pockets.

22

Valley-fold behind the front layer.

23

Reverse-fold to form the feet.

24

Crimp to form the knees.

25

Turn over.

26

The Unfortunate Fisherman has been effectively fished. To complete the meal, **turn the model over again.**

27

Roll each leg up and out of sight forming many mountain folds.

28

Turn the model over.

29

The Unfortunate Fisherman has been fully eaten, part of this fish's complete and nutritious breakfast. For more detailed instructions for how to feed the fish, see steps 30-36.

Proper Technique for Feeding the Fish

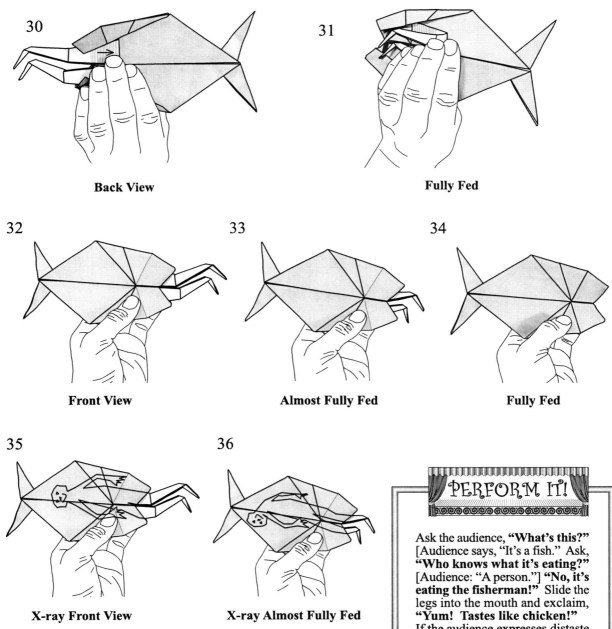

30 Back View

31 Fully Fed

32 Front View

33 Almost Fully Fed

34 Fully Fed

35 X-ray Front View

36 X-ray Almost Fully Fed

You see, it's really not so bad if you just use your imagination. But if fish gobbling humans is too disconcerting, what else could we make the fish be eating. **Ideas:** pretzel, spaghetti, letters of the alphabet, two worms in love (heart shaped), a couple of sea horses – uh oh, now we're back to being too disconcerting!

Unfortunate Fisherman **181**

Blue Moon

By Jeremy Shafer ©2004

Idea by Ian Hudson, age 12, of Harwinton, CT

Rather Simple

Smell sold Separately

"I spend my days just mooning, so sad and blue…" (from Grease, the musical)

This is not your ordinary everyday blue moon... This one is truly blue!

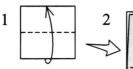

1 For a blue moon, begin with a blue sheet of paper, white side up. Valley-fold in half.

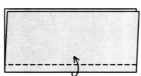

2 Valley-fold the bottom edge to taste.

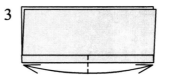

3 Mark the center of the bottom edge by valley-folding in half.

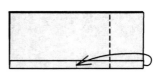

4 Valley-fold to the center mark.

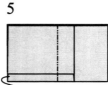

5 Mountain-fold.

6 Valley-fold the left edge to the raw edge, while swinging the rear flap all the way to the left.

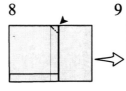

7 Valley-fold and unfold through all layers.

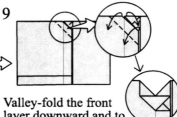

8 Reverse-fold the front corner.

9 Valley-fold the front layer downward and to the left, and squash the rear layer to the right.....like this.

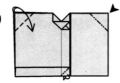

10 Valley-fold the left side. Reverse-fold the right side. Mountain-fold the bottom corner.

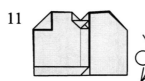

11 **Turn over top-to-bottom** and shape bottom to taste.

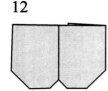

12 **The moon is ready to rise and shine:** "Good mooning to you, and have a good *afternoon* too!"

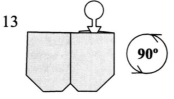

 90°

13 Butt wait, there's more! Hold the model gently between your lips where indicated by the arrow and blow in between the two layers for a fartastically funny noise. For the cleaner more publishable version, rotate the model 90° counterclockwise transforming it into a...

PERFORM IT!

Ask the audience, **"What's this?"** [Audience tries to guess.] Reply, **"It's a funny-looking moon. No it's a butt, I mean a *B*!"** (step 14) **"It's a *B* that goes 'Bzzz.'"** Make the funny farting noise (step 13). Embarrassingly say, **"Excuse me, I guess it is a butt! Everyone plug your nose! BUT, enough! On to the next model!"**

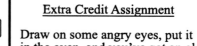

14 ... "B that goes Bzzz."

Extra Credit Assignment

Draw on some angry eyes, put it in the oven, and you've got an old British favorite: **Hot Cross Buns!**

How dare you sell me for a penny!

Pop-up Housewife Intermediate

By Jeremy Shafer ©2009

This model could be dangerous to society, for men might choose not to marry, since now they can simply fold their very own pop-up housewife.

1

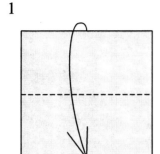

Colored side up, valley-fold in half top-to-bottom.

2

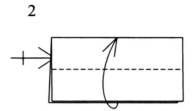

Valley-fold the top layer. **Repeat behind.**

3

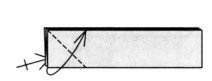

Valley-fold one flap. **Repeat behind.**

4

Valley-fold one flap edge-to-edge. **Repeat behind.**

5

Valley-fold edge-to-edge on all layers.

6

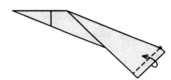

Valley-fold on the black dot.

7

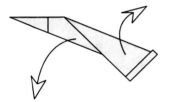

Completely unfold the model.

8

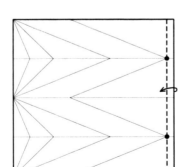

Valley-fold on the black dots.

9

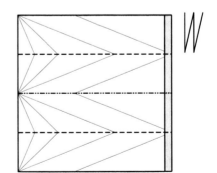

Pleat on existing creases.

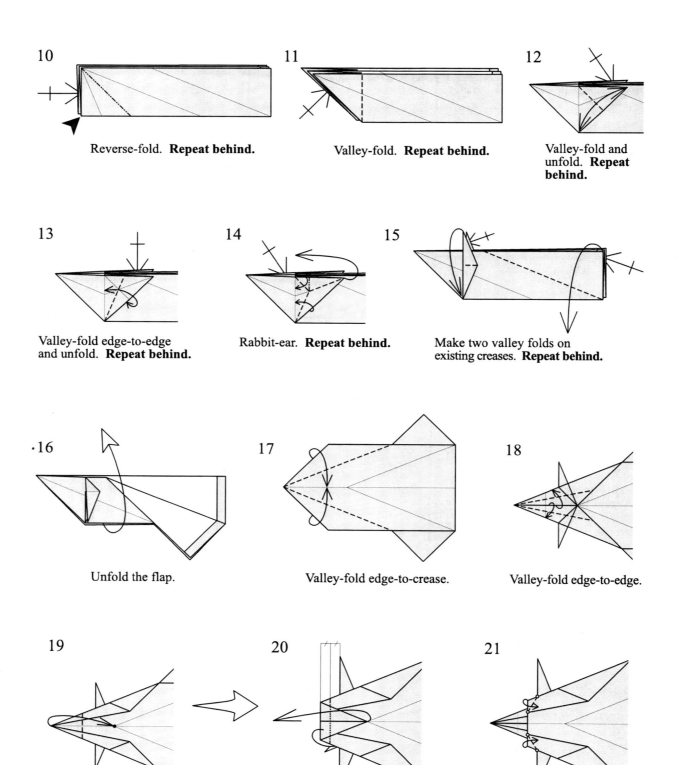

10 Reverse-fold. **Repeat behind.**

11 Valley-fold. **Repeat behind.**

12 Valley-fold and unfold. **Repeat behind.**

13 Valley-fold edge-to-edge and unfold. **Repeat behind.**

14 Rabbit-ear. **Repeat behind.**

15 Make two valley folds on existing creases. **Repeat behind.**

·16 Unfold the flap.

17 Valley-fold edge-to-crease.

18 Valley-fold edge-to-edge.

19 Valley-fold to the black dot.

20 Mountain-fold the left edge, letting the front flap swing leftward.

21 Valley-fold on the white dots.

22

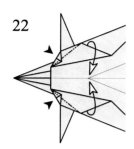

Unfold the two
flaps and flatten.

23

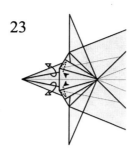

Unfold the two flaps and flatten.

24

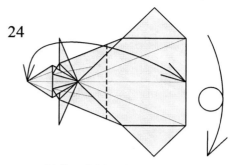

Valley-fold and unfold.
Turn over top-to-bottom.

25

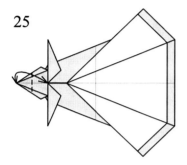

Valley-fold and unfold.

26

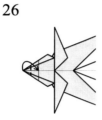

Valley-fold.

27

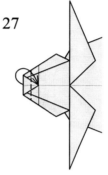

Valley-fold.

28

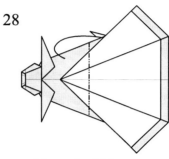

Mountain-fold on the
existing crease.

29

Valley-fold on
the black dots.

30

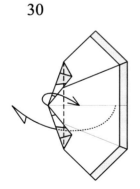

Valley-fold while
letting the rear
flap swing out to
the left.

31

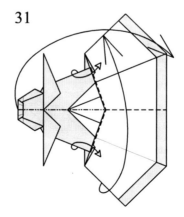

The housewife is recognizable!
Following the arrows, fold the
head and arms flap to the right
while valley-folding the dress
in half.

32

Cut-away View

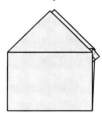

Normal View

The housewife is inside
the house, so you could
call the model complete,
but there is one more
tricky fold that will greatly
improve its appearance.
So, unfold to step 31.

33 Mountain-fold.

34 Reverse-fold on the black dots.

35 Undo only the part of the reverse fold indicated by the dotted lines. For a more precise explanation for how to do this fold, look down into the cloud.

36 The Housewife is done but lying on her back. Go back to the house position (step 32).

Steps 33-36 Alternate Method

33a Turn over.

33b Push in the indicate edge while folding the model in half.

33c Like this. Go back to the house position (step 32).

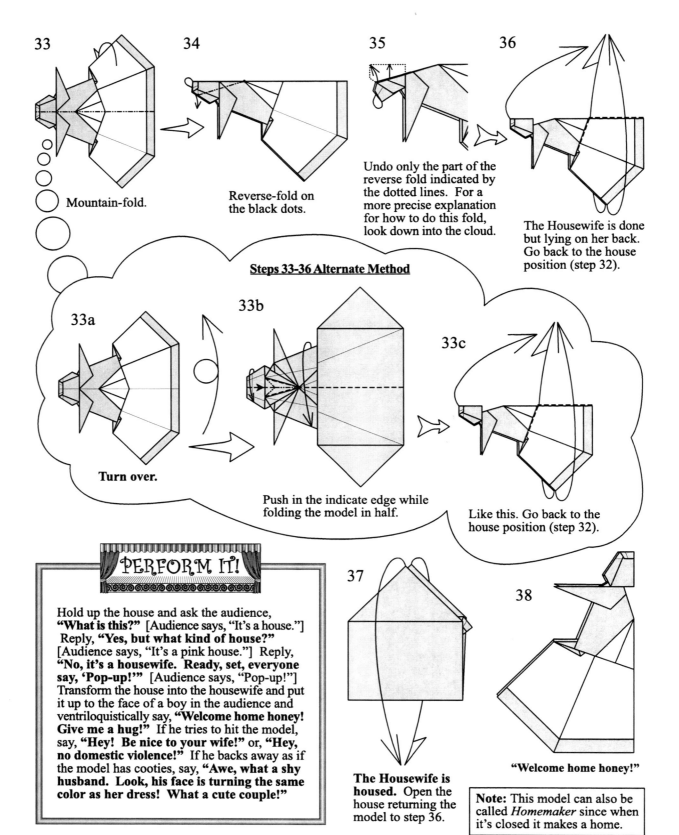

PERFORM IT!

Hold up the house and ask the audience, **"What is this?"** [Audience says, "It's a house."] Reply, **"Yes, but what kind of house?"** [Audience says, "It's a pink house."] Reply, **"No, it's a housewife. Ready, set, everyone say, 'Pop-up!'"** [Audience says, "Pop-up!"] Transform the house into the housewife and put it up to the face of a boy in the audience and ventriloquistically say, **"Welcome home honey! Give me a hug!"** If he tries to hit the model, say, **"Hey! Be nice to your wife!"** or, **"Hey, no domestic violence!"** If he backs away as if the model has cooties, say, **"Awe, what a shy husband. Look, his face is turning the same color as her dress! What a cute couple!"**

37 **The Housewife is housed.** Open the house returning the model to step 36.

38 "Welcome home honey!"

Note: This model can also be called *Homemaker* since when it's closed it makes a home.

Pop-up Househusband

By Jeremy Shafer ©2009

Watch out men, you too have competition! Like the Housewife, this model is dangerous too! Ironically, in most politically correct circles, it would be taboo to show the origami housewife unaccompanied by her manly counterpart, the Househusband.

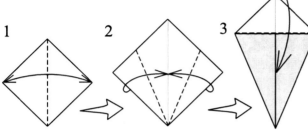

1
White side up, valley-fold in half diagonally and unfold.

2
Valley-fold two edges to the crease.

3
Valley-fold.

"Welcome home honey... Dinner's in the microwive!"

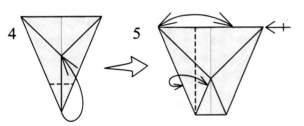
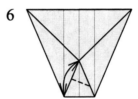
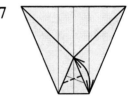

4
Valley-fold.

5
Valley-fold and unfold.
Repeat on the right side.

6
Valley-fold and unfold.

7
Valley-fold and unfold.

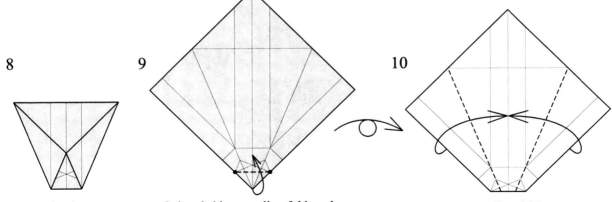

8
Completely unfold the model.

9
Colored side up, valley-fold on the black dots. **Turn over.**

10
Valley-fold.

Househusband **187**

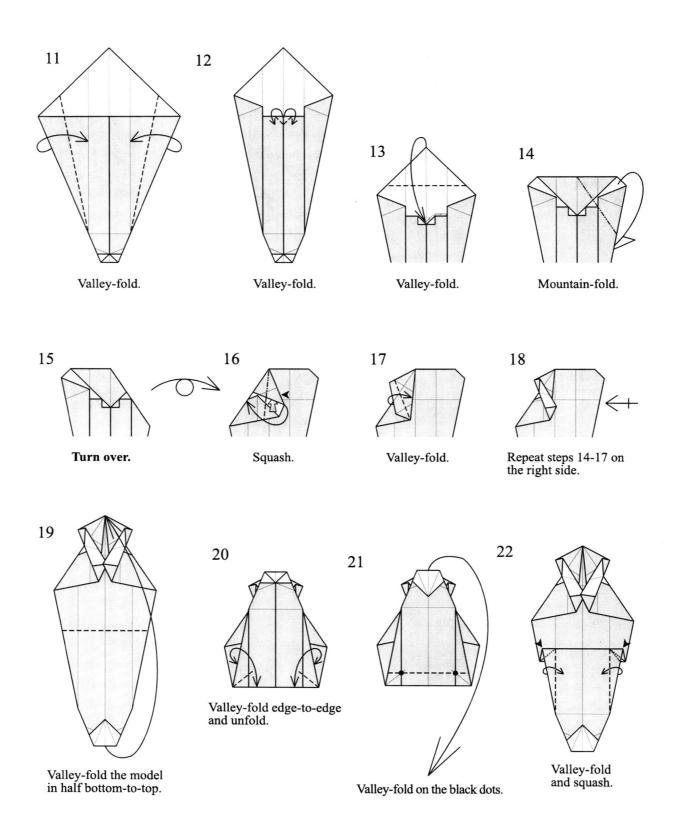

11

Valley-fold.

12

Valley-fold.

13

Valley-fold.

14

Mountain-fold.

15

Turn over.

16

Squash.

17

Valley-fold.

18

Repeat steps 14-17 on
the right side.

19

Valley-fold the model
in half bottom-to-top.

20

Valley-fold edge-to-edge
and unfold.

21

Valley-fold on the black dots.

22

Valley-fold
and squash.

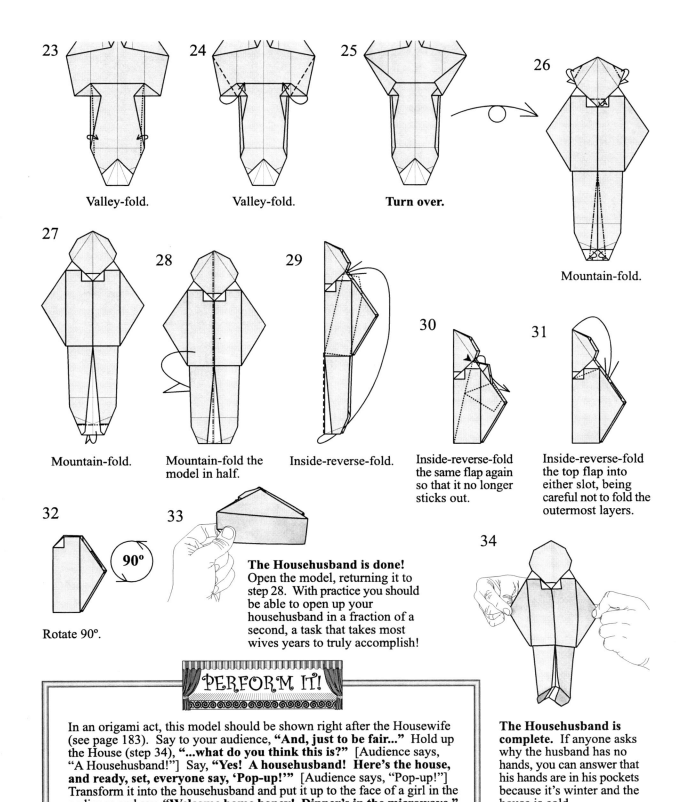

23 Valley-fold.

24 Valley-fold.

25 Turn over.

26 Mountain-fold.

27 Mountain-fold.

28 Mountain-fold the model in half.

29 Inside-reverse-fold.

30 Inside-reverse-fold the same flap again so that it no longer sticks out.

31 Inside-reverse-fold the top flap into either slot, being careful not to fold the outermost layers.

32 Rotate 90°. **90°**

33 **The Househusband is done!** Open the model, returning it to step 28. With practice you should be able to open up your househusband in a fraction of a second, a task that takes most wives years to truly accomplish!

PERFORM IT!

In an origami act, this model should be shown right after the Housewife (see page 183). Say to your audience, **"And, just to be fair..."** Hold up the House (step 34), **"...what do you think this is?"** [Audience says, "A Househusband!"] Say, **"Yes! A househusband! Here's the house, and ready, set, everyone say, 'Pop-up!'"** [Audience says, "Pop-up!"] Transform it into the househusband and put it up to the face of a girl in the audience and say, **"Welcome home honey! Dinner's in the microwave."**

34 **The Househusband is complete.** If anyone asks why the husband has no hands, you can answer that his hands are in his pockets because it's winter and the house is cold.

One Piece Flipper

©1997 by Sy Chen   Based on David Mitchell's four piece Pig Base modular version.

This model transforms again and again, cycling through four different positions. For an extra special effect, fold from paper with pictures printed onto it. Calendar paper works especially well. You can also fold it from a dollar bill and call it, 'Rolling in Money,' or 'Rolling in Dough.'

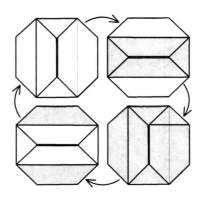

1
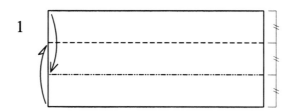

Start from duo-color 3 by 6.5 (or longer) rectangle with either side up; divide the short side into thirds.

2
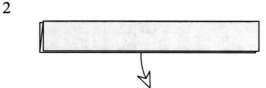

Unfold the rear flap.

3
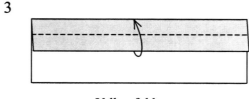

Valley-fold.

4

Valley-fold.

5
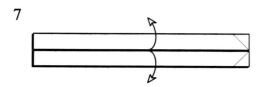

Valley-fold.

6
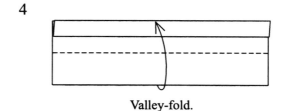

Valley-fold and unfold
THROUGH ALL LAYERS.

7

Unfold the two flaps.

8

On the left side, valley-fold and unfold. Mountain-fold the right side behind on the black dots. **Turn over.**

9

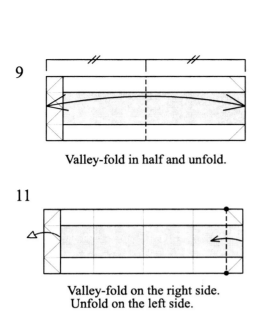

Valley-fold in half and unfold.

10

Valley-fold and unfold.

11

Valley-fold on the right side.
Unfold on the left side.

12

Valley-fold and unfold in half.

13

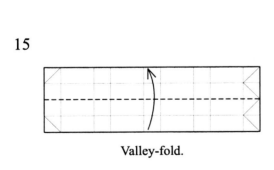

Valley-fold and unfold.

14

Unfold. **Turn over.**

15

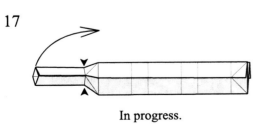

Valley-fold.

16

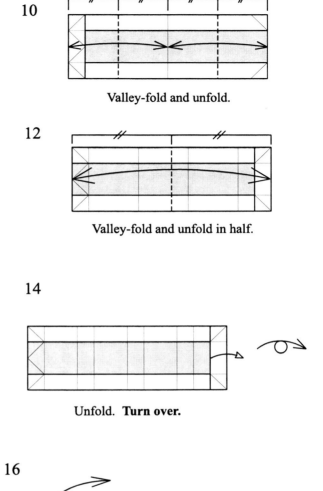

Squeeze the top and bottom edges
together and squash the flap upward.

17

In progress.

18

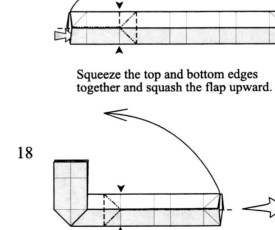

Squeeze the top and bottom edges
together and squash the flap upward.

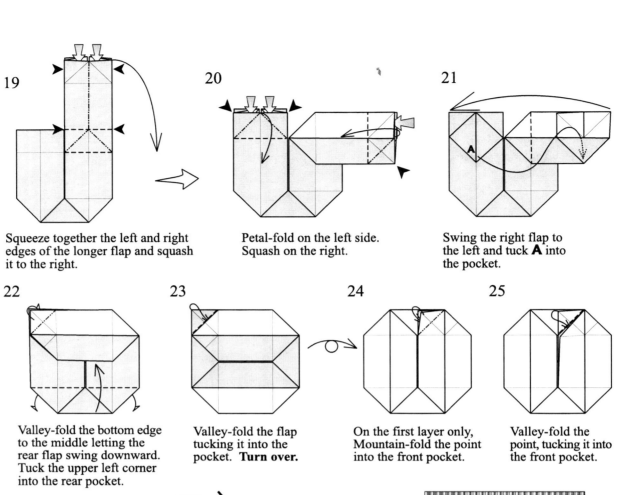

19
Squeeze together the left and right edges of the longer flap and squash it to the right.

20
Petal-fold on the left side. Squash on the right.

21
Swing the right flap to the left and tuck **A** into the pocket.

22
Valley-fold the bottom edge to the middle letting the rear flap swing downward. Tuck the upper left corner into the rear pocket.

23
Valley-fold the flap tucking it into the pocket. **Turn over.**

24
On the first layer only, Mountain-fold the point into the front pocket.

25
Valley-fold the point, tucking it into the front pocket.

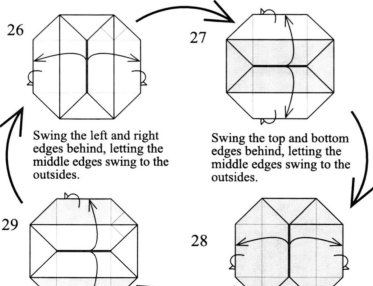

26
Swing the left and right edges behind, letting the middle edges swing to the outsides.

27
Swing the top and bottom edges behind, letting the middle edges swing to the outsides.

28
Swing the left and right edges behind, letting the middle edges swing to the outsides.

29
One more flip and then repeat steps 26-29 ad nauseam!

PERFORM IT!

Hold the model up and say, **"This is a model that can do continuous double flips! Ready, set, everyone say, 'Flip!'"** [Audience says, "Flip"] Flip it (step 26) and then say **"Again, everyone say, 'Flip!'"** Keep going a few more flips, and finish by saying, **"OK, that's enough! I think it has totally flipped out!"**

Frowny Abe Peep Show

Super Simple

By Jeremy Shafer
©2005

A long forgotten attribute of Abe Lincoln was his feracious frown. Fold this model, and get an up-close look at how Abe might have looked on one of his off days.

1

Make diagonal valley creases that touch the pupils of Abe's eyes.

2

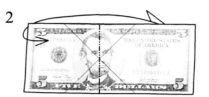

Make a vertical mountain crease at the intersection of the valley folds.

3

Fold on the existing creases forming a Waterbomb Base. (See Waterbomb Base, page 18.)

4

Valley-fold and unfold. **Repeat behind.**

5

Valley-fold.

6

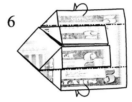

Mountain-fold.

7

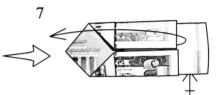

Valley-fold the flap. **Repeat behind.**

8

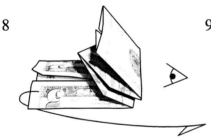

Unfold the rear flap. Hold the shorter flap in your left hand and the longer flap in your right hand and look into the pocket.

9

The Grumpy Abe Peep Show is ready to be shown. Pull the ends apart and look at Abe's contortedly frowny face.

10

Abe during a frowning tantrum.

11

Watch out! No billed president is safe from the Frowny Peep Show!

PERFORM IT!

This routine is best performed for a small audience because they really need to take turns individually. Ask the audience, **"What is this?"** [Audience says "A $5 dollar bill"] Reply, **"Yes, but that's not all! It's also a miniature peep show of Abraham Lincoln himself. Who wants to peep into the dollar and see a really funny-looking Abe Lincoln?"** Let the audience take turns looking at Frowny Abe. Conclude, **"No wonder he's was so famous! He's so funny looking!"**

Happy Sad Dollar 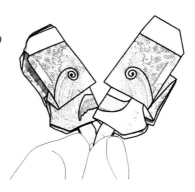 Intermediate

By Jeremy Shafer ©2001   Model inspired by a design challenge from Joel Bauer

George Washington is not alone! This model reveals that there are more faces than just his on the US one dollar bill!

1

Begin "ONE" side up.
Valley-fold and unfold in
half and unfold. **Turn over.**

2

Valley-fold the long sides to the
center crease.

3

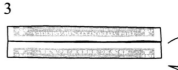

Turn over.

4

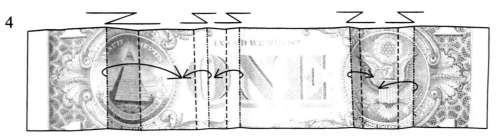

Make the indicated pleats.

5

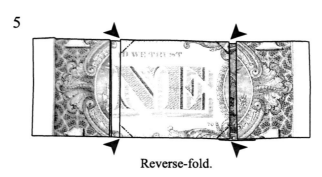

Reverse-fold.

6

On the center section mountain-fold the top and bottom
edges behind. To do this, you need to make little reverse
folds at the left and right of the mountain folds.

7

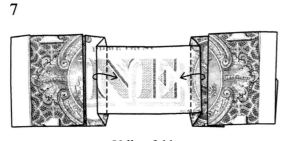

Valley-fold.

8

Turn over.

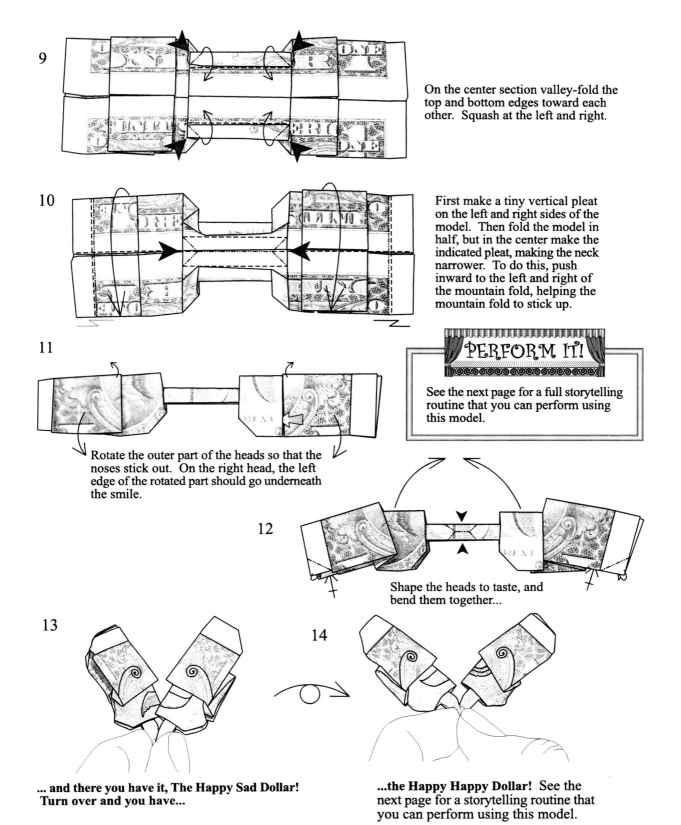

9

On the center section valley-fold the top and bottom edges toward each other. Squash at the left and right.

10

First make a tiny vertical pleat on the left and right sides of the model. Then fold the model in half, but in the center make the indicated pleat, making the neck narrower. To do this, push inward to the left and right of the mountain fold, helping the mountain fold to stick up.

11

Rotate the outer part of the heads so that the noses stick out. On the right head, the left edge of the rotated part should go underneath the smile.

PERFORM IT!

See the next page for a full storytelling routine that you can perform using this model.

12

Shape the heads to taste, and bend them together...

13

... and there you have it, The Happy Sad Dollar! Turn over and you have...

14

...the Happy Happy Dollar! See the next page for a storytelling routine that you can perform using this model.

One Dollar Story (Intermediate)

By Jeremy Shafer ©2010

Now that you've hopefully folded the Happy Sad Dollar, here's a story I came up with to present it to an audience. This story is best presented close-up to young children with at least some adults present too.

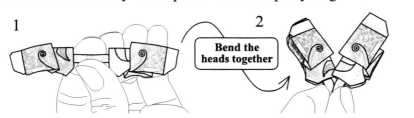

1

Once upon a time, there were two really important men – Mr. Bull, and Mr. Bear. They worked together in a tall building on a busy street called Wall Street. They were the heads of the company! They were so rich they even looked like money!

2 Bend the heads together

But they were very different. Mr. Bull was always happy and loved to spend his money, especially on shoes and stocks, I mean...[pause]... stockings. Mr. Bear, on the other hand, was always gloomy and liked to keep all his money in the bank.

3 Turn over

One day they started arguing face-to-face about who's smarter with their money, and to tell you the truth, they looked kinda funny...

4 Expose the other half of the "O" in ONE

...so funny that even Mr. Bear started smiling.

5

Then all of sudden, a big storm hit Wall Street. Mr. Bull opened the window and checked on his collection of stockings hanging out on line. Oh no! They had fallen to the ground in a downward spiraland landed on top of astockbroker who'd jumped out the window. Mr. Bullcried out, "What a sad day on Wall Street!"

6 Return to the smile

But the next morning, the stockings were back up, and so Mr. Bull was happy again.

7 180° Sad or Happy

Mr. Bear, on the other hand, had mixed feelings about this. He didn't know if he was sad or happy. After all, they weren't his stockings!

8 Turn over

But just to give this story a happy ending, they both lived happily ever after...

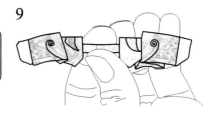

9

...except for Mr. Bear who was always gloomy, I mean, **almost** always!

The END

Question Mark!

This a model can raise many interesting questions and bring forth many surprising answers. In fact, it can be used to punctuate any interrogation or exclamation!

(Intermediate) By Jeremy Shafer ©2002

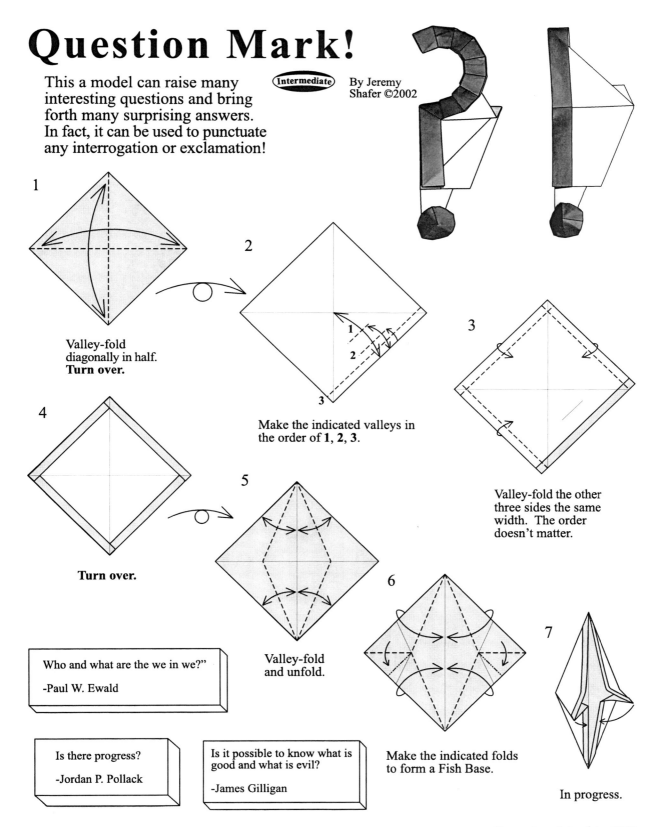

1

Valley-fold diagonally in half. **Turn over.**

2

Make the indicated valleys in the order of **1, 2, 3**.

3

Valley-fold the other three sides the same width. The order doesn't matter.

4

Turn over.

5

Valley-fold and unfold.

Who and what are the we in we?"

-Paul W. Ewald

Is there progress?

-Jordan P. Pollack

Is it possible to know what is good and what is evil?

-James Gilligan

6

Make the indicated folds to form a Fish Base.

7

In progress.

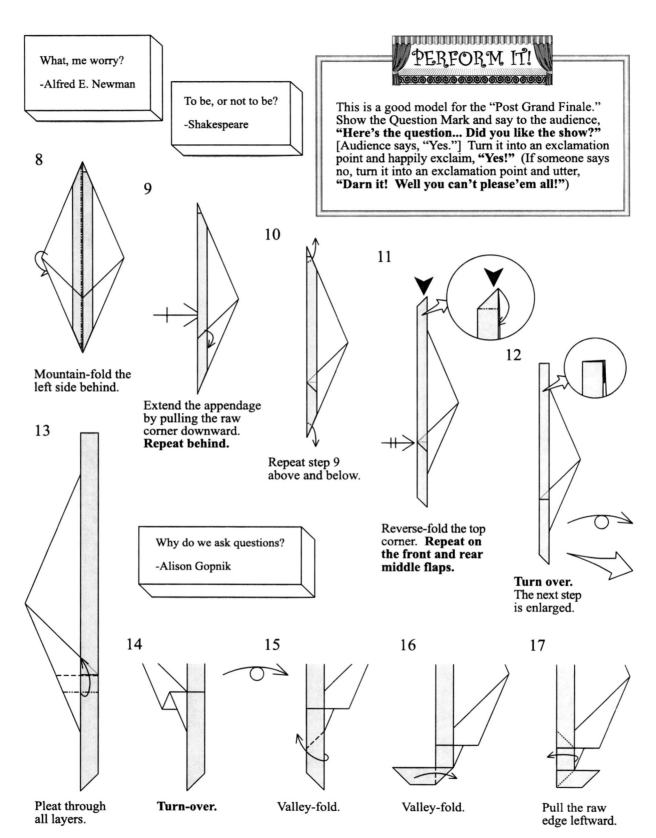

What, me worry?

-Alfred E. Newman

To be, or not to be?

-Shakespeare

8

Mountain-fold the
left side behind.

9

Extend the appendage
by pulling the raw
corner downward.
Repeat behind.

10

Repeat step 9
above and below.

11

Reverse-fold the top
corner. **Repeat on
the front and rear
middle flaps.**

12

Turn over.
The next step
is enlarged.

PERFORM IT!

This is a good model for the "Post Grand Finale."
Show the Question Mark and say to the audience,
"Here's the question... Did you like the show?"
[Audience says, "Yes."] Turn it into an exclamation
point and happily exclaim, **"Yes!"** (If someone says
no, turn it into an exclamation point and utter,
"Darn it! Well you can't please 'em all!")

13

Pleat through
all layers.

Why do we ask questions?

-Alison Gopnik

14

Turn-over.

15

Valley-fold.

16

Valley-fold.

17

Pull the raw
edge leftward.

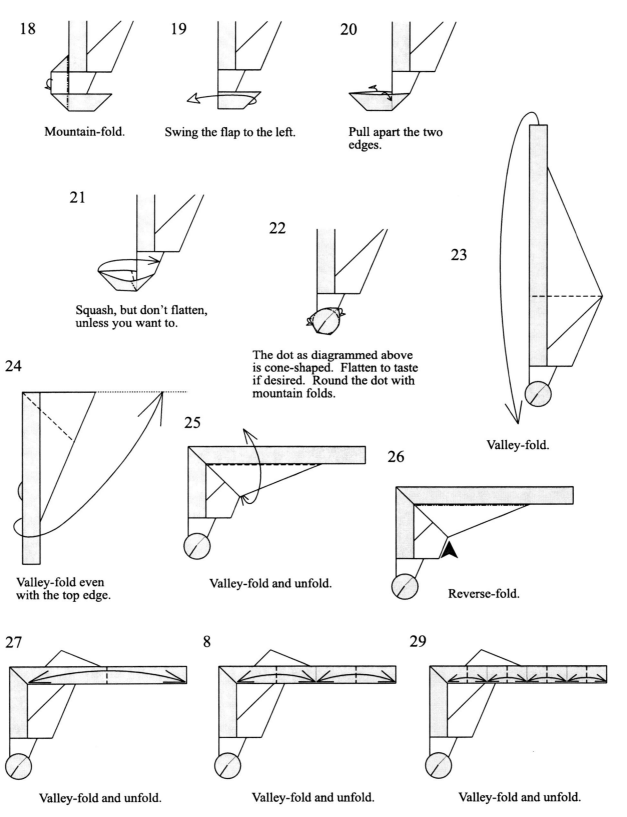

18 Mountain-fold.

19 Swing the flap to the left.

20 Pull apart the two edges.

21 Squash, but don't flatten, unless you want to.

22 The dot as diagrammed above is cone-shaped. Flatten to taste if desired. Round the dot with mountain folds.

23 Valley-fold.

24 Valley-fold even with the top edge.

25 Valley-fold and unfold.

26 Reverse-fold.

27 Valley-fold and unfold.

8 Valley-fold and unfold.

29 Valley-fold and unfold.

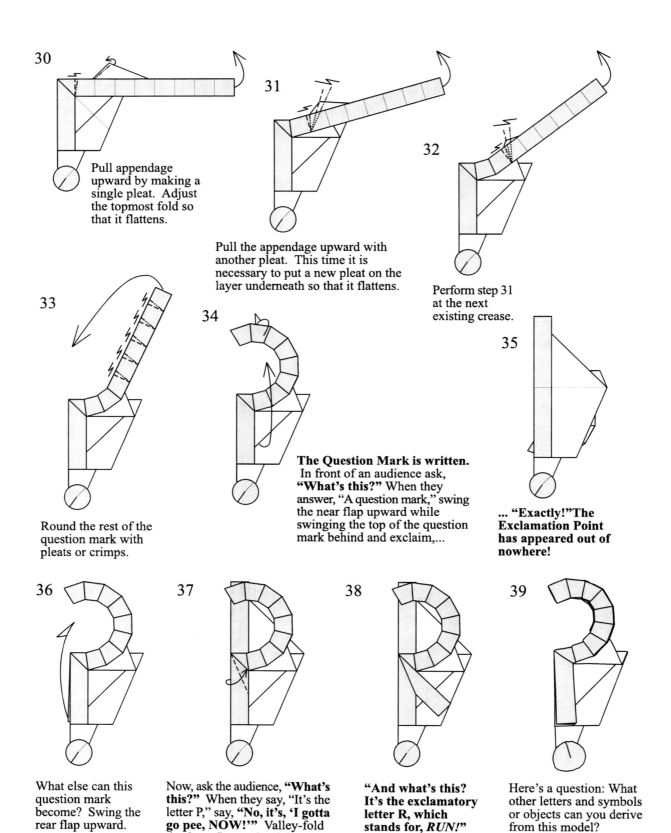

30

Pull appendage upward by making a single pleat. Adjust the topmost fold so that it flattens.

31

Pull the appendage upward with another pleat. This time it is necessary to put a new pleat on the layer underneath so that it flattens.

32

Perform step 31 at the next existing crease.

33

Round the rest of the question mark with pleats or crimps.

34

The Question Mark is written. In front of an audience ask, **"What's this?"** When they answer, "A question mark," swing the near flap upward while swinging the top of the question mark behind and exclaim,...

35

... **"Exactly!"The Exclamation Point has appeared out of nowhere!**

36

What else can this question mark become? Swing the rear flap upward.

37

Now, ask the audience, **"What's this?"** When they say, "It's the letter P," say, **"No, it's, 'I gotta go pee, NOW!'"** Valley-fold the front flap to the right.

38

"And what's this? It's the exclamatory letter R, which stands for, *RUN!*"

39

Here's a question: What other letters and symbols or objects can you derive from this model?

Flashers

Flashers are pleated origami patterns in which the paper winds around the center, like a vortex. When folded from foil, they 'flash' in the light as they are opened and closed. Chris Palmer and I stumbled upon the basic Flasher (page 210) while playing with Toshikazu Kawasaki's rose patterns, which, like Flashers, spiral about the center. The question quickly arose, "What other pleat patterns can be turned into Flashers?," and we set out on a quest for new Flasher designs. Around the same I was studying math at UCSC and I decided to try to use my Flasher studies as the basis for my math senior seminar. The seminar, which was attended by a sizeable group of UCSC math professors and grad students, really only scratched the surface of Flashers and mathwise wasn't over anyone's head, but at least everyone agreed that the Flasher patterns were pretty!

Since then, I've stopped trying to analyze the math of Flashers, but I've continued scratching the surface and have come up with numerous new Flashers to add to the six Flashers I published in *Origami to Astonish and Amuse*. So, this chapter is dedicated to Flashers!

But what role do Flashers play in performance origami? For me, Flashers are my Grand Finale. When folded from very large paper, they really command the audience's attention, and have the added benefit that in their contracted state they don't take up much space! For my origami grand finale, I simply call out to the audience, **"Everyone say, 'Ooh La La!,'"** to which I open a giant origami Flasher (hence, the title of this book). This is followed by, **"Everyone say 'La La Ooh!'"** to which I close it.

I find Flashers intriguing and limitless, and I love how they can be evenly squished into such a small area. I hope that this chapter will inspire you, the folder, to continue scratching the vast surface of Flashers, or least fold some Flashers, so that you too can say, **"Oo La La!"**

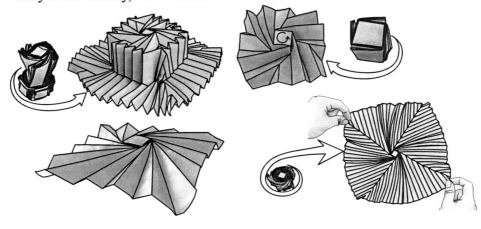

Iso-Area Twist Brochure

Jeremy Shafer
©2008

This is the origami brochure I designed for my advertising campaign to libraries and schools. It's an iso-area twist (step 19) folded in half to look like a book. On pages 203 and 204 is the actual brochure, which can be pulled out of the book, cut out and folded. There are many models such as tatos, pinwheels, envelopes and cards which, with a little graphic design, can be transformed into brochures. Compared to conventional "junkmail" advertising, sending origami brochures is unique, more personalized and should ultimately get more attention.

Note: Although this model doesn't have *Flasher* in the title, it is essentially the center of the Iso-area Flasher, and is a good first Flasher to fold.

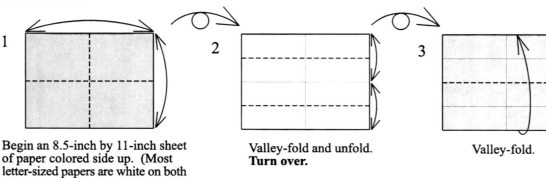

1. Begin an 8.5-inch by 11-inch sheet of paper colored side up. (Most letter-sized papers are white on both sides, but for clarity we'll pretend they aren't.) Valley-fold and unfold in half both ways. **Turn over.**

2. Valley-fold and unfold. **Turn over.**

3. Valley-fold.

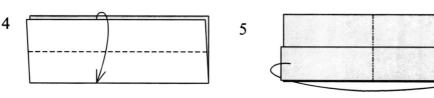

4. Valley-fold one edge down.

5. Mountain-fold in half on all layers.

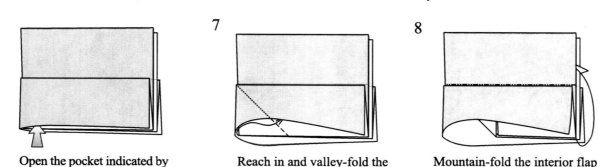

6. Open the pocket indicated by the arrow.

7. Reach in and valley-fold the interior flap.

8. Mountain-fold the interior flap on the existing crease. Continue to step 9 on page 205.

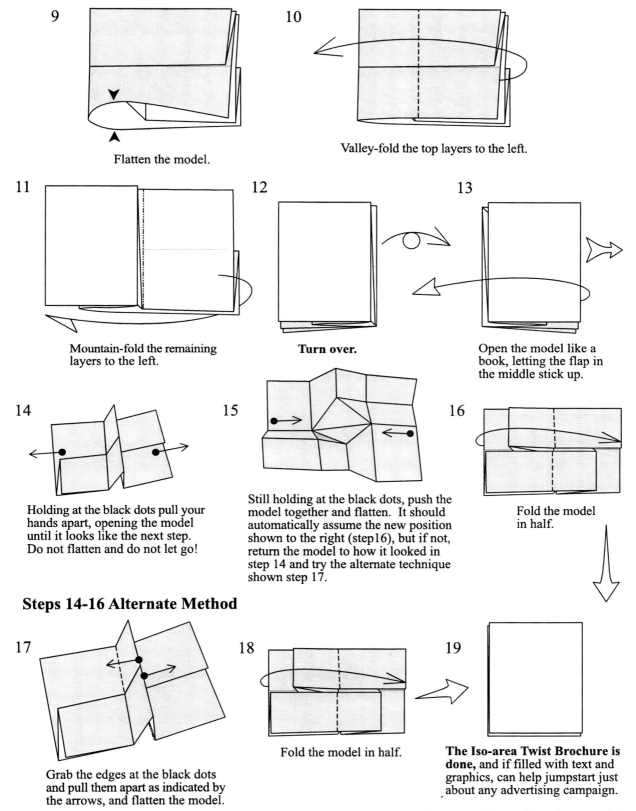

9

Flatten the model.

10

Valley-fold the top layers to the left.

11

Mountain-fold the remaining layers to the left.

12

Turn over.

13

Open the model like a book, letting the flap in the middle stick up.

14

Holding at the black dots pull your hands apart, opening the model until it looks like the next step. Do not flatten and do not let go!

15

Still holding at the black dots, push the model together and flatten. It should automatically assume the new position shown to the right (step16), but if not, return the model to how it looked in step 14 and try the alternate technique shown step 17.

16

Fold the model in half.

Steps 14-16 Alternate Method

17

Grab the edges at the black dots and pull them apart as indicated by the arrows, and flatten the model.

18

Fold the model in half.

19

The Iso-area Twist Brochure is done, and if filled with text and graphics, can help jumpstart just about any advertising campaign.

Iso-Area Flasher

Jeremy Shafer ©2001

Designed jointly by Chris Palmer and Jeremy Shafer, based on Kawasaki's iso-area twist folding
(Origami for the Connoisseur)

Intermediate

Here is a smaller simpler version of the basic Flasher. The diagrams include a simpler procedure for folding an Iso-Area Twist (steps 7-13).

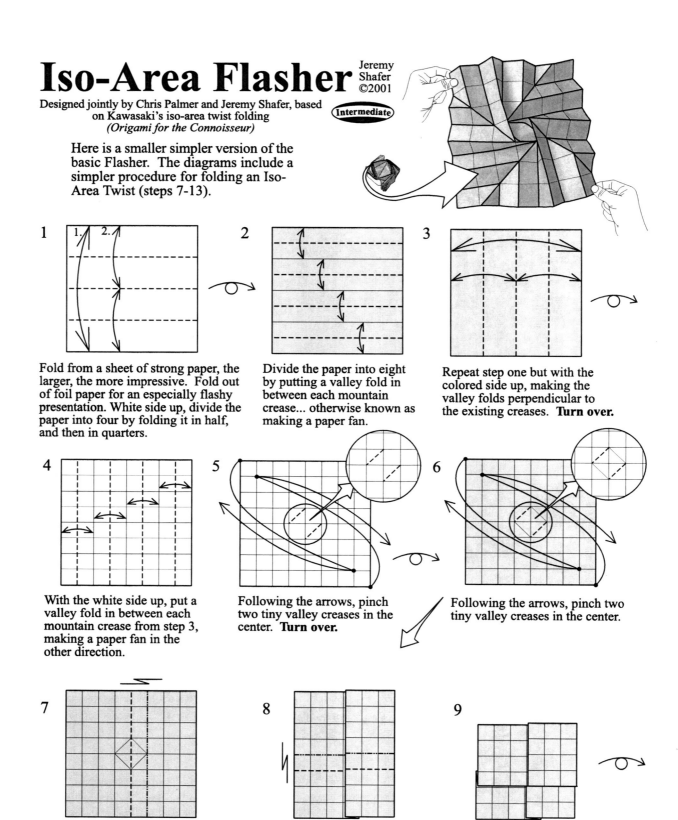

1 Fold from a sheet of strong paper, the larger, the more impressive. Fold out of foil paper for an especially flashy presentation. White side up, divide the paper into four by folding it in half, and then in quarters.

2 Divide the paper into eight by putting a valley fold in between each mountain crease... otherwise known as making a paper fan.

3 Repeat step one but with the colored side up, making the valley folds perpendicular to the existing creases. **Turn over.**

4 With the white side up, put a valley fold in between each mountain crease from step 3, making a paper fan in the other direction.

5 Following the arrows, pinch two tiny valley creases in the center. **Turn over.**

6 Following the arrows, pinch two tiny valley creases in the center.

7 Pleat.

8 Pleat.

9 Turn over.

10

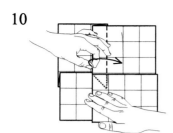

Holding the lower half flat with one hand, grab the edge with the other hand and fold it to the right on existing creases...

11

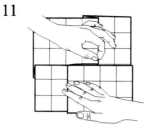

...like this. **Turn over.**

12

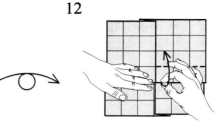

Holding the left half flat with one hand, grab the edge with the other hand and pull it upward on existing creases...

13

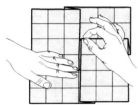

...like this. The Iso-Area Twist Square Base is complete.

14

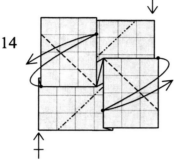

Following the arrows, make the diagonal valley creases. **Repeat behind for the mountain folds.** Note that these creases do not hit the raw corners of the model.

15

Make the indicated folds starting from the center and moving out. The diagonal folds will get formed naturally by squeezing together the existing horizontal and vertical folds. It's easiest to pleat each of the four quadrants separately before collapsing the model. After all of the folds are in place, twist the center making the sides come together as if they are getting sucked up into a spiraling, black hole.

16

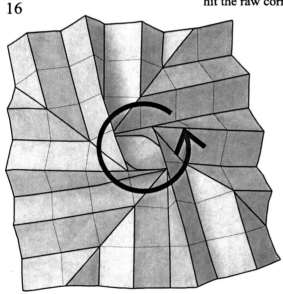

The Flasher open. Push inward on the sides and twist the center counterclockwise. **Wetfolding approach:** Once together, tie rubber bands around the model, dunk it in water, and set it out to dry in the sun (or warm place inside). This process will make the model spring closed by itself. The same process should be used on all Flashers and Flasher Labyrinths.

17

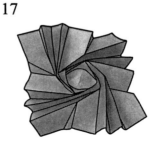

Flasher closing.

18

Finished Flasher Closed. Open and close rapidly to flash-dazzle the audience.

Turbo Flasher Intermediate

By Jeremy Shafer ©2005

This is an extra compact Flasher variation with double the RPM's of the other Flashers. That means that the center makes almost two complete revolutions in the process of opening. Now that's revolutionary!

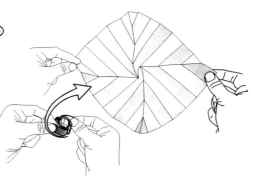

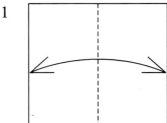

1

White side up, valley-fold and unfold.

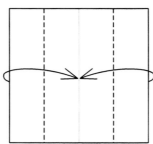

2

Valley-fold.

3

Valley-fold.

4

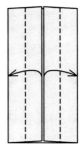

Turn over.

5

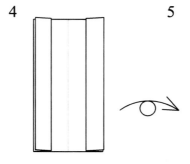

Valley-fold.

6

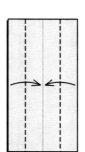

Completely unfold.
Turn over.

7

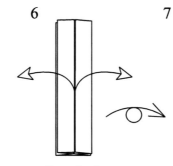

Repeat steps 1-6 to form the horizontal creases.

8

Mountain-fold, or, if you don't object to cutting, cut off the top strip (the paper above the mountain fold).

9

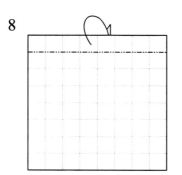

Valley-fold four unit squares.

10

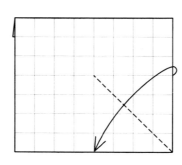

Pleat.

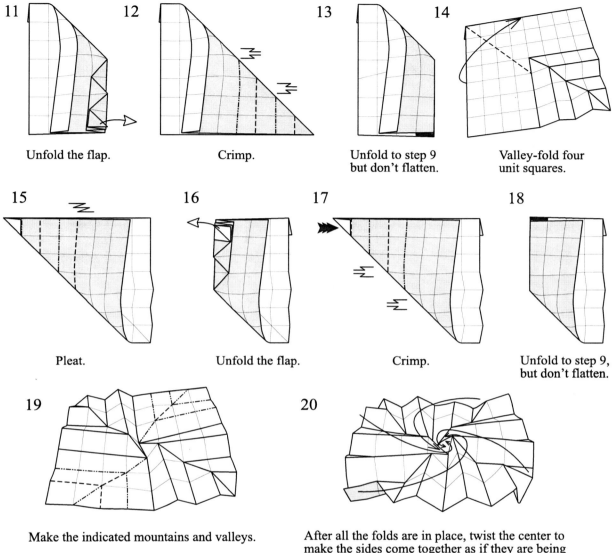

11
Unfold the flap.

12
Crimp.

13
Unfold to step 9
but don't flatten.

14
Valley-fold four
unit squares.

15
Pleat.

16
Unfold the flap.

17
Crimp.

18
Unfold to step 9,
but don't flatten.

19
Make the indicated mountains and valleys.

20
After all the folds are in place, twist the center to
make the sides come together as if they are being
sucked into a spiraling black hole.

21

The Turbo Flasher is ready to pull open.

Wet Folding Approach. Tie rubber bands
around the closed Flasher, dunk it in water, and
set it out to dry in the sun. This process will
make the model spring closed by itself.

22

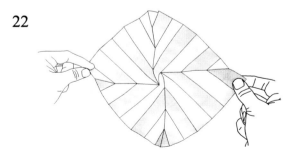

Turbo Flasher open. If folding out of shiny paper, face
the shiny side of the paper to the audience. To make an
Super Turbo Flasher, fold the model again, but start by
making a 16X16 grid of creases instead of an 8X8 grid.

Original Flasher (Intermediate)

By Jeremy
Shafer ©1994

This is the original Flasher model Chris Palmer and I designed together, using as a base Kawasaki's iso-area twist folding (*Origami for the Connoisseur*).

1

With the white side up, divide the paper into eighths by folding it in half, then in quarters and then in eighths. **Turn over.**

2

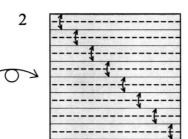

With colored side up, divide the paper into sixteenths by putting a valley fold in between each pair of mountain creases, making a paper fan.

3

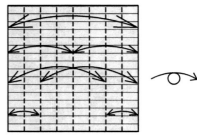

Repeat step 1 with the colored side up, making the valley folds perpendicular to the existing creases. **Turn over.**

4

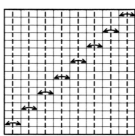

With the white side up, put a valley fold in between each pair of mountain creases from step 3, making a paper fan in the other direction.

5

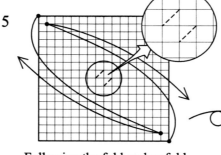

Following the fold-and-unfold arrows, pinch two tiny valley creases in the center. **Turn over.**

6

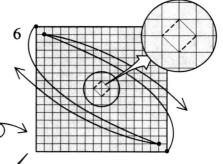

Following the arrows, pinch two tiny valley creases in the center.

7

Using existing creases, make the indicated mountain and valley folds. This will cause the little square in the center to make a quarter turn. Toshikazu Kawasaki calls this fold an 'iso-area square twist.' 'Iso-area' means, 'both sides look the same but are opposite in color and orientation.'

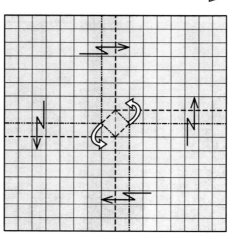

8

Iso-area square twist in progress.

9

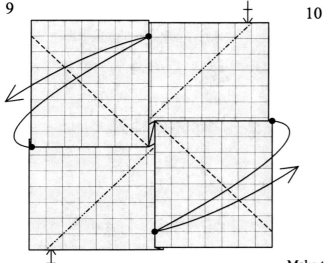

Following the arrows, make the diagonal valley creases. **Repeat behind for the mountain folds.** Note that these creases do not touch the corners of the model.

10

Make the indicated folds, starting from the center and moving out. The diagonal folds will form themselves naturally as you squeeze together the existing horizontal and vertical folds. It's easiest to pleat each of the four quadrants separately before collapsing the model. After all of the folds are in place, twist the center to make the sides come together as if they are being sucked into a spiraling black hole.

11

Thoughts Behind the Folds

For a long time, I had a passionate desire to fold a model that would expand and contract. I shared my obsession with my very good friend and folder, Chris Palmer. Together, we had many unfruitful, head-banging sessions. Then Chris came back from the OrigamiUSA Convention ('94), with Kawasaki's new rose base, which he sensed held the solution to our problem. In one collaborative evening the Flasher was born.

Finished Flasher open. Mathematically speaking this model has a very interesting property. Imagine the fold pattern extended infinitely in all four directions on an infinitely large piece of paper that had zero thickness. When all the folds are made, the infinite paper would have shrunk down to a finite area. **Wetfolding approach:** Tie rubber bands around the closed Flasher, dunk it in water, and set it out to dry in the sun. This process will make the Flasher, when opened, spring closed by itself.

PERFORM IT!

I like to fold this model from a sheet of 10-inch foil. Holding up a giant Flasher Big Bang (*Origami to Astonish and Amuse*), I ask the audience, **"Are you ready for the Grand Finale?"** No matter how loud they respond, I answer, **"I don't think you're ready, but you are ready for the Baby Grand Finale,"** and I pull out a tiny foil Flasher. As I open and close it, I say, **"You are getting sleepy! You will fall under my spell! Just kidding!"** (Sometimes the kids really do pretend to fall asleep!)

12

Finished Flasher closed. Open and close rapidly to flash-dazzle the audience. This model can also be used in storytelling as an explosion, a whirlpool, or a time machine.

Indecisive Flasher

By Jeremy Shafer ©2001

Here are two Flasher designs that can't make up their minds which way to turn; The rotating center switches directions in the course of opening. Begin by folding the Original Flasher (page 210). Alter the mountains and valleys as indicated.

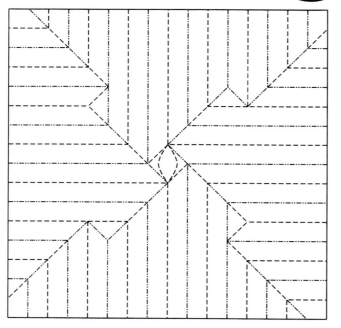

Note: Both of these Flashers were designed by making the Original Flasher and altering some of the creases. Both were inspired, or rather force fed to me, by Chris Palmer.

He called me up one day and said, **"I had a dream last night about a Flasher that in the middle of opening switched directions. Can you please do it, Jeremy?"** Ten minutes later I called him back to tell him I had done it. He then said, **"Good Grasshopper; now I want you to make one that switches directions at least twice. Then diagram both of the Flashers and email them to me."**

I replied, **"As you wish, Master!"**

And that is how the Oscillating Flasher came about. In fact, it switches directions so frequently that its center hardly moves at all -- it just vibrates.

I suspect there's a wealth of new Flasher patterns waiting to be discovered simply by using this idea of switching directions, or just by dreaming.

Oscillating Flasher

By Jeremy Shafer ©2001

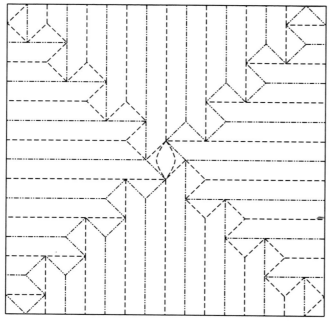

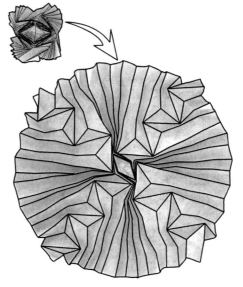

Oscillating Flasher

Radial Flasher

This Flasher has totally radical radial pleats, like OMG dude!

By Jeremy Shafer
©2007

1

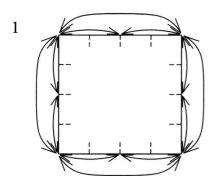

White side up, divide all four sides into fourths by employing pinch marks.

2

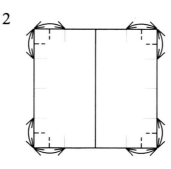

Make pinch marks as indicated.

3

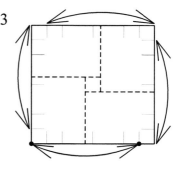

Valley-fold dot-to-dot. The folds lines should end near the middle as indicated.

4

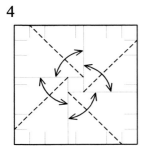

Valley-fold and unfold crease-to-crease.

5

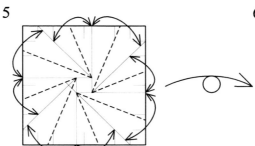

Valley-fold and unfold crease-to-crease. **Turn over.**

6

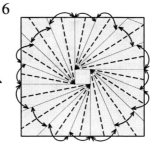

Valley-fold and unfold crease-to-crease.

7

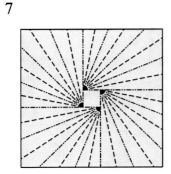

Make the indicated mountains and valleys on existing creases. As you make the folds, the center square rotates counterclockwise and the rest of the paper wraps around it.

8

The Radial Flasher Closed

9

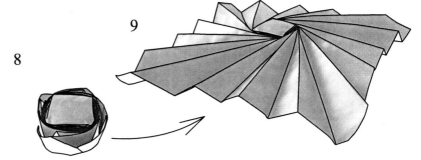

The Radial Flasher Open, emitting rays of sunshine!

Wetfolding approach: See page 207, step 16.

Quadruple Iso-Area Flasher

Also known as "Four Leaf Clover Flasher"

By Jeremy Shafer ©2001

Fold four Flashers from one sheet of paper! **Prerequisite:** Make sure you can fold the Iso-Area Flasher (page 206). This model is like folding four Iso-Area Flashers and taping them together, but minus the tape! Note that two of the four Flashers spiral in the opposite direction.

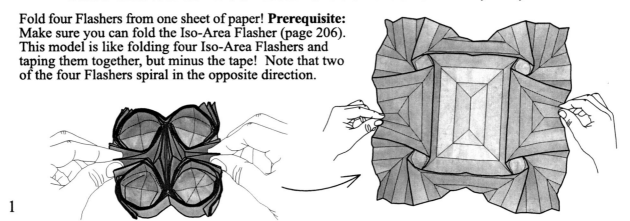

1

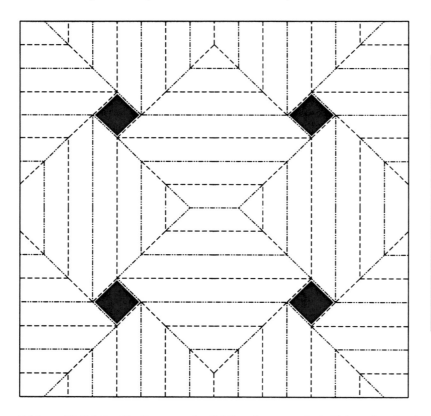

Make a 16 X 16 grid of creases, by folding the paper in half, into fourths, into eighths and then into sixteenths. It will be easiest if all folds are valleyed and mountained. Make the indicated folds so that the model closes up into a four-leaf clover shape. The black squares are the centers of the Flashers.

Tessellated Iso-Area Flasher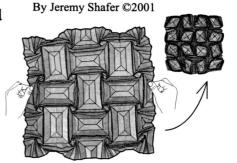

Why stop at four? The Iso-Area Flasher can be tessellated infinitely, but to be practical, let's stop at sixteen!

By Jeremy Shafer ©2001

1

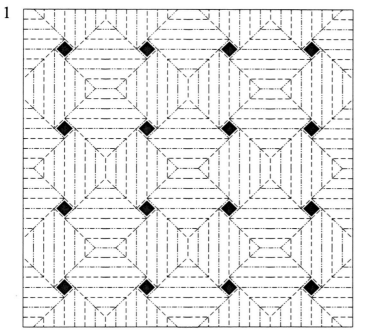

This model consists of sixteen Iso-Area Flashers joined at the sides. For best results, begin with a 28-inch square of Wyndstone Marble. Precrease a 32 X 32 grid. Make the indicated folds.

PERFORM IT!

Say to the audience, **"This is sixteen Flashers in one and they are all going to open at the same time! Ready, set, everyone say Ooh La La!"** [Audience says "Ooh La La!"] Pull the model apart and say, **"It's actually a Giant Manta Ray swimming over your heads!"** (As the model is pulled apart it becomes concave like a swimming ray.)

2

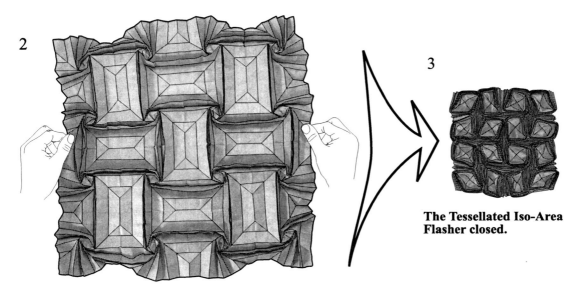

3

The Tessellated Iso-Area Flasher closed.

The Tessellated Iso-Area Flasher open.

Easy Flasher By Jeremy Shafer ©2007

This Flasher is relatively easy because it does not require first folding an iso-area twist at the center.

1

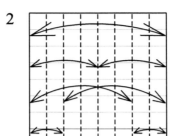

With the white side up, divide the paper into eighths by folding it in half, then into fourths and then into eighths. Mountain-fold and valley-fold every crease.

2

Repeat step 1, making new creases that are perpendicular to the existing creases.

3

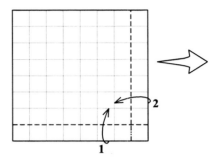

At this point, you could cut off a one unit strip from the bottom and right sides to form a 7X7 grid, but instead, in the name of origami purism, valley-fold the bottom and right sides.

4

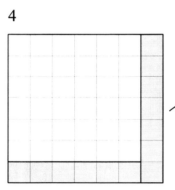

Turn over.

5

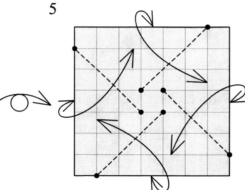

Valley-fold edge-to-crease and unfold. These creases extend from black dot to black dot. It will make it easier in the next step if these valley folds are mountained as well.

6

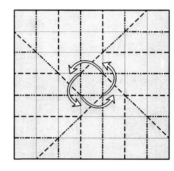

Using existing creases, make the indicated mountain and valley-folds. This will cause the middle square of creases to turn clockwise.

7

In progress. Ok, it's not as easy as folding a paper cup, but it is easier than folding the Flasher Hat.

8

The Easy Flasher is done.
Warning: Opening and closing this model repeatedly may put you or your loved ones into a trance. Use responsibly.

Wetfolding approach: See page 207, step 16.

Big Easy Flasher Intermediate

By Jeremy Shafer ©2007

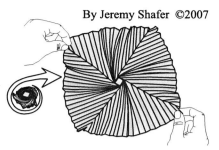

Disclaimer: This model does not need to be made big, is not necessarily easy, and has nothing to do with New Orleans.

Successfully folding the Easy Flasher (page 216) is a prerequisite for folding this model. Start by making a 27 X 27 grid of creases. The easiest way to do this is to fold a square into a 32 X 32 grid (by folding it in half, into fourths, etc), and then cut off 5 units from the height and 5 units from the width. But then you end up with a smaller model and the dissatisfaction of having had to cut the paper. So here (steps 1-20) is a method of folding a 27 X 27 grid of creases without cutting.

1
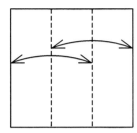

White side up, valley-fold and unfold in thirds.

2

Here's one way to fold thirds. Holding as shown, fiddle with the folds until they line up.

3
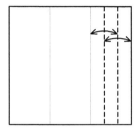

Now divide the right third into thirds.

4
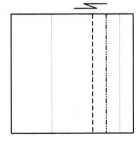

Pleat.

5
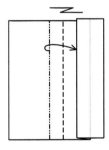

Pleat

6

Turn over top to bottom.

7
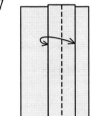

Valley-fold and unfold.

8
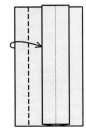

Valley-fold.

9

Turn over top to bottom.

10
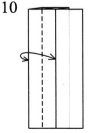

Valley-fold and unfold.

11
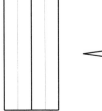

Completely Unfold.

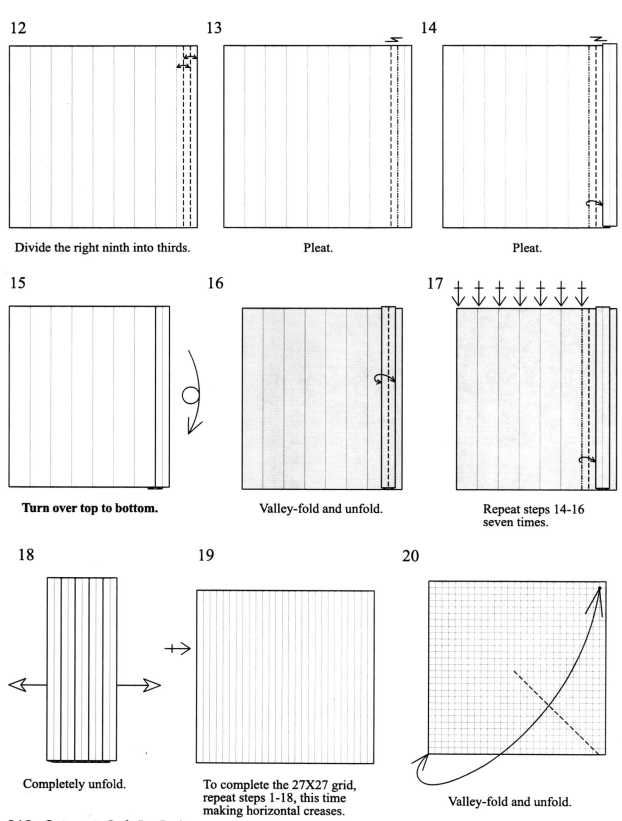

12

Divide the right ninth into thirds.

13

Pleat.

14

Pleat.

15

Turn over top to bottom.

16

Valley-fold and unfold.

17

Repeat steps 14-16
seven times.

18

Completely unfold.

19

To complete the 27X27 grid,
repeat steps 1-18, this time
making horizontal creases.

20

Valley-fold and unfold.

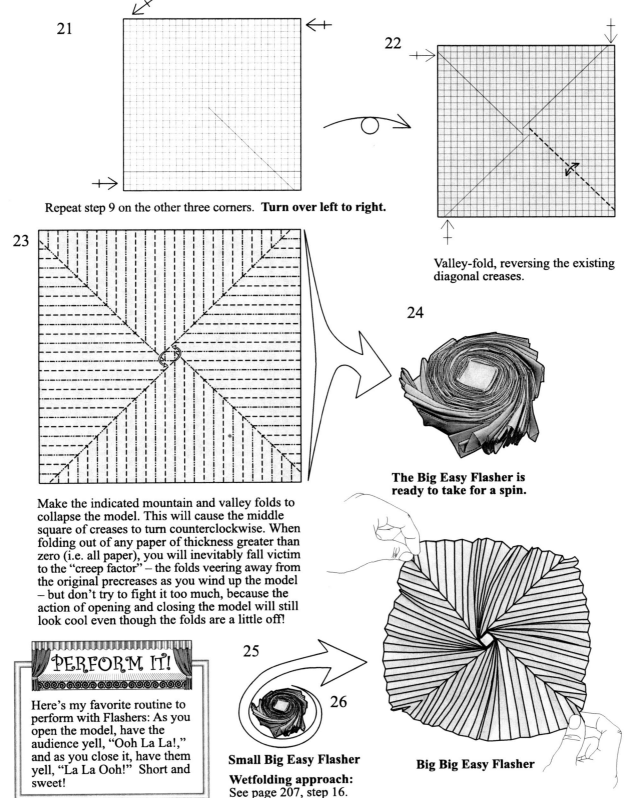

21

Repeat step 9 on the other three corners. **Turn over left to right.**

22

Valley-fold, reversing the existing diagonal creases.

23

Make the indicated mountain and valley folds to collapse the model. This will cause the middle square of creases to turn counterclockwise. When folding out of any paper of thickness greater than zero (i.e. all paper), you will inevitably fall victim to the "creep factor" – the folds veering away from the original precreases as you wind up the model – but don't try to fight it too much, because the action of opening and closing the model will still look cool even though the folds are a little off!

24

The Big Easy Flasher is ready to take for a spin.

PERFORM IT!

Here's my favorite routine to perform with Flashers: As you open the model, have the audience yell, "Ooh La La!," and as you close it, have them yell, "La La Ooh!" Short and sweet!

25

26

Small Big Easy Flasher

Wetfolding approach: See page 207, step 16.

Big Big Easy Flasher

Big Easy Flasher **219**

Easy Flasher Tessellation

As origami Flasher tessellations go, this one is as easy as
it gets. However, it's no piece of cake, hence its name,
Easy Flasher Tessellation, not *Piece of Cake*!

By Jeremy Shafer ©2007

1

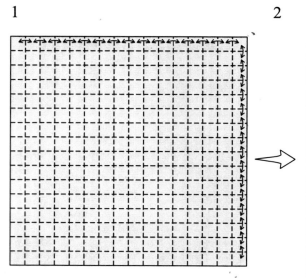

This model is like four Easy Flashers (page 116)
taped together, but minus the tape. Fold a square
into a 16 X 16 grid by folding it in half, into
fourths, into eighths and then into sixteenths.
It will be easiest if all folds are valleyed and
mountained.

2

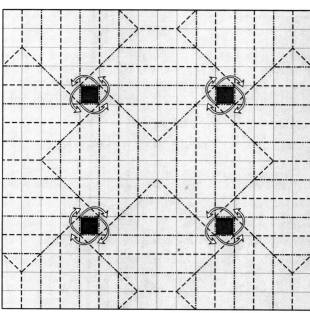

Starting at the sides and working your way toward the center,
make the indicated mountain and valley folds on existing
creases. As the model collapses, two black squares will turn
clockwise, and the other two will turn counterclockwise.

3

Easy Flasher Tessellation Closed

4

Easy Flasher Tessellation Open

PERFORM IT!

Show the closed model to the audience and say, **"This is
a very playful Flasher. Do you know what its favorite
game to play is? Four Square!"** Open and close the
model repeatedly and say, **"This version of Four Square
is so much more fun than the old Four Square, and the
best part – nobody gets out!"**

Not So Easy Flasher Tessellation

Most origami tessellation masters would probably still call this model easy, but for the rest of us, a *Not So* in front of the *Easy* is definitely in order!

By Jeremy Shafer
©2007

1

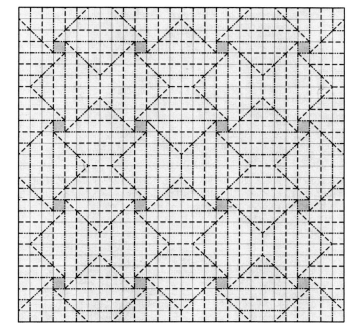

Fold the square into a 32 X 32 grid by folding it in half, into fourths, into eighths, into sixteenths and then into thirty-seconds. It will be easiest if all folds are valleyed and mountained. Make the indicated folds, first tackling the corners, then the four sides, and then gradually moving toward the center.

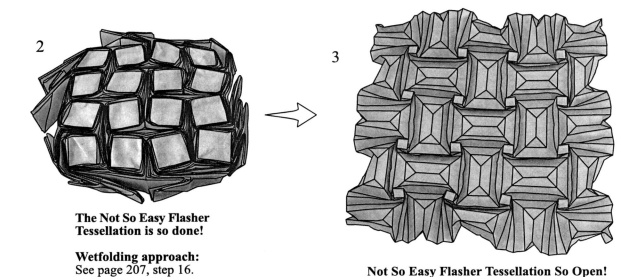

2

The Not So Easy Flasher Tessellation is so done!

Wetfolding approach:
See page 207, step 16.

3

Not So Easy Flasher Tessellation So Open!

Simple Flasher Labyrinth

By Jeremy Shafer ©2001

(Intermediate)

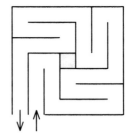

Well, this model is really not that easy to fold, but it is simple relative to most of the other Flashers in this book. It works well with any size paper and any type, though understandably you might want to avoid papers with intricate designs already on them! Folded from 4-foot square, it can be worn as a hat.

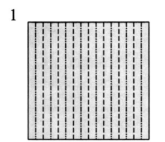

1 Colored side up, pleat the square into sixteenths by folding it in half, into fourths, into eighths and then into sixteenths.

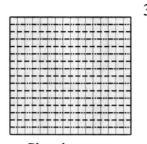

2 Pleat the square into sixteenths in the other direction.

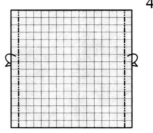

3 Mountain-fold the left and right sides behind.

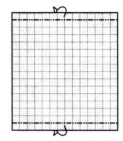

4 Mountain-fold the top and bottom sides behind.

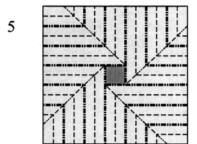

5 Make the indicated mountains and valleys forming a Flasher similar to the Easy Flasher on page 216. The diagonal creases get formed as you push the Flasher together. Open the Flasher.

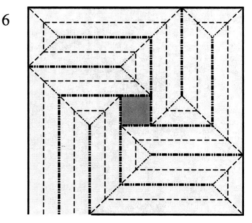

6 Alter the folds made in step 5 as indicated above. The resulting labyrinth is the path between the thick mountains.

7

Simple Labyrinth Flasher Open

For added viewing clarity, I recommend drawing the pattern onto the model as pictured above.

8

Simple Flasher Labyrinth Closed

Idea: Try making this model into a table or perhaps an octopus amputee.

PERFORM IT!

This model can be presented to an audience as a marble maze. Get four volunteers to each grab a corner and, working together, try to navigate a marble through the labyrinth.

Quadruple Simple Flasher Labyrinth

Rather Complex

By Jeremy Shafer
©2001

Here is a Flasher Labyrinth composed of four simple Flasher Labyrinths joined at the sides. In order to achieve a single path that goes through all of the labyrinths, the creases around the center are altered. Once you have folded this model, it should become clear how the Super Tessellated Flasher Labyrinth on page 254 could be folded.

1

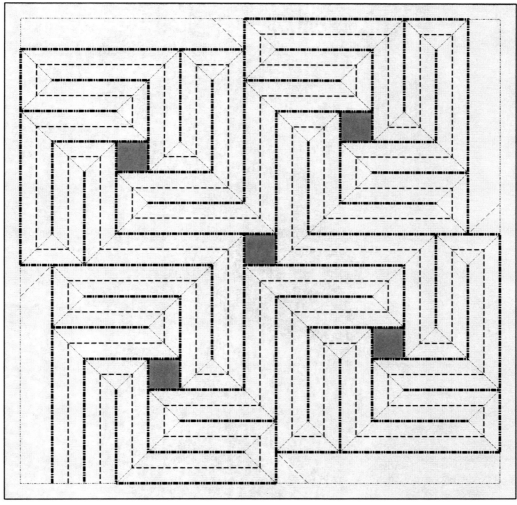

For best results, begin with a 28-inch square of Wyndstone Marble. Precrease a 32 X 32 grid by folding it in half, into fourths, into eighths, into sixteenths and then into thirty-seconds. Either cut off a one unit border or fold it behind. Then, simply make the indicated folds and your done! I suggest drawing the labyrinth pattern onto the model, as shown on page 224, so that the audience (and you!) can easily see the paths of the labyrinth.

2

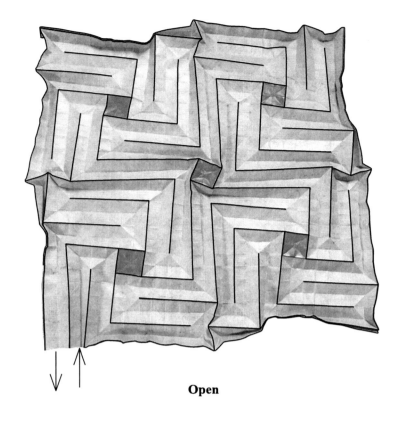

Open

3

Closed

The Tessellated Simple (but really not so simple) Flasher Labyrinth is finished.
It could also be called an 'Alien Spider Labyrinth Walker' – a very distant relative
of Lukesky Walker.

Kokopelli Labyrinth Walker

By Jeremy Shafer ©2002

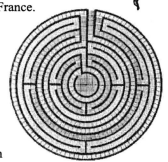

This model is a figure of a curvy dancer when folded but the but when you pull the appendages apart it takes on the pattern of a labyrinth

Kokopelli Labyrinth

The Kokopelli Labyrinth shown to the left is a variation I made up of the Bayeux Labyrinth, shown to the right, a 13th century labyrinth found at the Cathedral in Bayeux, France.

1

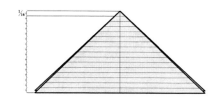

To fold the Kokopelli Labyrinth, first fold a Waterbomb Base and then divide its height into 16ths by first folding it in half (top to bottom), then into fourths, into eighths and, finally, into sixteenths. It's best if all creases get mountained and valleyed. Next, completely unfold!

Bayeux Labyrinth

2

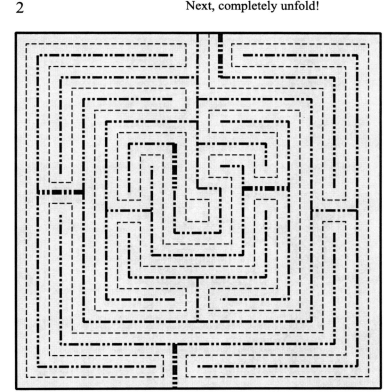

Using the existing creases as a framework, make the indicated folds, starting at the sides and moving inward and pushing the sides together as you go. The five extra-bold mountain segments are new folds but they do line up with existing creases elsewhere on the paper.

3

Curve the appendages to taste and the Kokopelli Labyrinth Walker is complete. You might say that the finished model looks nothing like the traditional Kokopelli figure to the right (except that they're both curvy), but since Kokopelli is a deity, I would assume it has the power to take on any shape, so the title of this model is completely justified!

Easy Flasher Hat

Rather Complex

By Jeremy Shafer
©2007

This model is easy only in comparison to the original Flasher Hat (Origami to Astonish and Amuse, page 114), which requires making about five times as many folds. Nonetheless, it is still quite difficult. I recommend using a 28-inch square of Wyndstone paper or other strong paper.

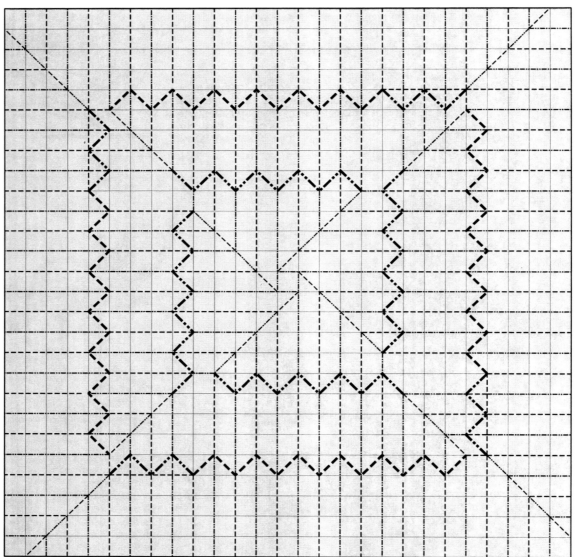

Start by folding the Big Easy Flasher (page 217), but don't close it up all the way, because the creep will alter the creases unnecessarily (this model stands a better chance than the Big Easy Flasher of ending up almost on the grid of creases). Then unfold the model and make the indicated mountain and valley folds, starting with the boldly diagrammed folds. Push the model together. **Wetfolding approach:** See page 207, step 16.

Flasher Skimmer Hat

By Jeremy Shafer
©2007

This model is basically the same as the Easy Flasher Hat except that the crown edge and inside edge of the brim are composed of crimps instead of reverse folds, giving the edges sharper 90° angles akin to a skimmer hat.

Rather Complex

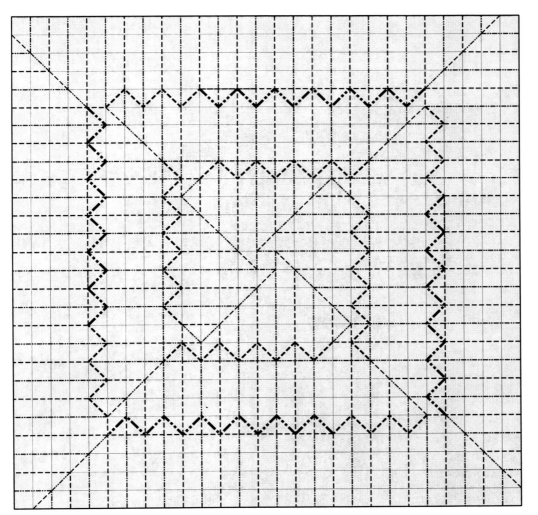

Start by folding the Big Easy Flasher (page 217), but don't close it up all the way, because the creep will alter the creases unnecessarily (this model stands a better chance than the Big Easy Flasher of ending up almost on the grid of creases). Then unfold the model and make the indicated mountain and valley folds, starting with the boldly diagrammed folds. Push the model together. **Wetfolding approach:** See page 207, step 16.

Flasher Bowler Hat

By Jeremy Shafer ©2007

Super Complex

This Flasher Hat is easier than the original Flasher Hat, as there are not as many diagonal creases. It's also slightly more round around the head, hence the name.

1

2

Simple Flasher Hat Closed

Begin by creasing a 31-by-31 grid with every crease being both mountained and valleyed. Don't give yourself a headache... begin by folding a 32 X 32 grid of creases and cut off a one-unit strip from the top edge and from the right edge. If you are opposed to cutting, fold the one-unit strips instead. Starting at the sides and moving inward, pinch the diagonal creases (you might want to pencil them in first). Then, working on one section at a time (moving inward again), make all the indicated folds, gradually pushing the model together as you go. **Wetfolding approach:** See page 207, step 16.

Flasher Barrister's Wig (Adult) Super Complex

This model was designed a challenge from David Lister of England. It alternatively can be called Long Hair. In my act I put the hat on a kid (usually a boy) and say, "I know you always wanted to have long blonde hair, but you were to lazy to grow it!

Now I'm a Judge and a good Judge too!

By Jeremy Shafer ©2005

A 28-inch square makes a nice wig size. The side shown in the diagram below will become the top of the hat.

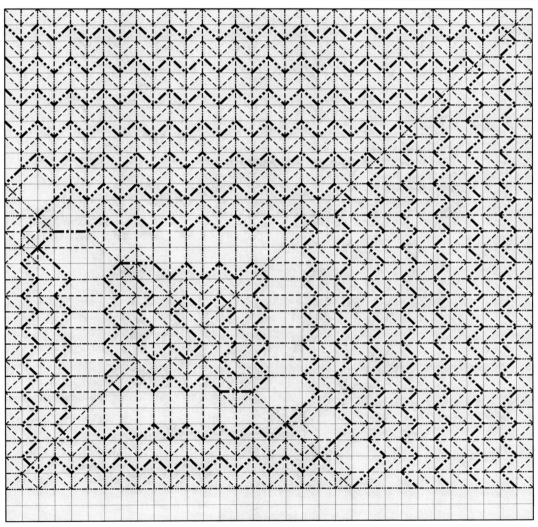

Begin by creasing a 32-by-32 grid with every crease being both mountained and valleyed. Next, valley-fold the square diagonally in half both ways. Then pleat a diagonal grid that divides both diagonals of the square by 64. Make a mountain fold two units from the bottom edge (or simple cut off the bottom two units) to form a rectangle. Make the indicated folds starting with the boldly diagrammed mountains. Push the model together. **Wetfolding approach:** See page 207, step 16.

Datura Flower*

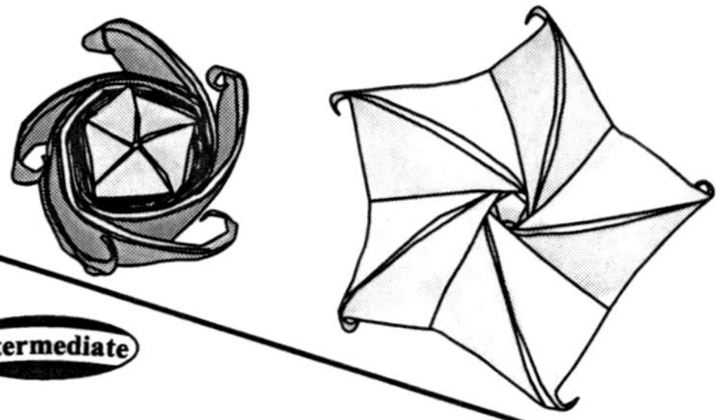

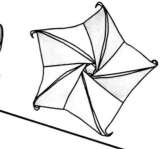

The Datura is a poisonous flower, whose bud when opening holds a striking resemblance to the origami Flasher, hence the creation of this model.

Jeremy Shafer ©2008 (**Intermediate**)

It looks pretty, but, trust me, it doesn't taste pretty!

1

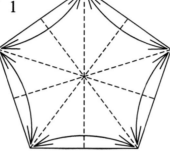

Begin with a pentagon. You can trace and cut out either pentagon on this page. The larger pentagon can be cut out of a 10-inch square (use a straight edge to reconstruct the cut-off corners). The smaller pentagon can be cut out of a 8.5-inch square. White side up, valley-fold in half all five directions.

2

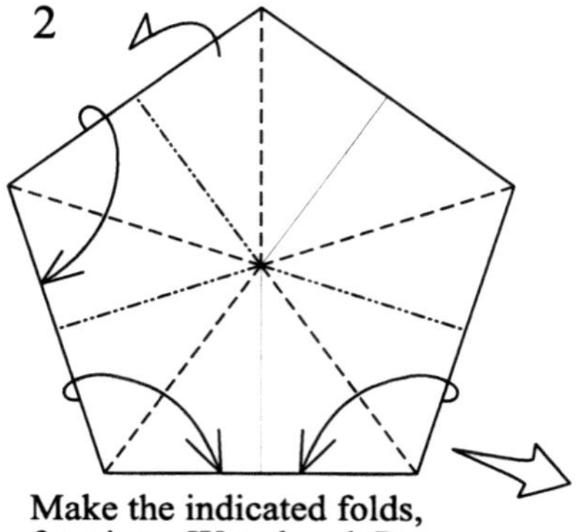

Make the indicated folds, forming a Waterbomb Base.

3

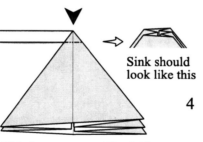

1/8

Sink should look like this

Sink the top corner. The fold line is 1/8th of the height.

4

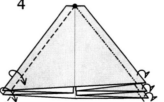

Valley-fold the left edges together on the black dot. Mountain-fold the right edges on the black dot.

5

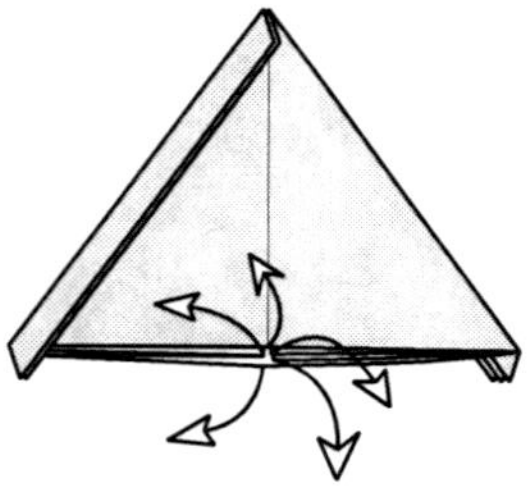

Spread open the bottom edges of the model and, white side up, flatten, forming a tiny pentagon in the middle.

* This model is based on the twist folding techniques developed by Toshikazu Kawasaki.

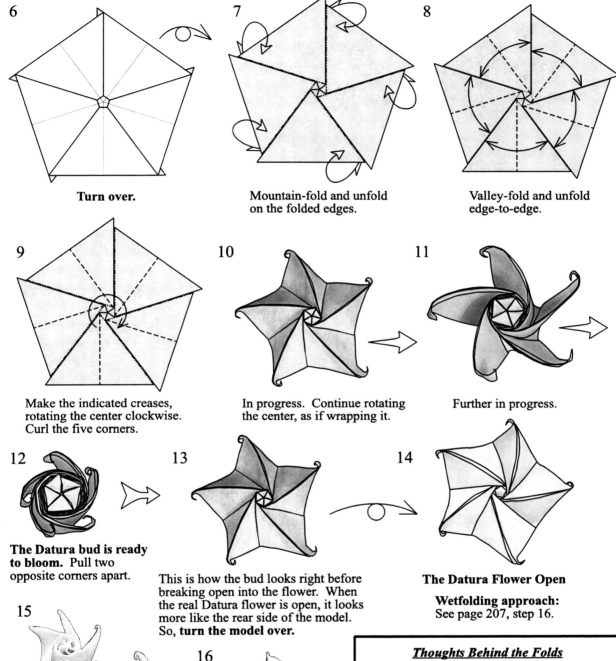

6

Turn over.

7

Mountain-fold and unfold
on the folded edges.

8

Valley-fold and unfold
edge-to-edge.

9

Make the indicated creases,
rotating the center clockwise.
Curl the five corners.

10

In progress. Continue rotating
the center, as if wrapping it.

11

Further in progress.

12

**The Datura bud is ready
to bloom.** Pull two
opposite corners apart.

13

This is how the bud looks right before
breaking open into the flower. When
the real Datura flower is open, it looks
more like the rear side of the model.
So, **turn the model over.**

14

The Datura Flower Open

Wetfolding approach:
See page 207, step 16.

15

Real Datura Flower
Starting to Open

16

Real Datura Flower Open

Thoughts Behind the Folds

The idea to fold a Datura Flower, came from
surfing the Internet. I came upon a picture
of a budding Datura, to which I exclaimed,
"Wow, it's Flasher Flower!" Nature had already
figured out the Flasher millions of years ago!
To find out more about datura flowers go to
http://en.wikipedia.org/wiki/Datura
Photo Source: Flickr: VeganChai:
http://www.flickr.com/photos/veganchai/sets

Biaxial Flasher Supreme

By Ushio Ikegami ©2002

山折り ——— 太い線   MOUNTAIN——BOLD

uıɥʇ ——— ʎǝllɐʌ   細い線 ——— 谷折り

First, fold a 24 X 24 grid of creases, by folding the paper into thirds, into twelfths, and finally into twenty-fourths. Then, use that grid to fold a diagonal grid of creases, being careful to only make the diagonals that contain the diagonal creases in the diagram; for example, don't make the two diagonals of the square. Finally, make the indicated mountains and valleys and push it all together! This structure is similar to the Flasher Supreme (*Origami to Astonish and Amuse* page 112) except that midway through the opening of it, the axis of rotation suddenly turns 90°! The paper's thickness is a problem even in this level of simplicity {**Author:** ...or utter complexity!}, so expanding it is smooth but contracting it is not. **Author's note:** Folding this model is harder than it looks! **Recommended prerequisite:** Fold the Flasher Barrister's Wig! (page 229)

232 *Origami Ooh La La!*

Octahedral Flasher

By Ushio Ikegami ©2002

Insanely Complex

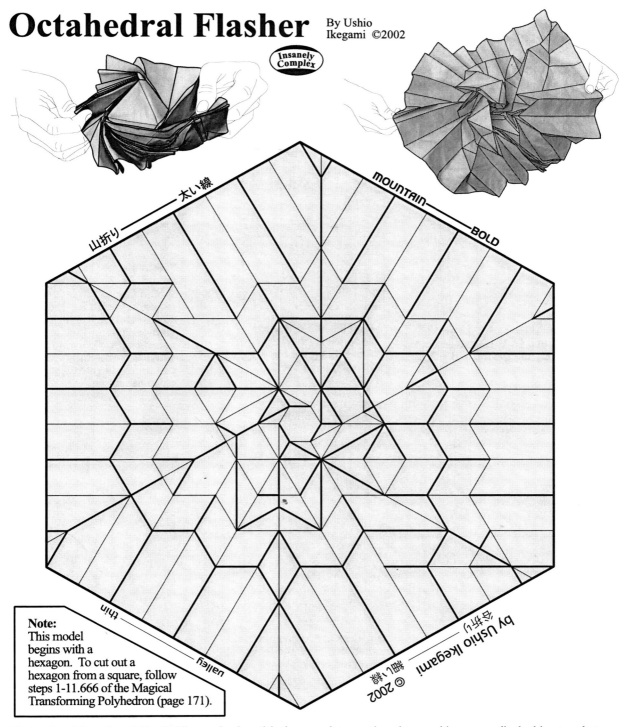

太い線 — MOUNTAIN — BOLD

山折り

Note:
This model begins with a hexagon. To cut out a hexagon from a square, follow steps 1-11.666 of the Magical Transforming Polyhedron (page 171).

thin

valley

細い線 — by Ushio Ikegami ©2002 — 谷折り

First make a triangular grid by dividing each edge of the hexagon into equal sections, making perpendicular bisectors that traverse the paper. Then, using the triangle grid as a framework, make the indicated creases. This model has 3 rotation axes which is related to octahedral symmetry. Because of paper thickness constraints inherent in Flashers, the amount of rotation on each individual axis is minimal and might be difficult to see. Folding this will probably be quite a challenge. I recommend cutting out the hexagon from a square 15-inches or larger. **Author's note:** ...And I recommend drawing the mountains and valleys on to the piece of paper, if you wish to have any luck folding it!

Flasher Bowl

In addition to its primary use as a kitchen bowl (be sure to use firm waterproof paper!), this model also works as an adjustable hat or yarmulke, and, at nighttime, as an extra-strength dream catcher.

1

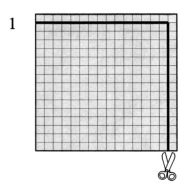

Begin by folding a 15 X 15 grid of creases (fold a 16 X 16 grid and cut one unit off from the top and side).

2

Fold the above Flasher and open it. (Stuck? Try first folding the Easy Flasher, page 216.)

PERFORM IT!

Choose a volunteer to wear the Flasher Bowl and say, **"Hold out your arms and spin."** As the volunteer is spinning, say, **"Everyone give a big hand for the space satellite!"** Pull out your cell phone, look at it and exclaim, **"Wow, the satellite is working! My cell phone is getting a stronger signal!"**

3

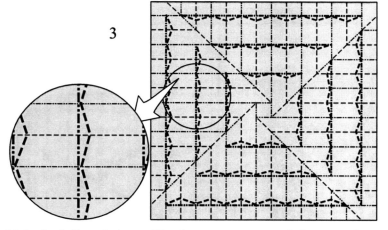

Make the indicated pleats. The above crease pattern is just one of many possible configurations of pleats. The angles between the mountains and valleys determine the amount of the curvature on the bowl.

4

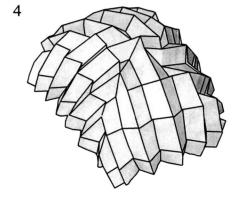

The Flasher Bowl is licked clean and turned over to dry. It could also be used as an inflatable emergency medical dome... for mice.

Thoughts Behind the Folds

I designed this model in 2001 for the company, FTL Happold, a subcontractor of NASA. I was contracted to design an origami Advanced Inflatable Airlock (AIA) for possible use as an Extravehicular Mobility Unit (EVA) for the Second Generation Reusable Launch Vehicle (RLV), in other words, an expandable room for astronauts to play in that will attach to the new space shuttle. They ended up going in a different direction (some sort of modular design), but at least I got a new origami hat out of it!

Triangular Flasher Deluxe

By Jeremy Shafer ©2001

1

This is a triangular version of the Flasher Deluxe, an unpublished Flasher that uses the same pleat pattern as the the Barristers Wig (page 229) but is planar instead of hat-shaped. This model is a stepping stone to the Tetrahedron Flasher (next page). On a slightly wandering side note, "The Big Easy Flasher (page 217) could be a stepping stone to make a Cubic Flasher by attaching six Big Easy Flashers together, but that would require taping. Now, back to the model at hand... Start with an Equilateral Triangle (page 248). Divide each side into thirty two by folding the triangle in half – which will divide one side into two – and then dividing that side again, again, again and again until you've divided it into thirty-two. All creases should get both mountained and valleyed. Using the triangular grid as a framework, make all of the indicated mountains and valleys starting at the sides and moving toward the middle. The bold mountains and valleys show the Flasher's spiral form, but the fine-lined mountains and valleys are just as important. The black triangle is the center of the flasher but is not in the exact middle of the triangle.

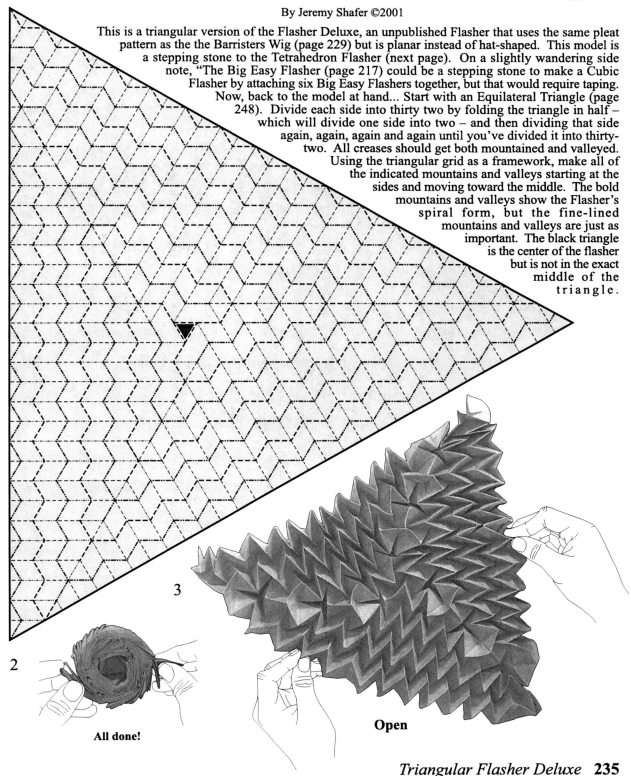

3

2

All done!

Open

Tetrahedron Flasher

By Jeremy Shafer
©2001

Taking the Triangular Flasher Deluxe one step further, or rather one dimension further, here is the Tetrahedron Flasher. It's a tetrahedron whose faces are each a Triangular Flasher Deluxe (prerequisite for folding this model). It was an extremely difficult model to make, but even more difficult would be to diagram it in a step-by-step manner. So here is just the crease pattern, which was relatively easy to diagram, thanks to computer copy and paste. Start with an Equilateral Triangle (page 248) with sides at least 30 inches in length. Make a triangular grid of creases by first dividing the left side into 81 equal parts (for a total of 80 horizontal creases). The best way to do this is to divide into thirds, ninths, twenty-sevenths, and finally into 81. Repeat on the top right side, resulting in a grid of rhombi. **Do not** repeat on the lower right side or else you will end up with a grid of hexagons and triangles. Instead, complete the triangular grid by folding on the intersections of the grid of rhombi. Next, simply make the indicated creases and collapse. The shaded hexagons become the points of the tetrahedron and the black triangles become the centers of the Flasher faces. The model locks naturally by overlapping the edges, but although there are many solutions, none of them are easy, so consider it a puzzle. Finally, you will need to make airholes at the four corners so the model can open. Good luck, or rather, skill!

Note. If you are not an origami purist, you could cut out the pattern along the bold black line and tape the edges together instead of overlapping them. If you choose this method, you might as well start from a square and divide one side into 64ths and construct a triangular grid on the gray-lined square shooting off the page. That is much easier than 81sts, and the bold black line still falls inside the square.

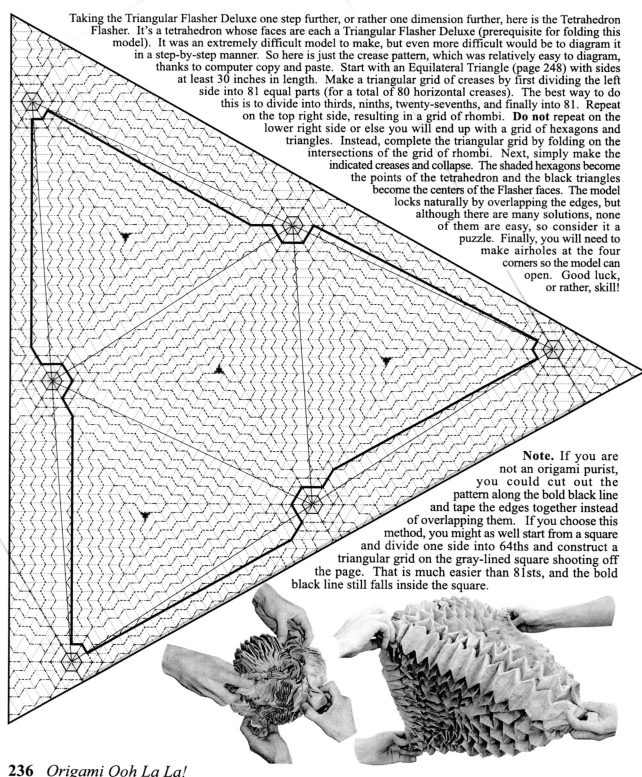

Intricate Designs

When showing origami in public, one way to get "Oohs and Aahs" is by showing intricate designs. A much easier way is to call out to the audience, "Everyone say, 'Ooh and Aah!'" Together, these two techniques can yield some very sincere and loud Oohs and Aahs!

Horse Saddle (Intermediate)

By Kurt Apple (11 years old) ©2006
Diagrammed by Jeremy Shafer from
written instructions at right.

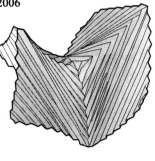

Here is a hyperbolic parabola that not only can be called a horse saddle, but actually looks like one too! It looks rather intricate, but it's actually relatively easy to fold.

Written Instructions (email) by Kurt Apple:

Hi Jeremy,

O.K. I don't even need to send a photo because this is such an easy origami piece. I had extremely vivid dreams of looking at origami books and looking at a particular piece over and over until I wanted to try to make it and it turned out to be wonderful. Well, lets get to the instructions. For the first time, it is easiest to make it with a square, but it probably doesn't matter for you. Make a square base, then open it and place it on the surface vertical and horizontal mountain folds facing you. Make a blintz base, then open it up. The last 4 folds you made are important for 1/2 the folds you are going to make in all. Pleat corners to about 16th folds, or, for higher complexity, 32nd, 64th, or 128th folds. Do not open up. After you do that to all the corners, fold on folds you used for the square base. It should look like a waterbomb base with pleats on bottom edges. After those, sink fold sink folds the same distance apart as the corner pleats were to each other. Sink-fold sink folds all the way to the center of the square or whatever you are using............ Open all corner pleats up and stretch it out a little and (drumroll).................. VUALLAAAAAAAAAA!!!!! It should look kinda like a giant ruffles chip. I really hope you understand this because trying to make origami instructions without pictures is WAAAAAAAAAAAAAAY harder than I could even imagine. Bye for now, *Kurt Apple*

1

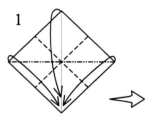

White side up,
fold a Square Base.

2

Completely unfold.

3

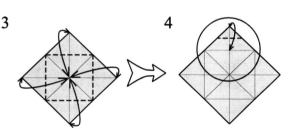

Blintz!

4

Valley-fold and unfold.

5

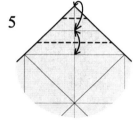

Valley-fold
and unfold.

6

Valley-fold and unfold.
Turn over.

7

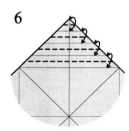

Using existing creases,
pleat like crazy!

8

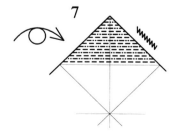

Repeat on the other
three corners.

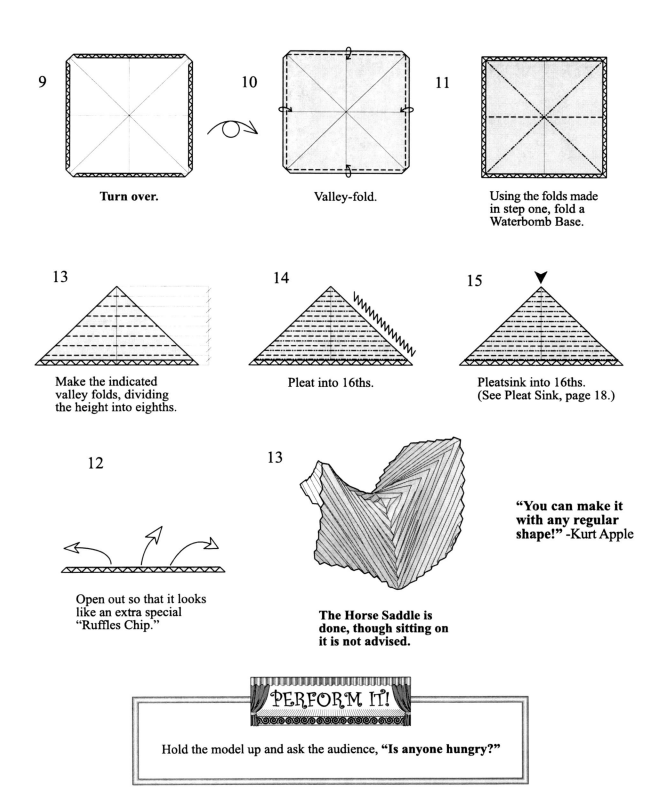

9

Turn over.

10

Valley-fold.

11

Using the folds made
in step one, fold a
Waterbomb Base.

13

Make the indicated
valley folds, dividing
the height into eighths.

14

Pleat into 16ths.

15

Pleatsink into 16ths.
(See Pleat Sink, page 18.)

12

Open out so that it looks
like an extra special
"Ruffles Chip."

13

**The Horse Saddle is
done, though sitting on
it is not advised.**

**"You can make it
with any regular
shape!"** -Kurt Apple

PERFORM IT!

Hold the model up and ask the audience, **"Is anyone hungry?"**

Iso-Area 4X4 Checkerboard

 Rather Complex

By Jeremy Shafer
©2003

This model, adapted from the Original Flasher, is a checkerboard on both sides. In addition to being used as a decoration, it also makes a great coaster – the non-rolling kind!

1

Begin by folding the Original Flasher (page 210). Hold it in its open position as shown above. Flatten all the folds in each of the four bold rectangles, push the rectangles together, and flatten the model, resulting in a form similar to step 9 of the Original Flasher.

2

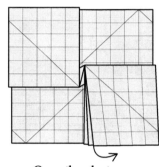

Open the pleats on the bottom edge.

3

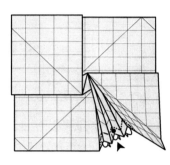

Mountain-fold near the raw edge and then apply pressure on the black dot to collapse the model flat.

4

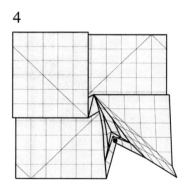

In progress.

5

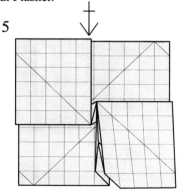

Repeat steps 2-4 on the top edge.

6

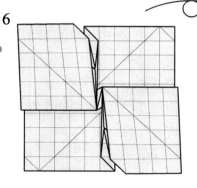

Turn over.

PERFORM IT!

Showing the model, ask the audience, **"What is harder than folding a 4 X 4 Checkerboard?** [Audience answers, "What?"] Say, **"A Checkerboard on both sides! Anyone want to play checkers?"**

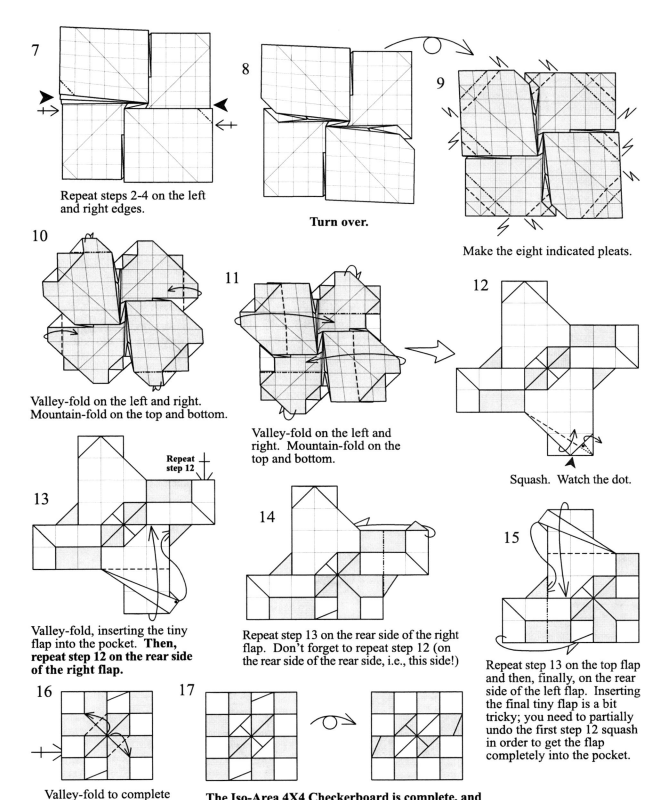

7 Repeat steps 2-4 on the left and right edges.

8 Turn over.

9 Make the eight indicated pleats.

10 Valley-fold on the left and right. Mountain-fold on the top and bottom.

11 Valley-fold on the left and right. Mountain-fold on the top and bottom.

12 Squash. Watch the dot.

Repeat step 12

13 Valley-fold, inserting the tiny flap into the pocket. **Then, repeat step 12 on the rear side of the right flap.**

14 Repeat step 13 on the rear side of the right flap. Don't forget to repeat step 12 (on the rear side of the rear side, i.e., this side!)

15 Repeat step 13 on the top flap and then, finally, on the rear side of the left flap. Inserting the final tiny flap is a bit tricky; you need to partially undo the first step 12 squash in order to get the flap completely into the pocket.

16 Valley-fold to complete the checkerboard. **Repeat behind.**

17 The Iso-Area 4X4 Checkerboard is complete, and almost completely the same on the both sides!

Magic Carpet

By Alex
Ratner ©2001

Overworked genies will really appreciate this model as it
takes much less work to produce than most magic carpets.

1

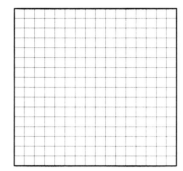

Make a 16X16 grid of creases by folding the
paper in half, in fourths, eighths and, finally,
sixteenths in both directions. The creases can
be any combination of mountains and valleys.

2

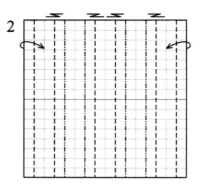

Make the indicated
vertical mountain
and valley folds.

3

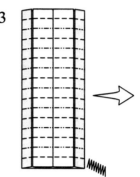

Pleat horizontally on the
existing creases and unfold.

4

Make diagonal valley
creases on all layers.

5

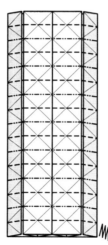

Pleat the model
horizontally and
open partially.

6

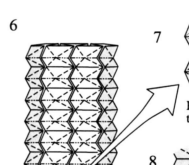

Zoom in on
the corner.

7

Reverse-fold on
the front layer

8

One pair of reverse-folds is done; make
the remaining 23. **Turn over, and
make another flurry of reverse folds.**

9

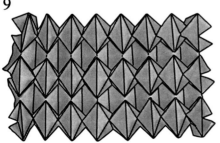

**The ideal
companion to
your car, the
Magic CarPet
is complete.**

PERFORM IT!

Perform this routine indoors. Say to the audience,
**"This is a magic carpet that flies, but not just
any magic carpet. It's a wall-to-wall magic
carpet. You wanna see?"** [Audience says,
"Yes"] Touch the model to a wall and then throw
it against the opposing wall.

Defines points to a Logarithmic Spiral

Rather Complex

Folds out into a table too!

Bermuda Triangle Vortex

By Jeremy Shafer ©2003

Inspired by a similarly patterned model by Alaisdair Post-Quinn.

'Tis a jolly infinite progression to entertain any fanatical origami tessellationist!

One square no cuts!? You gotta be crazy!...
... in order to successfully fold this model.

1

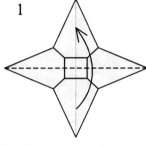

For best results use Japanese foil or kami fifteen inches square or larger. Begin by folding the Magical Levitating Star (page 145). Valley-fold in half.

2

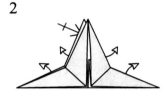

Unfold to step 8 of the Magical Levitating Star.

3

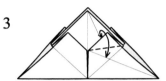

Valley-fold and unfold edge-to-crease.

4

Reverse-fold.

5

Valley-fold the flap downward.

6

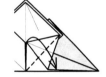

Valley-fold another flap downward.

7

Valley-fold one flap leftward.

8

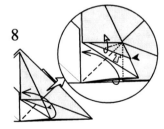

Swing the white flap upward and flatten the model.

9

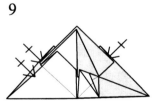

Repeat steps 3-8 on the left side. **Repeat steps 3-9 behind.**

10

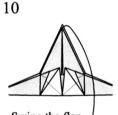

Swing the flap downward.

11

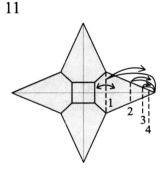

Make four valley creases in the indicated order.

PERFORM IT!

Show the model and say, **"This is the Bermuda Triangle Vortex. It's folded from one square no cuts! Don't look at it too closely or you too will be sucked up into the Bermuda Triangle Vortex!"**

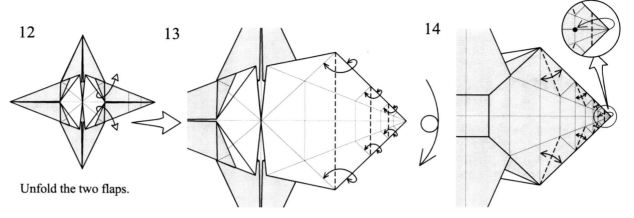

12

Unfold the two flaps.

13

Make the indicated valley creases.
Turn over top to bottom.

14

Make the indicated valley creases.
Valley-fold the rightmost point to
the nearest crease.

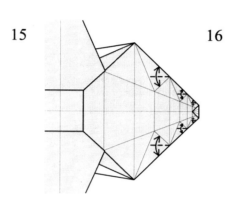

15

Make the indicated
valley creases.

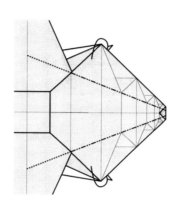

16

Mountain-fold the flaps.

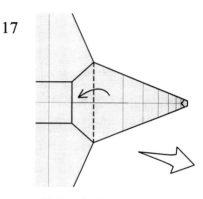

17

Valley-fold.

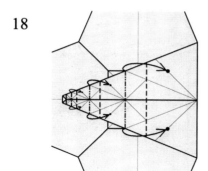

18

Pleat the flap as indicated.
The mountain folds which are
on existing creases get folded
rightward to the black dots,
forming the valley folds.

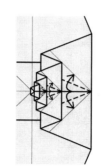

19

Spread the raw edges apart
reverse-folding on the
existing creases to form
three white right triangles
of different sizes.

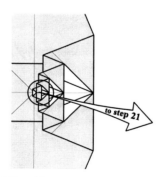

20

Like this. Focus on
the tip of the flap.

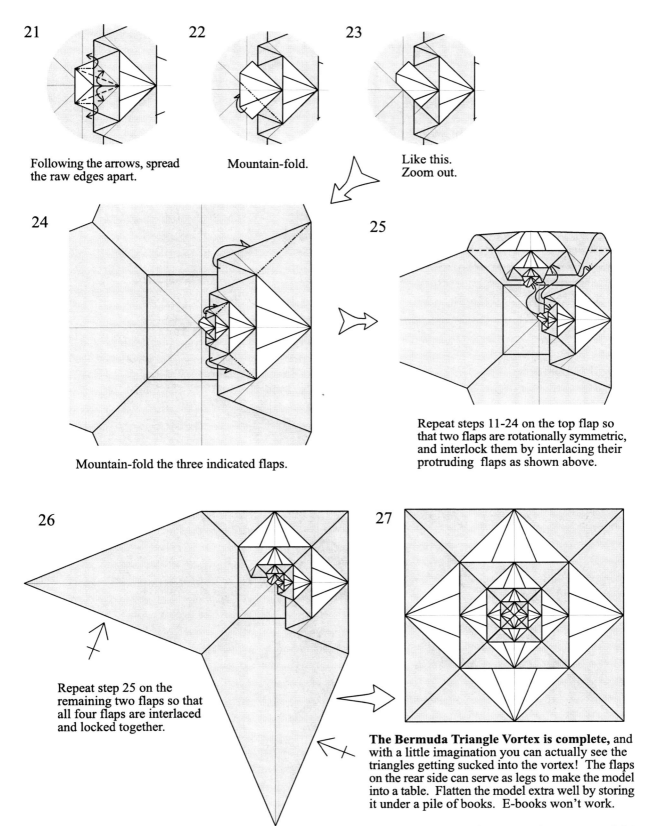

21

Following the arrows, spread the raw edges apart.

22

Mountain-fold.

23

Like this.
Zoom out.

24

Mountain-fold the three indicated flaps.

25

Repeat steps 11-24 on the top flap so that two flaps are rotationally symmetric, and interlock them by interlacing their protruding flaps as shown above.

26

Repeat step 25 on the remaining two flaps so that all four flaps are interlaced and locked together.

27

The Bermuda Triangle Vortex is complete, and with a little imagination you can actually see the triangles getting sucked into the vortex! The flaps on the rear side can serve as legs to make the model into a table. Flatten the model extra well by storing it under a pile of books. E-books won't work.

Pinwheel BARF Flyer

Rather Complex — By Jeremy Shafer ©1995

This is a model I designed one night in 1995 while trying to explain decreeping* to Chris Palmer who was just getting into origami at the time. He went on to become a master decreeper and origami tessellationist. Begin by creasing a 16 X 16 grid and then make the indicated folds.

Note: This model was used as a flyer for the Bay Area Rapid Folders (BARF) origami club in San Francisco, and also as a logo (see right) for the *Bay Area Rapid Folders Newsletter*, which I publish.

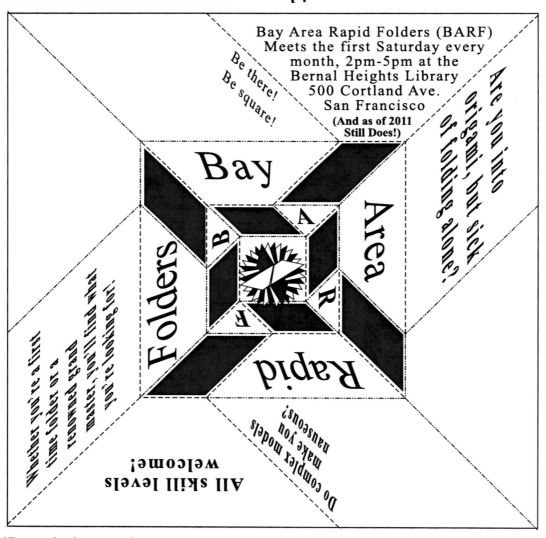

Bay Area Rapid Folders (BARF)
Meets the first Saturday every month, 2pm-5pm at the Bernal Heights Library 500 Cortland Ave. San Francisco
(And as of 2011 Still Does!)

Be there! Be square!

Are you into origami, but sick of folding alone?

Bay

Area

Folders

Rapid

Whether you're a first time folder or a renowned grand master, you'll find what you're looking for!

All skill levels welcome!

Do complex models make you nauseous?

*Decreeping is rearranging several trapped layers of paper so that no layer is wrapped around another.

Hexagonal BARF Flyer

Rather Complex

By Chris Palmer ©1995 – Variation of Pinwheel BARF Flyer (page 246)

This model is another relic of the collaborations of Chris Palmer and I in the mid 1990's. Begin with a hexagonal piece of paper. To cut out a hexagon from a square, follow steps 1-11.666 of the Magical Transforming Polyhedron (page 171). Crease a 16 X 16 X16 grid and make the indicated folds.

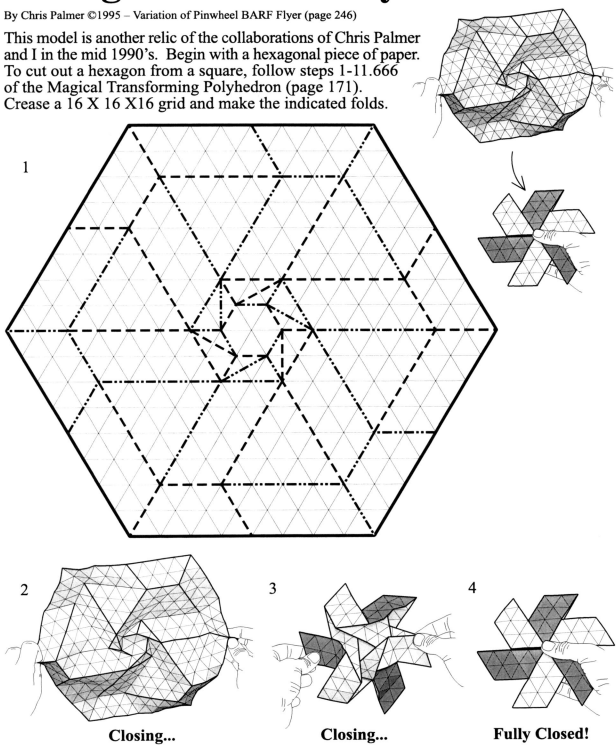

1

2

Closing...

3

Closing...

4

Fully Closed!

Hexagonal BARF Flyer **247**

Staircase Tessellation By Jeremy Shafer ©2004

Who knows... Maybe this model will be used in the future to make stadium seating. Or perhaps it will be used in the music video remake of the song, Stairway to Heaven, played on the accordion. In any case, these stairs will provide many minutes of pleating fun for any tessellation-inclined origami enthusiast.

1

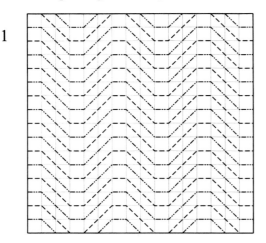

Pleat the paper into a 16 X 16 grid of creases (see page 210). Make the indicated mountains and valleys!

2

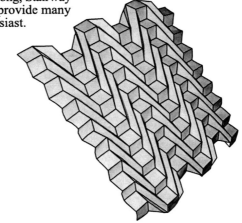

The Staircase Tessellation is complete. Pull the left and right sides apart and back together and you'll notice that half of the staircases move upward and the other half move downward. Stare at Stairs for several hours, and you will be several hours older.

Equilateral Triangle (Super Simple) Diagrams by Jeremy Shafer ©2003

Turn a square into an equilateral triangle in just three cuts!...   **... or in just one cut!**

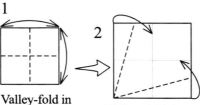

1

Valley-fold in half and unfold in both directions.

2

Valley-fold the corners so that they touch the existing creases.

3

Valley-fold on the black dots.

4

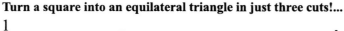

Completely unfold the model...

5

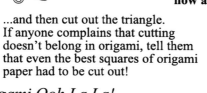

...and then cut out the triangle. If anyone complains that cutting doesn't belong in origami, tell them that even the best squares of origami paper had to be cut out!

6

The square is now a triangle.

1

Valley-fold in half vertically and unfold. Valley-fold in half diagonally.

2

Valley-fold both layers on the black dot corner-to-crease, and unfold.

3

Valley-fold on the black dot, folding the diagonal edge onto itself, and unfold.

4

Valley-fold on the black dot, crease-to-crease.

5

Cut on all layers along the existing crease (dotted line) and completely unfold.

6

Done!

Koch Snowflake Fractal

By Jeremy Shafer ©2003

Super Complex

Turn a Star of David into a Koch Snowflake Fractal!

The Koch Snowflake, is a fractal discovered by Swedish mathematician, Helge Von Koch (1870-1924).

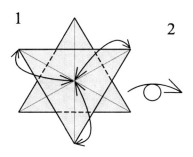

1

Begin with the Star of David (page 96). Valley-fold three corners and unfold. **Turn over.**

2

Valley-fold.

3

Zoom in.

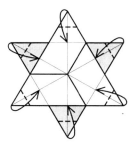

4

Valley-fold and unfold the shaded triangle in half both ways.

5

Valley-fold on the black dot.

6

Repeat steps 3-5 on the remaining five points.

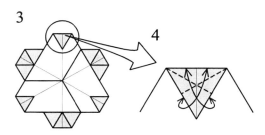

7

Pleat!

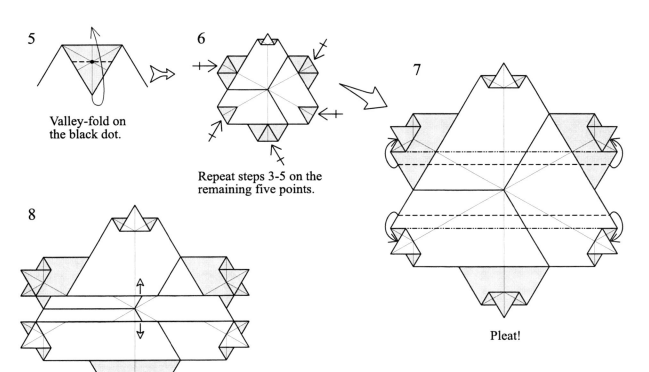

8

Unfold to step 7.

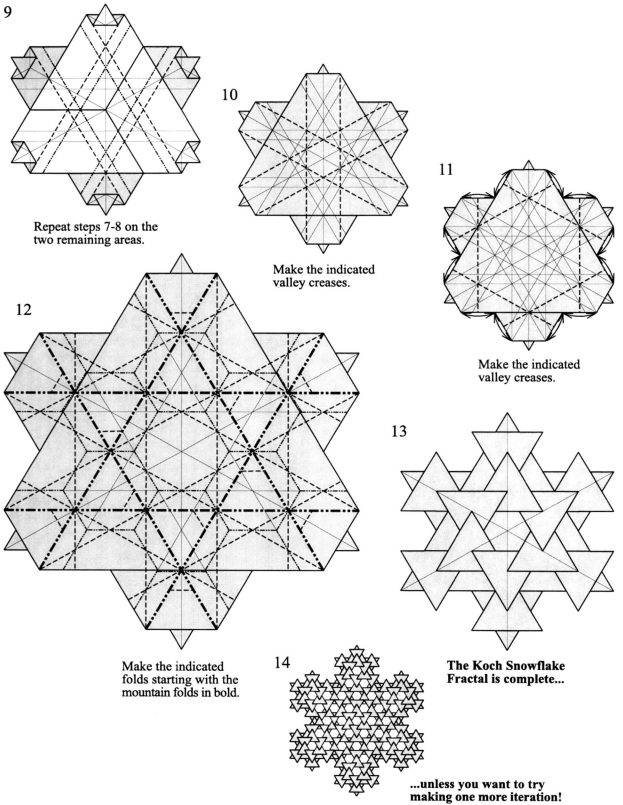

9 Repeat steps 7-8 on the two remaining areas.

10 Make the indicated valley creases.

11 Make the indicated valley creases.

12 Make the indicated folds starting with the mountain folds in bold.

13 The Koch Snowflake Fractal is complete...

14 ...unless you want to try making one more iteration!

Spring into Inaction

By Jeremy Shafer, ©2001

Here's a model that is similar to Jeff Beynon's "Spring into Action" in its folding method, but looks like a star and behaves instead more like a standard spring. Except for its mild springiness it isn't really an action model, hence it's name, "Spring into Inaction."

Begin with a 1 by 2.165 rectangle (or a 12-inch by 26-inch rectangle). Divide its width into 12 and its length into 15. Make the indicated folds. Regard the final assembly as a puzzle whose desired final result is pictured above. May the folds be with you!

PERFORM IT!

Say to the audience, **"This is a pile of stacked stars. Which do you think has more stars... this model or the Milky Way Galaxy?"** [Audience says, "The Milky Way Galaxy."] Respond defensively, **"Ya, but the Milky Way Galaxy was not folded from one piece of paper no cuts! God cheated... he used lots of pieces!"**

Star of David Tessellation

By Jeremy Shafer, ©2003

(Variation of a tessellation by Toshikazo Kawazaki)

Here is a tessellation I discovered in 1994 soon after teaming up with Chris Palmer. Not long after my discovery, I discovered that a slightly more condensed version had already been discovered a decade earlier by Toshikazu Kawasaki.

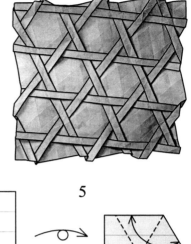

1

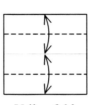

White side up, valley-fold in half and unfold.

2

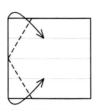

Valley-fold and unfold.

3

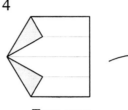

Valley-fold the corners to the creases.

4

Turn over.

5

Valley-fold edge-to-edge and unfold.

6

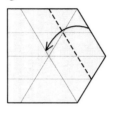

Valley-fold.

7

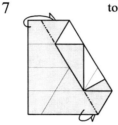

Mountain-fold the flap.

8

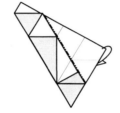

Mountain-fold the flap again.

9

And again.

10

Unfold to step 6.

11

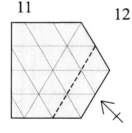

Repeat steps 6-10, completing the triangular grid.

12

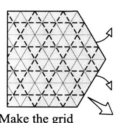

Make the grid finer by putting a valley crease inbetween every existing crease. Completely unfold.

13

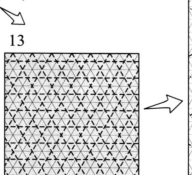

Make the grid finer by putting a valley crease inbetween every existing crease.

14

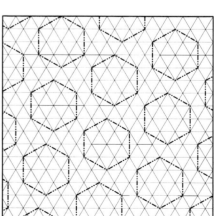

Pinch hexagons of mountain creases as indicated.

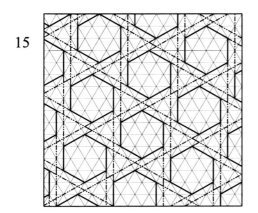

15

Make the indicated mountain folds.
Each mountain fold originates at the
corner of one hexagon and terminates
at the corner of a nearby hexagon.

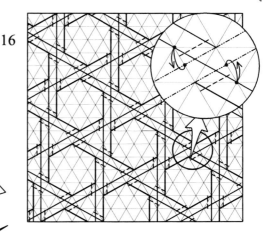

16

Make the indicated valley segments. Focusing on
the enlarged circle, first make one of the existing
mountain folds and fold it over dot-to-dot and unfold
to form the valley segment. Repeat on the other
side of the path and all around as indicated.

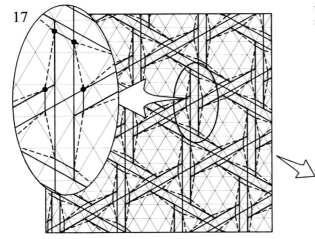

17

Form valley creases that connect the black dots. Repeat all
around as indicated. You might consider making these folds as
mountains from the other side, but, if you're in a hurry, skip to
step 18 and just push the model together making sure the pleats
in step 16 hold together. The valley folds above will form
naturally when the model is flattened.

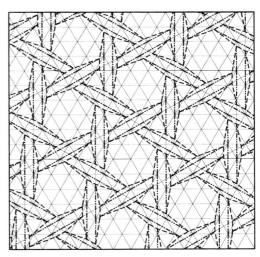

18

Finally, make the indicated folds, pushing
the model together and flattening.

19

**The Star of David Tessellation
is done. Turn over.**

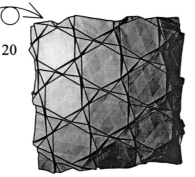

20

**Back side: Twist triangles
and twist hexagons.**

21

Holding it up to light produces
another nice pattern.

Star of David Tessellation **253**

Super Tessellated Not at All Simple Flasher Labyrinth

Insanely Complex

By Jeremy Shafer ©2001

Simple Labyrinth Flasher

The figure above is the path created when you fold the Simple Labyrinth Flasher (see page 222). Below is the path created when you fold the Quadruple Simple Labyrinth Flasher (see page 223). Just to illustrate that this model can be tessellated infinitely, at the right is the Simple Labyrinth Flasher multiplied by 32. Notice how there is still just one path that goes through the whole labyrinth. At the bottom of the page is the crease pattern and instructions for folding it. Although I don't really expect anyone to actually fold it, I do expect you to gaze at it up close and get mesmerized.

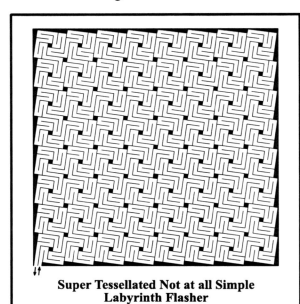

Super Tessellated Not at all Simple Labyrinth Flasher

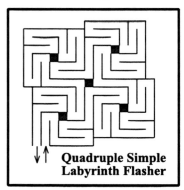

Quadruple Simple Labyrinth Flasher

Fold a 126 X 126 grid of creases. The easiest way to do this is to fold a 128 X 128 grid of creases and cut off two units. Then cut off or fold off the grey area. Make the indicated mountains (bold lines) and valleys (thin lines). Finally, draw the labyrinth pattern onto the paper by tracing all of the mountains, take a picture of the completed work, and email it to me so that I can have a picture of the model to include in the next edition of this book.

BANG! (I just thought I'd end this book with a bang!)

14 Units

98 Units

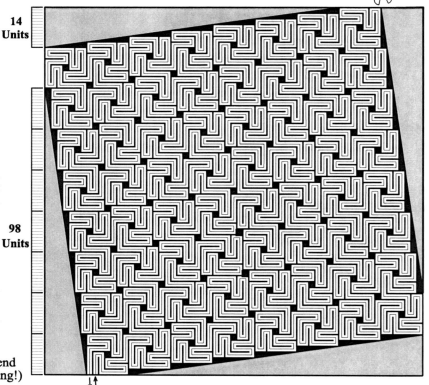

CPSIA information can be obtained at www.ICGtesting.com
Printed in the USA
LVOW05s1959240813

349496LV00002B/21/P